SCHOOL
–TO–
WORK

by
Arnold H. Packer
Marion W. Pines

with

M. Frank Stluka
Christine Surowiec

EYE ON EDUCATION

EYE ON EDUCATION
P.O. BOX 3113
PRINCETON, NJ 08543
(609) 395–0005
(609) 395–1180 fax

ISBN 1-883001-18-8 ˙

Library of Congress Cataloging-in-Publication Data

Packer, Arnold H.
        School-to-work / by Arnold H. Packer, Marion W. Pines.
            p.   cm.
        Includes bibliographical references (p.).
        ISBN 1-883001-18-8
        1. School-to-work transition—United States. 2. Career education—United
States. 3. Education, Cooperative—United States. 4. Industry and
education—United States. 5. Vocational education—United States. 6.
Internship programs—United States. 7. Vocational guidance—United States.
I. Pines, Marion W., 1924– . II. Title.
LC1037.5.P24 1996
370.11'3'0973—dc20   95-26115
                                                                                                      CIP

10 9 8 7 6 5

Editorial and production services provided by Richard H. Adin Freelance Editorial
Services, 9 Orchard Drive, Gardiner, NY 12525 (914-883-5884)

Also Available from Eye On Education:

THE LIBRARY OF INNOVATIONS

Educational Technology: Best Practices from America's Schools
by William C. Bozeman and Donna J. Baumbach

Block Scheduling: A Catalyst for Change in High Schools
by Robert Lynn Canady and Michael D. Rettig

Research on Educational Innovations
by Arthur K. Ellis and Jeffrey T. Fouts

Research on School Restructuring
by Arthur K. Ellis and Jeffrey T. Fouts

**The Performance Assessment Handbook
Volume 1: Portfolios and Socratic Seminars**
by Bil Johnson

**The Performance Assessment Handbook
Volume 2: Performances and Exhibitions**
by Bil Johnson

Innovations in Parent and Family Involvement
by William Rioux and Nancy Berla

The Directory of Innovations in High Schools
by Gloria G. Frazier and Robert N. Sickles

The Educator's Guide to Implementing Outcomes
by William J. Smith

THE LEADERSHIP AND MANAGEMENT SERIES

The Principal's Edge
by Jack McCall

Hands-on Leadership Tools for Principals
by Ray Calabrese, Gary Short, and Sally Zepeda

The Administrator's Guide to School-Community Relations
by George E. Pawlas

**The School Portfolio:
A Comprehensive Framework for School Improvement**
by Victoria L. Bernhardt

Schools for All Learners: Beyond the Bell Curve
by Renfro C. Manning

**Transforming Education Through Total Quality
Management: A Practitioner's Guide**
by Franklin P. Schargel

Quality and Education: Critical Linkages
by Betty L. McCormick

DEDICATION

This book is dedicated to Renée and Sam.

ABOUT THE AUTHORS

Dr. Arnold Packer, Senior Fellow at the Johns Hopkins University Institute for Policy Studies, directs the SCANS/2000 Program. As former Assistant Secretary in the U.S. Department of Labor, his responsibilities included policy, evaluation, and research. He is also the former Executive Director of SCANS, and the coauthor of *Workforce 2000*.

Marion Pines, also Senior Fellow at the Johns Hopkins University Institute for Policy Studies, is Project Director for Maryland's Tomorrow. Previously, she chaired the National JTPA Advisory Committee. She was the first recipient of the Augustus F. Hawkins Award for individual leadership in advancing our nation's development of human resources.

Associate Author **Frank Stluka** is the Senior Research Associate at the Institute for Policy Studies SCANS/2000 Program. He conducts training, research, and program development on a variety of education and human resource development issues.

Contributing Author **Chris Surowiec** completed her M.A. at the Institute for Policy Studies in 1994.

TABLE OF CONTENTS

PREFACE AND ACKNOWLEDGMENTS

The nation faces no larger problem than the continuing stagnation and even decline in the wages of most workers. Coupled with the rapid increase in the share of income captured by the highest earning workers, a future America that is a nation of have and have-nots becomes a distinct possibility. This is not the America most of us want for the 21st century.

There are various theories of what is causing the phenomena—technological change, international competition, and so on. There are also debates as to what can reverse the trend. Out of this confusion one thing is clear. Those better equipped for the workplace of the next century will have a better chance of succeeding.

School-to-Work Transition, or School-to-Careers if you prefer, is one practical solution. Success will require a sound vision of what is to be done and an effective way of doing it—state-by-state and community-by-community. The vision and the tools for successful implementation have to be shared by thousands of employers and thousands of schools. Millions of individual teachers and work supervisors must insure that youngsters learn while at work and work while at school.

This book is intended to assist that process for all those involved. It provides both theory and case studies—a vision and a description of the experience of those who have been implementing programs.

We want to acknowledge our partners in this effort. We especially owe more than can be recounted to Lana May, our Research Associate. Without her wisdom and tireless efforts on all aspects of this work the book would never have gotten done. We also thank June Lee and Rebecca Freeman, students at the IPS, for their work in creating the index, and Eric Artson, Jonathan England, and Jessica Ziegler-Madden who completed the practitioners' directory.

We also are indebted to Bob Sickles, our publisher and editor, who first suggested this project. Finally, we want to acknowledge the practitioners and participants whose work is chronicled in the case studies. This, at least in part, is their book.

We also want to thank our respective spouses, Renée and Sam, whose encouragement and support were called upon time and again as we prepared this manuscript.

Arnold Packer
Marion Pines

INTRODUCTION

I admit that Plato's world was not ours, that his scorn of trade and handicraft is fantastic, that he had no conception of a great industrial community such as the United States, and that such a community must and will shape its education to its own needs. If the usual education handed down to it does not suit it, it will certainly before long drop this and try another.

— Matthew Arnold[1]

Like most slogans that fit on a bumper sticker, *"the school-to-work transition"* is a phrase that needs explaining to be understood. Indeed, there are other, albeit longer expressions, that may be better. Try: *"The purpose of school is to help youngsters become responsible, productive, fulfilled adults."*

Responsible adulthood in our democratic society includes being "a good citizen" in the broadest sense of the word. Good citizens understand enough of our history and the background of other cultures to follow and participate in national debates. They are economically, scientifically, and mathematically literate. They grasp enough philosophy and ethics to maintain a civil society. Education is incomplete without this background; it should not be sacrificed to rush the transition from school to work.

If the demands of citizenship are defined by society at large, each individual's need for personal fulfillment is unique. A well-rounded education should expose students to literature, music, and the visual arts, enabling them to appreciate cultural amenities, from a good book to a good meal. These are the resources they will need to face life's existential dilemmas — from how to escape boredom to facing mortality.

---

[1] Quoted in Jacques Barzun, *The American University*, New York: Harper and Row, 1968.

Yet most of us, even those few blessed with a trust fund or married into affluence, find that being a responsible, productive, fulfilled adult requires having a "good" job. Although a job will not necessarily guarantee fulfillment, we will feel cheated if our education leaves us unemployed.

This book, then, is about a learning enterprise that prepares all students for paid work of all kinds: for ambitious careers that provide fame and fortune and for more modest outcomes that "only" provide satisfaction, security, and a decent living. Only half the students who begin high school go on to postsecondary education. Taking into consideration nonbaccalaureate programs and overall attrition, only half these postsecondary entrants — about one-fourth the total cohort — actually receive a 4-year degree.[2] The learning systems described in this book apply to all students, including those who will get a baccalaureate degree, those who obtain some postsecondary education, those who end their formal education after obtaining a high school diploma, and those who drop out of the traditional high-school.

As we near the end of the 20th century, school still fails too many young people. They leave unprepared for adult life. Too many drop out of high school. Diplomas, for those who graduate, are no longer reliable tickets into remunerative careers, nor are their afterschool or summer jobs rewarding. Yet, with effort and commitment, many of these work experiences could be restructured to provide young people more meaningful opportunities to develop conceptual, practical, and social competencies.

This book's purpose is to present options for educators, employers, students, parents, and communities. It will deal with the changes needed:

♦ **in school,** in the curriculum and teaching strategies that constitute school-based learning;

♦ **at work,** in the tasks assigned to students in their part-time or summer jobs;

♦ **in counseling** so that students understand the potential and requirements of various careers;

---

[2] Manpower Development Research Corporation (MDRC), *Learning Through Work: Designing and Implementing Quality Worksite Learning for High School Students,* January 1994:1.

- **in the connections** between secondary and postsecondary education, between school and employment, between teachers and worksite supervisors; and

- **in the community**, providing mentoring support to meet students' and young earners' other self-development needs.

The book has three parts. Part I proposes changes in the educational system that could better prepare students for a good job. Part II presents 23 promising practices where such changes have been made in all or a part of a local system. Part III describes four statewide plans and distills the lessons from these promising practices.

PART I:
THE CHANGES NEEDED TO INTEGRATE WORK AND SCHOOL

1

CHANGING SCHOOL SO THAT ALL CHILDREN ACQUIRE WORKPLACE KNOW-HOW

*The single most important thing about any enterprise is that results
exist only on the outside. . . . The result of a school is a student
who has learned something and put it to use ten years later.*
— *Peter Drucker*

THE PROBLEM: FALLING EARNINGS

The market value of a high school diploma is falling. Between 1973 and 1993, the entry-level wages for male high-school graduates fell 30% while that for women fell 18%.[1] The chances that a man between the ages of 25 and 54 with a high school diploma (but no college) will earn less than enough to support a family of four above the poverty line has been growing for over 20 years. The percentage of such low-wage workers increased from 12% in 1979 to 18% in 1992. Among young workers, the share of low-wage workers

---

[1] L. Mishel and J. Bernstein, *The State of Working America — 1994–95,* Washington, DC: Economic Policy Institute, 1994:147.

increased from 23% to 47% in the same years. Among African-American men with 12 years of schooling, the proportion with low earnings grew from 20% in 1969 to 43% in 1989; among Hispanic men from 16% to 36%; and among white men from 8% to 23%.[2] (*See* Fig. 1.1). Too many youngsters with a high school diploma proceed into a decade of short-time dead-end jobs before finally settling down as they approach 30. Indeed, the National Longitudinal Survey of Youth revealed that over 35% of 30-year-old men have held their current jobs for less than 1 year, a pattern correlated with significantly lower wages.[3] Globalization, job restructuring, and inadequate workforce preparation — all share responsibility for these disturbing trends.

Changing the context and content of today's schooling would certainly help significantly. Today, teaching emphasizes memorization, abstract learning, and solo problem solving without modern tools. A real-world context would emphasize team solutions, applied learning, and using tools ranging from reference books to computers.[4] Improvement requires changing at least three things about school:

♦ **The Curriculum**: What courses should be required, how should course content be determined, what choices should be available, and what should be left out?

♦ **The Teaching Strategy**: How should information be transmitted?

♦ **The Context**: Recognizing that much learning occurs outside of the classroom, how can the synergy between school and learning-rich experiences be created?

---

[2] Secretary's Commission on Achieving Necessary Skills (SCANS), *Learning a Living: A Blueprint for High Performance. SCANS Report for America 2000*, Washington, DC: U.S. Department of Labor, 1992. Data on women over this period is confounded by the dramatic increase in women working during this period.

[3] Paul Osterman, "Is There a Problem with the Youth Labor Market?" (unpublished manuscript, MIT, 1992). Cited by Richard Kazis in *Improving the Transition from School to Work*, Cambridge, MA: Jobs for the Future.

[4] Lauren Resnick, *Education and Learning to Think*, National Academy Press, 1987.

FIG. 1.1. THE PROPORTION OF MALE HIGH SCHOOL GRADUATES UNABLE TO SUPPORT A FAMILY*

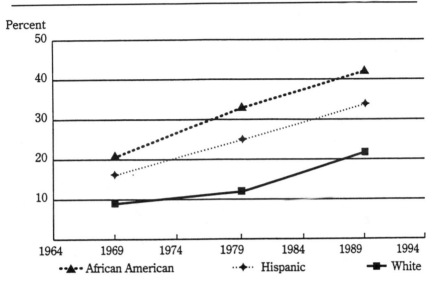

*Males, ages 25–54, with 12 years of education whose own earnings are less than poverty level for a family of four. Family income may be higher.

Source: Sheldon Danziger, "The Poor," in David Hornbeck and Lester Salamon., *Human Capital and America's Future* (Baltimore: Johns Hopkins Press, 1991), p. 148, and unpublished data for 1989.

THE STRUGGLE TO CHANGE

Many of the facts and problemsolving techniques that are learned in school will never be "put to work ten years later," as called for by Peter Drucker. Take "canoe mathematics" as an example: problems that deal with paddling upstream at x miles per hour while the current is y miles per hour are unlikely to be drawn upon outside the K–12 school experience.[5] Instances of this ilk can be encountered throughout the curriculum. Memorizing the periodic table and similar feats needed to pass a high school chemistry course are other examples. Written reports for school are assigned to be a stipulated minimum number of pages, so quantity of verbiage may take precedence over clarity, in contrast to effective work-based writing which is concise and

---

[5] For a scathing criticism of today's school-based math, *see* Michael H. Smith, *Humble Pi*, Buffalo, NY: Prometheus, 1994.

focused. School writing has an audience of one, the teacher, while figuring out the potential audience is the first task in "real" writing. (*See* Fig. 1.2.)

Why are the current curricula so inadequate for today's tasks? What fallacies and forces prevail against restructuring curricula? What conceptual pitfalls need to be kept in mind when considering the core curriculum?

One fallacy is the persistent belief that "you *may* encounter this problem." Much is kept in the curriculum even though the chance that the lessons will be used is nearly zero. Learning long division, for example, may be defended on the offchance that one will have to divide 36 into 4,283 at a time when the power fails and the computer is inoperative — never mind the battery-operated calculator. What will the student do if no equipment is available? For one thing, he can put off the problem to another day. A persuasive case can be made that long division is not only wasted effort, but that it steals time from learning the kind of mathematics which could help solve problems more likely to be confronted, such as estimating the answer so that the student can check whether the right numbers have been put into the calculator.

Consider whether trigonometry should be part of the mathematics *every* student is required to master, or whether the time is better spent on something else, say probability and statistics. To satisfy those who (rightly) say school is more than preparation for work, consider the knowledge needed to be a "responsible citizen." Good citizens know enough probability and statistics to comprehend public issues. They know how to interpret polling data or make a judgement about national (or personal) health insurance. They will, however, rarely need trigonometry to understand the daily news.

Should trigonometry be required in the belief that all of us need this knowledge to become "productive workers"? There is only so much time in a day and *most* students will have no future use for trigonometry. (There are more elementary and kindergarten teachers than engineers employed in the U.S.) Trigonometry is fine to offer as an elective, but it need not be mandatory. One does not have to pick on mathematics or trigonometry to make this point. Many things taught in science classes and other parts of the high school curriculum are retained because of tradition or because someone on the school board believes they *may* be useful. The issue is, as the body of knowledge grows, does the curriculum cover the most useful material for

FIG. 1.2. WRITING: THE SCANS PERSPECTIVE

What Today's Schools Teach	What the Workplace Requires.
Purposes for Writing	
• Central purpose is to display mastery of knowledge, skills, and format.	• Range of purposes (instrumental): to inform, persuade, clarify (or obscure), soften the blow, explain how to do something, tell others to do something, make a recommendation, sell.
Types of Writing Routinely Generated	
• Essays, book reports, poetry, stories, research papers, letters.	• Reports, brochures, letters, memos, proposals, surveys, ad copy, instructions, planning documents, messages, specifications, recommendations, logs, legal documents/ contracts, news releases, minutes, personnel evaluations.
Audience	
• Single audience: the teacher.	• A range of audiences, including people differing in needs, motivations, uses for the information, and knowledge of the topic, e.g., supervisors, clients, coworkers, subordinates, the general public.
Work Conditions	
• Deadlines and distractions controlled by the teacher.	• Deadlines and distractions often unavoidable.

Content

- Teacher assigns topics.
- Text reveals everything discovered.

- Ill-defined problems are
  worked through.
- Text tells what the reader
  needs to know.

Logic

- Theoretical; "academic."

- Problemsolving, pragmatic,
  goal-oriented.

Correctness

- Usage, handwriting, spelling,
  and punctuation are a focus
  for evaluation, accounting for
  50–100% of the document's
  value.

- Same factors are a given, not
  a focus for evaluation.

Source: Fort Worth Public Schools

tackling the problems a student will face in his life outside of school in the new century.

A second fallacy is the loyalty to mental gymnastics: certain exercises, such as learning Latin or proving geometric theorems are thought to "train the mind." The recent findings of cognitive scientists cast great doubt on this so-called far transferability. Good chess players can transfer a strategy they have learned in one chess game to another. But brilliant chess players who have learned to plan their future moves are not necessarily better at developing financial strategies.[6] This is not to say that learning Latin, or how to prove geometry theorems, or how to play chess is unworthy. Rather, for these and manifold other learning possibilities to be part of the

---

[6] John R. Anderson, *Cognitive Psychology and Its Implications*, New York: W.H. Freeman and Co., 1980. *See also* Thomas Bailey and Donna Merrit, *School-to-Work Transition and Youth Apprenticeship in the United States*, New York: Manpower Demonstration Research Corporation, 1993.

curriculum they will have to make it on their own, not because they "train the mind."

College requirements are an important force for inertia in high school curricula. Colleges, at least many of the better ones, require trigonometry and calculus. So the high schools teach precalculus to their better students. Then, the issue of tracking raises its ugly head. Indeed, there is an important movement that identifies geometry and algebra as the "gatekeepers" to college.[7] One might contend that calculus is kept in the curriculum to separate the men from the boys (or, more often, girls). The better math students thus work hard to take precalculus, and the best take Advanced Placement calculus. In college calculus, they go on to learn how to take integrals of trigonometric functions, thereby justifying the trig course. But except in rare cases, they will not use calculus to solve real world problems. Worse yet, mathematically challenged students struggle through the same process, putting in much more effort at the expense of developing skills in other fields where they may be more talented. Again, although calculus is a tempting target for such criticism, the same points can be made about foreign language instruction, science, and many other courses that are "required" on the college track.

The forces that divide academic and vocational courses should be bridged, or at least mitigated. Calls to combine vocational and academic courses are long-standing. Some progress has been made. But most reform efforts have concentrated on putting academic material in vocational courses (applied academics) rather than making mainstream academic courses more relevant to adult life. Despite the progress, one dictionary definition of "academic" still holds: "having no direct practical application." Vocational education, meanwhile, still often bears the stigma of being suitable only for those who are not academically talented, not on the college track. A curriculum designed to prepare students for life beyond their school years would do well to jettison instructional programs composed of disjunct academic and vocational "tracks" and replace them with more flexible, integrated learning options.

Tension between general competency and specific skills can be seen in the conflict between the academic and vocational curricula

---

[7] Sol H. Pelavin and Michael Kane, *Changing the Odds: Factors Increasing Access to College*, New York: College Entrance Examination Board, 1990.

or, at the college level, between liberal arts and preprofessional education. Academic courses tend to eschew "practical" knowledge, striving instead for "learning for its own sake" (and the sake of those who teach it). Vocational courses, meanwhile, tend to prepare students for very specific occupations. Indeed, vocational programs are often evaluated in terms of whether students enter the job for which they are trained.

To be fair, employers also find it difficult to reconcile the tension between their desire for general competency with their need for instantly productive workers. Within a single firm, the CEO and the Vice President for Human Resources may call for general competency, flexibility, and adaptability. But most line managers want specific skills so that new hires can be put to work quickly without extensive training.

All of these obstacles, plus the well-known resistance to discard old lesson plans, make curriculum change a challenge. Teachers, it is often said, teach the way they were taught in school. As we approach the year 2000, however, new winds may be gathering enough force to overcome this long-term stasis.

During the late 1980s, workforce issues moved from the sidelines to center stage. *Workforce 2000*[8], published in 1987, convinced many that human resources are the most important resources required for economic growth. Soon thereafter, *The Forgotten Half*[9] made policymakers aware of what dismal prospects await more than half of those emerging from high school, those who do not go on to college. Individuals without 4-year degrees are falling further behind each year. The troubling result, as cited previously and shown in Figure 1.1, is that fewer and fewer people can support a family at even a modest standard of living on a single salary.

The 70% of Americans without a baccalaureate degree may have been forgotten by many, but by no means are they gone. In 1990, *America's Choice*[10] laid out the options: high skills or low wages. The

---

[8] William B. Johnston and Arnold H. Packer, *WorkForce 2000*, Indianapolis, IN: Hudson Institute, 1987.

[9] W.T. Grant Foundation Commission on Work, Family, and Citizenship, *The Forgotten Half* (Final Report, 1988).

[10] Commission on the Skills of the American Workforce, *America's Choice: High*

Commission on the Skills of the American Workforce, which produced that work, set the stage for much of today's school-to-work and education and industry standards legislation, as well as introducing the concept of Certificates of Mastery (CIM) into the national dialogue on education reform. In 1991, another commission, the Secretary's Commission on Achieving Necessary Skills (SCANS), published its first report, *What Work Requires of Schools*.[11] At this point, national candidates were pledging to be "the education President" and corporate CEO's were promising "quality through training." By 1993, presidential candidates and leading CEOs who had failed to deliver were in early retirement.

The change in corporate thinking exerts significant pressure for curriculum change. Leading employers' attitudes toward their workers are undergoing metamorphosis as they adopt concepts brought to the fore by Edwards Deming and Juran and Total Quality Management, and updated by more recent gurus like Michael Hammer and James Champy in *Reengineering the Corporation*.[12] The idea of worker "empowerment" moved from New Age seminars in the 1970s to the Ford Motor Company in 1983. Training problem-solvers became the goal of corporate Human Resources departments in America's leading companies. Frontline workers who can think for themselves enable firms to restructure and downsize by eliminating middle management. The "scientific management" of Frederick Taylor — breaking jobs down so that any unskilled willing worker could do them, while the elite, college educated one-fourth of the workforce did the thinking and planning — was out. Deming and "high performance" were in. Clearly, this vision would be unreachable if workers were leaving high school functionally illiterate. Indeed, high performance workplaces require high performance schools. (*See* Fig. 1.3.)

Skills or Low Wages!, Rochester, NY: National Center for Education and Economy, 1990.

[11] Secretary's Commission on Achieving Necessary Skills (SCANS), *What Work Requires of Schools*, SCANS Report for America 2000, Washington, DC: U.S. Department of Labor, 1991.

[12] Edwards Deming, *Out of the Crisis*, Cambridge, MA: MIT, 1986; J. Juran, *Planning for Quality*, New York: McMillan, 1988; Michael Hammer and James Champy, *Reengineering the Cooperation*, New York: HarperCollins Publishers, 1993.

FIG. 1.3. CHARACTERISTICS OF TODAY'S AND TOMORROW'S WORKPLACE[13]

TRADITIONAL MODEL	HIGH PERFORMANCE MODEL
STRATEGY	
• Mass production • Long production runs • Centralized control	• Flexible production • Customized production • Decentralized control
PRODUCTION	
• Fixed automation • End-of-line quality control • Fragmentation of tasks • Authority vested in super-visor	• Flexible automation • On-line quality control • Work teams, multiskilled workers • Authority delegated to worker
HIRING AND HUMAN RESOURCES	
• Labor-management confronta-tion • Minimal qualifications ac-cepted • Workers as a cost	• Labor-management cooper-ation • Screening for basic skills abili-ties • Workforce as an investment
JOB LADDERS	
• Internal labor market • Advancement by seniority	• Limited internal labor market • Advancement by certified skills
TRAINING	
• Minimal for production work-ers • Specialized for craft workers	• Training sessions for everyone • Broader skills sought

[13] Source: "Competing in the New International Economy." Washington, DC: Office of Technology Assessment, 1990.

Perhaps to date all these new ideas have had more influence on the incomes of consultants who write articles and conduct seminars about them than on the average employer. Yet one should not underestimate the power of these new thoughts. Total quality management, in one version or another, has been adopted — with frequent lapses — by the country's most prestigious firms. These, in turn, through the volume of their transactions as well as by their example, can foment significant change across an entire industry. Suppliers to Ford or Motorola, for instance, must know their Deming.

The new thinking has also profoundly influenced the public sector. Consider Vice President Gore's work on "reinventing government," and the substantially heightened executive and legislative branch policy focus (both state and national level) on education reform. The aim of empowering workers finds expression in the effort to inaugurate site-based management of schools. It is also evident in the six education goals approved in 1989 by the National Conference of Governors, led by then-governor Bill Clinton, and endorsed by the Bush administration (and expanded to eight goals in *Goals 2000*).

The most germane of these goals for the school-to-work transition are goals #3 and #5, stating in part:

From Goal #3
American students . . . [will demonstrate] competency in challenging subject matter . . . every school in America will ensure that all students learn to use their minds well, so that they may be prepared for responsible citizenship, further learning and productive employment in our modern economy.

From Goal #5:
Every adult American will . . . possess the knowledge and skills necessary to compete in a global economy.

STANDARDS AND SCANS

These lofty goals led to the effort, begun in the Bush administration and accelerated by President Clinton's team, to develop and implement more rigorous educational standards. If this is to be a real effort and not just rhetorical grandstanding, curriculum change will be essential despite the forces of considerable resistance described earlier.

In the early 1990s, the federal government began to fund standards development in mathematics, science, the arts, and other academic subjects. The standards developed by the National Council of Teachers of Mathematics (NCTM) are a good example. NCTM calls for students who can learn to "reason" and "communicate mathematically," and apply mathematical concepts to solve real-life problems.[14] There has been a parallel standards-setting effort for science students under the auspices of the American Association for the Advancement of Science (AAAS) and for the arts, history, and so on.

The standards discussed so far relate to the "academic" side of the curriculum issue. Other pressures for curriculum change lurk on the "vocational" side. The federal government has funded industry groups to develop voluntary standards for their entry-level jobs. For example, the Hospitality Industry Consortium is a group of the important trade associations in this large industry. The Consortium includes the National Restaurant Association, The Hotel and Motel Association, the Bartender's Association, and others. The larger of these associations have, for quite a long time, supported curriculum development through their individual educational foundations. They also support the Center for Hotel, Restaurant, and Institutional Education (CHRIE). CHRIE received about $250,000 in 1993 and another $300,000 in 1994 from the U.S. Department of Labor to develop standards for a set of eight entry-level positions (back and front of the house positions in restaurants and hotels).

The Department of Labor awarded similar standards-development contracts to the American Electronic Association, National Federation of Retailers, and others. Most of these organizations published standards in 1994 and 1995. The Department of Education also awarded contracts to organizations that have or soon will publish standards. (*See* Fig. 1.4 for a list of the contracts awarded.) Efforts to delineate industrywide standards are institutionalized under the National Skills Standards Board created by the *Goals 2000 Educate America* Act of 1994.[15] The aim, under the *School-to-Work Opportunities* Act of 1994, is to have youngsters earn skills certificates certifying that they meet these industry skill standards.

---

[14] National Council of Teachers of Mathematics, *Professional Standards for Teaching Mathematics*, Reston VA, March 1991.

[15] *Goals 2000, Educate America Act.*

FIG. 1.4. STANDARDS DEVELOPMENT CONTRACTS

Organization	*Occupational Area*
National Retail Federation Washington, DC	Professional Sales Associate
Uniform & Textile Service Association Washington, DC	Production Workers and Maintenance Technicians (These occupations include most of the nondegreed workers in the industry)
National Tooling and Machining Association Ft. Washington, MD	Machining, Industrial Equipment, Tooling & Metalforming Technicians
National Electrical Contractors Association Bethesda, MD	Electrical Construction Worker, Electrical Line Construction Worker, and Electrical Residential Construction Worker
Center for Hotel, Restaurant, and Institutional Education Washington, DC	Front-Line Positions in Hospitality & Tourism Industry (Server, Host, Cashier, Busser, Front Desk Associates, Reservationist, Bellstand, and Concierge)
Far West Lab for Educational Research and Development San Francisco, CA	Health Care Core (Applying to All Workers in Health Services), and Four Occupational Clusters: Therapeutic, Diagnostic, Information Services, and Environmental Services
Education Development Center Newton, MA	Beginning-Level Bioscience Technical Specialists (Standards for Entry-level Specialists Cover 20 Related Occupations)
American Chemical Society Washington, DC	Entry-Level Chemical Laboratory Technicians and Process Technical Operators
American Welding Society Miami, FL	Entry-Level Welder (a Semiskilled Production Worker Requiring Significant Supervision)
Southern Association of Colleges and Schools Decatur, GA	Air-conditioning, Heating, and Refrigeration Technicians in Residential and Commercial Environments
Center for Occupational Research Development Waco, TX	Entry-Level Hazardous Materials Management Technician (Encompasses Several Job Titles)

Center for Occupational Research Development Waco, TX	Photonics Technicians (in Defense/Public Safety/Aerospace, Medicine, Computers, Communications, Manufacturing/Test & Analysis, and Environmental/Energy/Transportation)
Electronic Industries Foundation Washington, DC	Entry-Level Electronic Technicians (Covers Those Employed Within Basic & Applied Research, Product Development, Manufacturing, Marketing, Maintenance, and Repair of Electronic Components, Devices and Systems)
National Automotive Technicians Education Foundation Herndon, VA	Entry-Level Automobile, Autobody, and Medium/Heavy Truck Technicians
Foundation for Industrial Modernization Washington, DC	Computer-Aided Drafting and Design (CADD) Users Across All Industries
Foundation for Industrial Modernization Washington, DC	Technical Workers
National FFA Foundation Alexandria, VA	Agricultural Biotechnology Technician
Human Services Research Institute Cambridge, MA	Entry-Level Human Service Occupations (Case Managers, Job Coaches, and Residential Support Staff)
Laborers-AGC Education and Training Fund Pomfret Center, CT	Pipe Laying Work, Concrete Work, Lead Remediation, and Petro-Chemical Remediation
Grocers Research and Education Foundation Reston, VA	Customer Service/Stock Associate and Front-End Associate (Encompasses All Entry-Level Positions)
American Electronics Association Santa Clara, CA	Manufacturing Specialist, Administrative/Information Services Support, Pre/Post Sales
Graphic Arts Technical Foundation Pittsburgh, PA	Prepress/Imaging, Press, and Binding/Finishing/Distributing

The relationships between academic and vocational standards, and the various career paths which open up when these standards are achieved, are further discussed in Chapter 3. The emerging standards are a powerful force and a serious bid to change the curriculum in thousands of middle and high schools. Properly implemented, the standards should be an important step toward much more effective school-to-work transitions for participating students.

CURRICULUM: THE WHAT

Curriculum in Latin means a running course, as in a race. In school, it means the required fixed series of studies needed to reach an end. The end, the finish line in the race course that youngsters are forced to run, should be responsible, productive, fulfilled adulthood. Curriculum, then, should be designed for this end.

The ideal curriculum will help the student surmount a number of hurdles on that journey. It will reconcile the need for a sufficiently comprehensive general education — the academic side — with the need for more specific occupational preparation and orientation. Look at it from the school's point of view. How will Typical High School serve those who are going to a 4-year college and those who will more immediately enter the workforce without tracking the "college-bound" and the "work-bound"?

As a guideline, hark back to national goal #5: preparing students for " . . . responsible citizenship, further learning, and productive employment in our modern economy." The last can be achieved, without compromising the first two, by giving all students an opportunity to acquire "workplace know-how." This know-how is a set of generic competencies needed in most industries and on most rungs of a career ladder. The most ambitious effort to define workplace know-how has been SCANS, the effort of the Secretary's Commission on Achieving Necessary Skills.[16]

The Commission consulted experts and employers, but relied even more on lengthy interviews with workers and their immediate supervisors. The criteria of attainment developed through this process

---

[16] One of your authors was Executive Director of the Commission which was established by the Secretary of Labor in the Spring of 1990 and which completed its work in the Spring of 1992.

are applicable to a broad range of workplace situations. SCANS saw workplace know-how as defined by a set of five competencies and a three-part foundation. (*See* Fig. 1.5.) The SCANS recommendations start with three broad *foundation skills:*

♦ basic mastery of reading, writing, arithmetic and mathematics, as well as speaking and listening;

♦ thinking skills including creative thinking, problem solving, and decisionmaking — what it takes to apply knowledge to useful work, and;

♦ personal characteristics that render a worker trustworthy and able to work well with others.

FIG. 1.5. WORKPLACE KNOW-HOW

COMPETENCE—effective workers can productively use:

♦ **Resources** — allocating time, money, materials, space, and staff.

♦ **Interpersonal skills** — working on teams, teaching others, serving customers, leading, negotiating, and working well with people from culturally diverse backgrounds.

♦ **Information** — acquiring and evaluating data, organizing and maintaining files, interpreting and communicating, and using computers to process information.

♦ **Technology** — selecting equipment and tools, applying technology to specific tasks, and maintaining and troubleshooting technologies.

♦ **Systems** — understanding social, organizational, and technological systems, monitoring and correcting performance, and designing or improving systems.

THE FOUNDATION—competence requires:

♦ **Basic Skills** — reading, writing, arithmetic and mathematics, speaking, and listening.

♦ **Thinking Skills** — creative thinking, making decisions, solving problems, seeing things in the mind's eye, knowing how to learn, and reasoning.

♦ **Personal Qualities**—individual responsibility, self-esteem, sociability, self-management, and integrity.

These attributes comprise a firm foundation for workplace know-how. Staying with the construction analogy, a sound foundation is necessary, but not sufficient, for a successful project. The project's goal is more than work readiness. The youngster needs the know-how it takes to move into increasingly challenging and rewarding employment. Productive employees have the ability to organize concepts, mobilize resources, work amicably and effectively with others. SCANS defines these abilities needed in virtually every workplace as the five major *competencies.*

The need for workplace know-how is borne out in various state studies and in a very large survey of job-holders by American College Testing.[17] Jobs which require higher levels of the competencies are those which tend to pay a "living wage." In today's economy, mastery in these competencies is required to earn an adequate income.

The first of the five competencies concerns managing **resources.** From the most basic to the most complex level, efficiently allocating time, money, and personnel is an essential business skill, with multiple applications from manufacturing to retailing to professional services.

Second come **interpersonal** skills. Almost all workers need to function as part of a team, give and receive instructions, and serve clients or customers. Many have to negotiate and work well with people from culturally diverse backgrounds. Those who want to progress must know how to teach and to lead.

The third SCANS competency is the ability to acquire, evaluate, organize, and communicate **information.** More information, along with the extensive and fast-evolving information technology, makes rote learning obsolete. The notion that one gains all the information one needs early in life and spends the rest of life simply using it is no longer valid. The information explosion implies far more emphasis on self-directed, well-targeted, and critical information searches. Finding patterns in data and communicating the results marks the best financial analyst, the outstanding scientist or physician.

Technology is the fourth SCANS competency. Workers from clerks to gardeners, not to mention obvious examples like medical technicians and computer programmers, will have to master

---

[17] See the reports of the American College Testing on their *National Jobs Analysis Study* beginning with the "Overview of Methodology and Pedagogics" (Iowa City, IA: ACT, 1994).

increasingly complex technology. It is important to know the tools of one's occupation, but accelerating technological development makes it even more important to be able to evaluate and incorporate new tools into one's work as they become available.

Finally — in a sense tying the previous four competencies together — the high-quality employee needs to grasp the meaning of **systems**. This competency is the most difficult to pin down, but probably contributes most to increasing a worker's earning power. The master of systems understands how the parts of a hospital, factory, school, machine, or social organization fit together. More important, she can adjust, fix, or redesign the system so that it will achieve higher quality performance. Systems are subject to continuous improvement as they operate over time.

To sum up, workplace know-how is generic across industries, needed in hospitals and hotels, as well as manufacturing firms and retail stores. The competencies are also generic up and down the career ladder, although the problems get more complex as a worker gains responsibility and authority. An entry-level hospital administrator may schedule the use of an operating room, but much more experience is needed to schedule the activities of an entire hospital complex. One can learn how to develop a budget for a modest paint job or for building an entire office complex.

Moreover, these competencies are enduring. The Pharaohs had to manage resources of time, money, space, and staff when they built the pyramids; space pioneers of the next century will have to exercise the same skills when they plan an expedition to Mars. Much the same can be said about interpersonal skills. Consider negotiating. The bible speaks of the patriarch Abraham negotiating to buy his burial cave and one can be sure that our descendants will continue to value those who succeed at getting warring factions to agree.

The challenge for curriculum designers is to integrate these workplace competencies with the academic courses that students will have to take to advance to college. Students will have to meet the academic standards created under the Goals 2000 legislation and acquire workplace know-how simultaneously. How can this be done in the time available to schools? If academics and workforce preparation are considered completely separate realms, it cannot; there is simply not that much time in a day (or in the 12 years typically taken to move through elementary, middle, and high school). The trick is using the time spent at work and at extracurricular activities to support the goal of acquiring workplace know-how. Ideally, work and personal time should reinforce learning experiences that take place in the classroom and vice versa. Work readiness and solid academic grounding are complementary, not competing, objectives. And making the classroom a more work-relevant place argues for, not against, schools that adopt and meet reasonably rigorous academic standards.

NCTM's math standards and the AAAS science standards both encourage real-world problem solving. However, the standards statements are often unclear about the types of math or science problems that are to be solved. Will they be problems encountered only by professional mathematicians and scientists? Or are they to be — as urged by NCTM — problems common to many jobs; problems that could be solved better if mathematical or scientific knowledge were applied to them? It will be a lost opportunity if they continue to be contrived problems that neither professional mathematicians nor anyone else will encounter after leaving school.

Instead of learning "canoe mathematics," students could learn about the algebra associated with budgets. Through the process of developing a business plan, more algebra and more workplace know-how will be acquired simultaneously. That same project could give the student the opportunity to use a spreadsheet and make oral presentations to the "board of directors."

If precalculus is replaced with a course in making trade-offs, students will simultaneously learn the mathematics and the workplace know-how needed for efficiently allocating resources. Every day, adults make trade-offs between time and money when scheduling a project or setting inventory policy. They choose between labor and capital in investment decisions. Physicians decide between a medicine's efficacy and its side-effects. These problems are often solved by seat-of-the-pants methods which could be improved by applying mathematics — if students learned math concepts that are useful in their "real" world.

For example, a course in "Mathematics for Trade-off Decisions" might introduce the student to the principles of Newton's calculus. Endless sterile exercises would be displaced by an authentic demonstration of how mathematical principles are put to useful work. With the advent of computers, calculus has become even more arcane than it was previously. A good case could be made for spending more time on linear programming and less on taking integrals and differentials of trigonometric functions. Foreman and Steen, now at the Mathematics Science Education Board, make a plea for "concrete" mathematics."[18] Figure 1.6 lists a series of problems that a high-school graduate might be expected to solve if they learned "concrete" mathematics.

FIG. 1.6. REAL-WORLD PROBLEMS THAT ALGEBRA COULD HELP SOLVE

I.   ALLOCATING RESOURCES*
   A.   To Invest in Equipment
      1.   Justify an investment in an MRI machine
      2.   Investment in a new crane
      3.   A numerically controlled drill press
      4.   A computer
      5.   A hospital ship
   B.   To Invest in Human Resources
      1.   Making a career choice
      2.   As an education planner
   C.   For Space Layout
      1.   Lots in a land parcel
      2.   Satellite coverage
      3.   Hotel lobby
      4.   Concert audience
      5.   Retail store
   D.   To Make a Business Plan
      1.   A retail store
      2.   Entertainment
      3.   Housing construction and sales
      4.   Manufacturing
      5.   A new college department (or any new service)
   E.   To Schedule and Budget
      1.   Manufacturing production
      2.   A music theater
      3.   Health services
      4.   Travel
      5.   Construction project

---

[18] National Council of Teachers of Mathematics, *Mathematics for Work and Life* (forthcoming).

II   OBTAINING OR COMMUNICATING INFORMATION*
   A. Estimating market demand for
       1.   A consumer product
       2.   A radio show
       3.   A personal service
   B. Advertising
       1.   A professional service
   C. Polling
       1.   About a tax increase or other public policy

III INTERPERSONAL SKILLS*
   A. Negotiation
       1.   Affirmative action
       2.   Apportioning cost for a mistake made by a group of firms
       3.   Bidding as a convention site
       4.   A labor dispute over wages and benefits
       5.   The selling price for a piece of real estate

IV SYSTEMS*
   A. Hypothesis testing
       1.   Health test
       2.   Manufacturing quality
       3.   Maintenance troubleshooting
       4.   Debugging a computer program
       5.   Finding an accounting error
   B. Trade-offs
       1.   Providing scarce health services
       2.   Inventory
       3.   Hiring decisions
       4.   Transportation
       5.   Education curricula

---

* One of the SCANS competencies. See *"What Work Requires of Schools,"* Secretary's Commission on Achieving Necessary Skills, Washington, DC, 1991.

Science can include learning about systems that students are likely to encounter in the workplace. The study of environmental systems, for example, can include some understanding of systems theory that will be useful in careers dealing with the environment

— from farmer to environmental engineer. Building computer models of population growth in biology can be used to teach how other systems evolve, from the spread of epidemics like AIDS to the spread of technology like fax machines or the dispersion of ideas via advertising. Checking theories against empirical data to determine if a system is operating as expected is both good science education and widely applicable in the world of work.

For traditional "softer" academic courses, more imagination is needed to reconcile what is properly in their domain with skills that enhance careers. While courses in English literature should properly give the student an appreciation of Shakespeare and Milton, the course in writing may strive for goals more modest than emulating these authors. For many youngsters, the ability to organize thoughts in order to write a clear concise memo will suffice. History courses are not just cultural background; they are part of preparing students to fulfill their citizenship responsibilities. In this regard, teaching introductory economics and the associated statistical skills in conjunction with a current events or civics course would further that goal and simultaneously advance students' workplace know-how. Likewise, a foreign language such as Japanese serves as both cultural enrichment and a possible springboard to conducting business in Asia. Figure 1.7 lists some possibilities that were described in the final SCANS report.[19]

The school-to-work legislation asks students to concentrate on a career "major." Because of the generic character of workplace competencies, certainly at this relatively early level, the choice should not be seen as a narrowing of options for the student so much as a chance to explore in greater depth a field for which she[20] feels affinity. For example, a student interested in health may announce this choice by the 11th grade. She takes health-related courses and has related work experiences in her last 2 years of high school — perhaps starting even sooner and/or moving up to quite an advanced level if she is in a magnet school that emphasizes health. Upon graduation she may go to a community college for two postsecondary

---

[19] *See also* Secretary's Commission on Achieving Necessary Skills (SCANS), *Teaching the SCANS Competencies*, Washington, DC: U.S. Department of Labor, 1993.

[20] To avoid the awkward constructions "he/she" and "his/her," we will sometimes use the masculine and sometimes the feminine form of these pronouns.

years. The process might culminate with an associate degree in res-
piratory therapy, a 4-year degree in nursing, the 12 years or so needed
to become a neurosurgeon, or some combination of these credentials,
and career options. In this instance, the curriculum design should
provide the opportunity to learn workplace know-how, as well as
academic content, in the context (and language) of the health sector;
for example, scheduling in a doctor's office or a hospital admitting
office and communicating this schedule in a reliable concise memo.

To envision how these curricula might be delivered, think of
education in the next century. Computers are widely available. In
a math class students are studying the algebra of project planning
using planning software. Individual students begin by selecting health,
construction, manufacturing, or some other occupational field from
a menu. The students wrestle with allocating time, money, space,
and staff to solve a problem in a health, construction, or manufacturing situation. For many schools, the future could be now with
technology already available in computer labs.

The significance of technology in changing education is difficult
to forecast, but likely to be great. At one extreme are those, like Lewis
Perelman, who predict that electronic and chemical technology will
lead to "hyperlearning" and "the end of education" as we know
it in the near future.[21] Diane Ravitch, in a special issue of *The Economist*, hedges her bet by projecting a situation 150 years hence.[22] She
predicts teachers "will pick and choose among electronic programs."
With proper leadership, 150 weeks, rather than 150 years, could be
the timetable. It is already clear that computers give students an
opportunity to accomplish more in the classroom. Wordprocessing
programs enable drafts and redrafts of a paper that would otherwise
be written once, returned with red marks, and discarded.

This discussion of technology takes us beyond curriculum to
teaching strategy. Standards and curriculum development will specify
how many units and what type of math and science students are
required to learn. Innovative teaching — including innovative technology — will be instrumental in helping students absorb and master

---

[21] Lewis J. Perelman, *Schools Out, Hyperlearning, the New Technology, and the End
of Education*, New York: Morrow, 1992.

[22] Diane Ravitch, "When Schools Come to You," in *The Future Surveyed, 150 Economist
Years*, London: The Economist, [add date].

FIG. 1.7. ASSIGNMENTS THAT INTEGRATE THE SCANS COMPETENCIES INTO THE CORE CURRICULUM AREAS

Competency	English/Writing	Mathematics	Science	Social Studies/Geography	History
Resources	Write a proposal for an after-school career lecture series that schedules speakers, coordinates audio-visual aids, and estimates costs.	Develop a monthly family budget, taking into account family expenses and revenues and using information from the budget plan. Schedule a vacation trip that stays within the resources available.	Plan the material and time requirements for a chemistry experiment, to be performed over a two-day period, that demonstrates a natural growth process in terms of resource needs.	Design a chart of resource needs for a community of African Zulus. Analyze the reasons why three major cities grew to their current size.	Study the Vietnam War, researching and orally presenting findings on the timing and logistics of transporting materials and troops to Vietnam and on the impact of the war on the Federal budget.
Interpersonal	Discuss the pros and cons of the argument that Shakespeare's *Merchant of Venice* is a "racist" play and should be banned from the school curriculum.	Present the results of a survey to the class, and justify the use of specific statistics to analyze and represent the data.	Work in a group to design an experiment to analyze the lead content in the school's water. Teach the results to an elementary school class.	Debate the issue of withdrawing U.S. military support from Japan in front of a peer panel. Engage in a mock urban planning exercise for Paris.	Study the American Constitution and role-play the negotiation of the wording of the free states/slave states clause by different signers.
Information	Identify and abstract passages from a novel to support an assertion about the values of a key character.	Design and carry out a survey and analyze the data in a spreadsheet program using algebraic formulas. Develop a table and a graphic display to communicate the results.	In an entrepreneurship project, present statistical data pertaining to a high-tech company's production and sales. Use a computer to develop the statistical charts.	Using numerical data and charts, develop and present conclusions about the effects of economic conditions on the quality of life in several countries.	Research and present papers on the effect of the Industrial Revolution on the class structure in Britain, citing data sources used to arrive at conclusions.

Competency	English/Writing	Mathematics	Science	Social Studies/Geography	History
Systems	Develop a computer model that analyzes the motivation of Shakespeare's *Hamlet*. Plot the events that increase or decrease Hamlet's motivation to avenge the death of his father.	Develop a system to monitor and correct the heating/cooling process in a computer laboratory, using principles of statistical process control.	Build a model of human population growth that includes the impact of the amount of food available, on birth and death rates, etc. Do the same for a growth model for insects.	Analyze the accumulation of capital in industrialized nations in systems terms (as a reinforcing process with stocks and flows).	Develop a model of the social forces that led to the American Revolution. Then explore the fit between that model and other revolutions.
Technology	Write an article showing the relationship between technology and the environment. Use word processing to write and edit papers after receiving teacher feedback.	Read manuals for several data-processing programs and write a memo recommending the best programs to handle a series of mathematical situations.	Calibrate a scale to weigh accurate portions of chemicals for an experiment. Trace the development of this technology from earliest uses to today.	Research and report on the development and functions of the seismograph and its role in earthquake prediction and detection.	Analyze the effects of wars on technological development. Use computer graphics to plot the relationship of the country's economic growth to periods of peace and war.

Source: The Secretary's Commission on Achieving Necessary Skills, *Learning a Living: A Blueprint for High Performance* (Washington, DC, U.S. Department of Labor, 1992).

this material. It may even be essential. It is not just a matter of what to teach, but how to teach.

LEARNING IN CONTEXT: THE "HOW"

This year, thousands of high school students are sitting in traditional chemistry classes listening to their chemistry teacher lecture about molecules and compounds. Behind the teacher is a large chart of the periodic table of elements. Students are taking notes and, before their next big exam, they struggle to guess what Mr. Jones will ask on the test. Then they try to memorize the properties of the key molecular structures from a replica of the chart in their textbook.

Many students, especially the females, already have decided not to take Mr. Jones' chemistry course. If they are going to college, they have decided on some less rigorous (although no more interesting) course to meet the science requirements. Those not planning on college have decided not to take *any* science course. Some in Mr. Jones' class are wondering why they let their parents or academic advisor talk them into taking chemistry, knowing in their hearts that they never will see a periodic chart again if, by some stroke of fortune, they can ever get past Mr. Jones' fearful final.

Chemistry class is a different story at Southwest High School in Fort Worth, Texas. The class was asked to find the most effective, economical, and environmentally safe grass fertilizer for use on the grounds of 100 Fort Worth schools. Working together, the students prepared a plan, including a proposed timetable and budget, for doing the work. They wrote to the school district's Grounds and Maintenance (G&M) Department to find out about current fertilizing practices, and to local nurseries and fertilizer companies for information about fertilizers. They interviewed plant specialists to learn about different grasses and their fertilizer requirements and studied the chemical principles that describe how fertilizers work.

Once they did all the research and analysis and determined the best fertilizer, the students wrote the G&M Department to share their conclusions with them. The students either congratulated the department on its choice of fertilizer or urged a change in the G&M Department's practice. The Fort Worth students, working together to interview professionals in the outside world and engage in an interesting and meaningful project, were just as likely to learn the principles of chemistry as those in Mr. Jones' more traditional class.

They are more likely to remember what they learned, understand how chemistry is used in the real world, and become interested in science as a possible career.

To move away from the "hard subjects" of mathematics and science, we can examine what this approach means to teaching "softer" material such as writing. Figure 1.2 illustrated the difference between writing in school and writing at work. The most important difference is the purpose. At school the goal is to please the teacher and get a decent grade; at work it is to convey vital information, often in pursuit of solving a problem. The difference was erased in the Fort Worth chemistry class. A group of students who took on the project of writing to the G&M Department also had access to a writing teacher as a coach. The students learned workplace communication know-how in addition to acquiring writing skills.

The salient issue here is learning in context, a recommendation that goes back at least to Dewey. Learning in context is not, however, a sufficient description for what is needed. Contexts differ. William Glasser has written that children deserve a quality experience in their daily school lives. Sometime each day they should do their very best, not only rise to meet some standard. Elaborating on Maslow's hierarchy of needs, he speaks of four needs to be met: the need to belong — to love, share, and cooperate; the need for power; the need for freedom; and the need for fun.[23] These needs are met in few classrooms unless the teacher sets the right context.

Progressive education (unfairly) got a bad reputation for advocating nonintellectual pursuit of fulfillment. The nadir most likely came in the book, and later movie, *Auntie Mame*. The story's heroine puts her nephew in a "progressive" school where naked children walk about emulating the reproductive cycle of fish. Those who have read Dewey will decry the comedy. The implementation of progressive schooling was more often than not a serious departure from what Dewey advocated. The dangers of watered-down progressive education are, however, real. If context is as good as any other, if rigor can be avoided because no reliable and valid assessment is available, and if there are no clear paths through the educational racecourse, then it is likely that bad instruction will be found more often than good.

---

[23] William Glasser, *Control Theory*, New York: Harper and Row, 1984.

Three things should be kept in mind for effective learning in context as emphasized in the school-to-work transition curricula:

♦ *Producer Context* — The context, where possible, should be one in which students solve problems of the kind that employers are willing to pay to have solved. Instead of asking students to compute the change they will receive as customers in a restaurant, ask them to create a menu for a $15 prix fixe pretheater dinner.

♦ *Rigorous Assessment* — The results will have to be rigorously assessed so that students can earn skill certificates and diplomas that will give them access to careers. Employers have to value the pieces of paper that schools bestow; otherwise, students will not make the effort.

♦ *Articulated with the Next Career Step* — The work will have to fit the articulation requirements so that students can, if they want, go on to a 2- or 4-year college. The academic work should also fit employer requirements as specified in industry standards. Often, this will mean that school-based learning leads to a certificate that employers will honor. Again, this reflects an insight going at least as far back as Dewey: the primary worker in education must be the student.

The promising practices described in the Part II of this book provide practical examples of how school-based curriculum designers are reshaping programs. Chapter 2 describes a different kind of "curriculum," the curriculum at work where many high school and college students spend as much time during the year as they do at school. The issues of assessment, certification, and articulation are discussed in Chapter 3.

2

INTEGRATING STUDENTS' WORK EXPERIENCE: LEARNING-RICH WORK

As one worker from Tiger Creek mused: "If you don't let people grow and make decisions it's a waste of human life — a waste of human potential. If you don't use your knowledge and skills, it's a waste of life. . . ."

Shoshana Zuboff[1]

The "school-to-work" transition is a misleading phrase. "Transition" could be understood as passing from one condition (learning) to another (doing). The phrase conjures up the picture of two different worlds. A child leaves her mother's home to go to school and then, after graduating, she becomes an adult and goes to work. Graduation becomes a divide, separating a child's learning from an adult's world of earning a living.

This picture does not reflect the reality of the school years. Most youngsters work while in school. About two-thirds of all high school juniors and seniors hold jobs in the formal part-time labor force. Over half the employed seniors work more than 20 hours a week.[2] Some work an extraordinary 1000 hours or more during the school year — about as much time as they spend in the classroom.

---

[1] Shoshana Zuboff, *In the Age of the Smart Machine*, New York: Basic Books, 1988:414.

[2] L.S. Sternberg, S. Fegley, and S. Dornbusch, *Negative Impact of Part-Time Work on Adolescent Adjustment*, Philadelphia, PA: Temple University, Dept. of Psychology, 1992.

The picture of two separate worlds also distorts the changing nature of work. More and more learning will take place on the job; it will have to if lifelong learning is to be more than a motto. Firms like Xerox strive to remain competitive by becoming "learning organizations." Lack of job security, changing technology, and other changes in the economy make it imprudent for anyone to stop learning after graduation. For these reasons and more, "learning to learn" is the key to success for both the individual and her company.

Chapter 1 explored the subject of changes in school curriculum and teaching strategies. Now we turn our attention to changes at work needed to better integrate school and work. Reflecting more than school-to-work issues, the changes speak to the nature of work itself in the 21st century. Will we be a nation of "symbolic analysts" as Robert Reich[3] suggests; will we command the new computer technology to benefit ourselves and the global community? Or will we become nonthinking slaves to it, as Shoshana Zuboff asks? The Commission on Skills of the American Work Force posed the question as a choice between high-skills or low wages.[4] The outcome is still pending, yet one must believe that the optimistic outcome is possible if we as a nation make the right choices.

It is within our power to change school and work to bring about the "high performance" outcome. Generating momentum for those changes requires that school administrators and employers understand the convergence of their now anachronistically separate worlds. Only then will employers change what occurs at the part-time and summer jobs that youngsters fill while in school, transforming the tasks most youngsters now routinely perform into more learning-rich activities.

THE CONVERGENCE OF SCHOOL AND WORK

Corporate boards and school boards now face comparable challenges. Corporate boards, and the management teams they appoint, are inquiring: is our company becoming the learning organi-

---

[3] Robert B. Reich, *The Work of Nations: Preparing Ourselves for 21st Century Capitalism,* New York: Alfred A. Knopf, Inc., 1991.

[4] Commission on the Skills of the American Workforce, *America's Choice: High Skills or Low Wages!,* Rochester, NY: National Center for Education and Economy, 1990:135.

zation it should be to thrive in the 21st century? Parents, and the school boards they elect, are thinking: Are our schools preparing our children to earn a decent living in the new era?

Transformation is the subject discussed in today's corporate boardrooms, using phrases such as "continuous quality improvement," "high-performance learning organizations," and "market-driven quality." The new organizations alter the everyday experience of frontline workers and the role of supervisors. Flatter organizations, in which cross-trained frontline workers solve problems, replace hierarchical structures. Workers whose sole responsibilities were coming on time and doing as they were told, now join in the search for creative solutions. The new supervisor, now titled a coach, encourages colleagues to bring creativity to their work. In effect, he performs as a teacher making *learning-rich* work assignments. Figure 1.4, in Chapter 1, illustrates the workplace transformation.

Reform is a theme infusing education-related discussions for the past 10 years. Phrases like "site-based management" and "teacher professionalism" have become catchwords. The new schools alter both the students' experience and the teachers' role. Passive learning diminishes; teachers move away from the practice of filling students' heads with information to be recalled for multiple-choice or short-answer exams. The new teaching role is often described as teacher-as-coach, a "guide on the side" instead of a "sage on the stage." He guides groups of students who engage in structured learning activities or *learning projects*. The process greatly enhances student initiative and the opportunity for self-directed learning. Figure 2.1 illustrates school reform.

Neither transformation nor reform will come quickly. It will proceed in fits and starts, even in individual corporations and schools. Lip service will precede "walking the walk" as those in control cling to their accustomed power and habitual subordinates hesitate to take responsibility. But change and adaptation will take place; success will be flattered by imitation. Each year will bring more transformed workplaces and a greater number of reformed schools. As the reformed school and the transformed workplace converge, employers and educators will increasingly see that they share similar concerns. With a shared vision, communities will move forward to higher performance schools, workplaces, and neighborhoods.

Reforming schoolrooms and transforming workplaces demands new roles for teachers and supervisors. But the new roles of these

FIG. 2.1. CHARACTERISTIC'S OF TODAY'S AND TOMORROW'S SCHOOLS[5]

SCHOOLS OF TODAY	SCHOOLS OF TOMORROW
STRATEGY	
• Focus on development of basic skills • Testing separate from teaching	• Focus on development of thinking skills • Assessment integral to teaching
LEARNING ENVIRONMENT	
• Recitation and recall from short-term memory • Students work as individuals • Hierarchically sequenced—basics before higher order	• Students actively construct knowledge for themselves • Cooperative problem solving • Skills learned in context of real problems
MANAGEMENT	
• Supervision by administration	• Learner-centered, teacher-directed
OUTCOME	
• Only some students learn to think	• All students learn to think

two managers will be interestingly similar. (*See* Fig. 2.2.) Teachers will supervise and supervisors will teach. Teachers will assign meaningful projects to students and supervisors will make learning assignments for workers. Instead of the passage from a school regimen irrelevant to future work in a workaday world with no room for personal growth, there will be a gratifying integration of school and

---

[5] Source: The Secretary's Commission on Achieving Necessary Skills, *What Work Requires of Schools*. Washington, DC: U.S. Department of Labor, 1991.

FIG. 2.2. NEW VISIONS OF SCHOOL AND WORK

DOMAIN	Schoolroom	Workplace
GOAL	Reform So All Meet World-class Standards	Transform to Market-Driven Quality
1ST MANAGER	Teacher	Supervisor
FRONT LINE: Old way	Student as receptacle	Worker as machine
FRONT LINE: New Way	Student as Worker	Worker as Learner
MANAGER ROLE: Old Way	Inform, test, control	Manage, direct, control
MANAGER ROLE: New Way	Facilitate, lead, guide, assign learning projects	Coach, lead, make learning assignments
SUPPORT: Old Way	Curriculum, text, lesson plans	Fixed production plans, directives
SUPPORT: New Way	Project designs, technology, vision	Information systems corporate vision
INTEGRATE: Old Way	Unrelated individual courses	Unrelated work stations
INTEGRATE: New Way	Across subjects: inter-disciplinary	Across functions: cross-train
ORGANIZATION: Old Way	Teacher in front of 25-30 students	Assembly-line
ORGANIZATION: New Way	Work groups	Work groups

work. Learning to learn and lifelong learning will be hallmark concepts both at school and at work.

Many involved on both the school and work sides of the issue, of course, think that this picture is much too optimistic. Numerous business spokespersons call for "choice" as the only way to change school bureaucracies. Educators may refer to the influential report by the Commission on the Skills in the American Workforce, which found, in the late 1980s, only 5% of American firms worthy of being called "high performance."[6] As Bill Brock, one of the chairs of that Commission said, the good news is that many employers still think workers are sufficiently skilled and that is the bad news.

Yet, there are reasons to be optimistic. The 5% that are high performance firms are the industry leaders. In some cases they will force change on their suppliers. Only firms that practice total quality management can supply IBM, Boeing, or Ford. Vendors to Motorola must be candidates for the Baldridge award, which is given to those who practice these techniques in an exemplary way.[7] Even when coercion is lacking, firms will follow leaders that are successful. The high rate of productivity growth in manufacturing over many years suggests that high performance is catching on in that sector. High-performance ideas are also spreading to the service sector where firms as diverse as Federal Express and Ritz Carlton have received Baldridge awards. The now commonplace waves of "downsizing" and "right-sizing" are painful. But these actions require flattened organizational structures, less middle management, and heightened worker skills and initiative. The hoped for end result, once the restructuring has been accomplished, should eventually be higher wages and more fulfilling work.

Finally, one has to be optimistic because the alternatives are too bleak: an uncompetitive economy in an increasingly integrated world, falling wages for the majority of working people, and a society of very rich and very poor with a diminishing middle class. Some years ago, in a book entitled *Workforce 2000*, moderately optimistic predic-

---

[6] A hard and fast definition of high performance is elusive although many believe that, like pornography, they know it when they see it. American College Testing (ACT) is seeking to arrive at a definition in their work on national standards.

[7] The awards, named after the deceased Secretary of Commerce, Malcolm Baldridge, go to firms that seek total quality.

tions were made about the period between 1985 and 2000. Data from half way through that 15-year period show that the targets are still within reach if the book's recommendations are pursued more vigorously (*see* Fig. 2.3). *Workforce 2000*'s most relevant recommendation, in terms of the concerns addressed here, was to "improve all workers' education and skills."[8] Such an improvement would be best accomplished by changing *both* the school experience and that of the workplace where high school students already spend many hours of their lives.

THE PLACES WHERE YOUNGSTERS WORK

Millions of youngsters work part-time during the school year and full-time during the summer. Most of the jobs they hold during the school year are in for-profit organizations, generally in the so-called secondary labor market — restaurants, hotels, retail stores, and service stations. Classroom learning has little to do with performing these jobs. The disconnect also works in reverse. The jobs offer little or nothing in the way of learning experiences that can improve academic performance. As a highly noted example, McDonald's replaced numbers with food and drink pictures on its cash register keys. Afterschool jobs are often seen as competitive with school, with some justification for youngsters who work more than 20 hours weekly. However, a great number of teenagers want, need, and will continue to work in such positions. The situation prompts a creative search for latent learning possibilities in these jobs — and activating those possibilities to give young earners a more meaningful, fulfilling workplace experience.

Various traditional programs have sought to provide school-age youth with meaningful workplace experience. Cooperative education is the most long-established and widespread attempt to coordinate work and school. School-based coordinators enroll employers and make the connections. Students work for pay, usually close to the minimum wage. An estimated 520,000 students were enrolled in cooperative education in the 1979–80 year. The number fell sharply

---

[8] William B. Johnston and Arnold H. Packer, *Workforce 2000*, Indianapolis, IN: Hudson Institute, 1987.

FIG. 2.3. ECONOMIC INDICATORS

Evaluation of WF 2000 predictions at halfway point.

Variable	Workforce 2000	Actual
Real GNP ($bil., 87)	5310	5119
annual growth rate	2.9%	2.6%
GNP deflator	120.7	124.3
annual inflation rate	3.3%	3.6%
GNP/worker ($, 87)	44810	42908
annual growth rate	1.5%	1.1%
Employment (mil.)	118.5	119.3
Manu. emp. (mil.)	18.3	17.8
Interest rate (Moody's)	9	7.25
Trade surplus	-1	-95.3
Budget surplus	-123.2	-205.1

[1] Actual figures come from the August 1993 publication of Economic Indicators, and the Bureau of Labor Statistics.

Predictions for year 2000.

Variable	Workforce 2000[1]	Ec. Report '94[2]
Real GNP	6566	6186
annual growth rate	2.9%	2.4%
GNP deflator	154.2	151.86
annual inflation rate	3.3%	3.2%
GNP/worker	50122	46511
annual growth rate	1.5%	1.1%
Employment (mil.)	131	133
Manu. emp. (mil.)	17.2	N/A
Interest rate (Moody's)	7.2	N/A
Trade surplus	9.6	N/A
Budget surplus	-71.3	N/A

[1] Workforce 2000 predictions are based on growth from the 1985 statistics. The Economic Report predictions reflect growth from 1993.
[2] Employment figure predictions come from Bureau of Labor Statistics.

to 430,000 high school students in the 1989–90 year.[9]

Many students find work through agricultural education. In 1986, over 4.5 million young people between the ages of 9 and 19 belonged to 4-H clubs, sponsored by the federal Extension Service[10] and fostered by the Future Farmers of America. Apprentice relationships with employers are not a necessary, or even common, part of these agricultural programs.

School-based enterprises, where the school operates a business or activity, comprise another mode of creating work-based learning without directly involving employers. Students working in these enterprises often have an opportunity to become entrepreneurs and apply the skills and knowledge learned in their academic courses. Such applied academics also figure in carefully structured efforts, known as cognitive apprenticeships, developed at the University of Pittsburgh. Many other school-based projects, not so formally structured or well-publicized, also attempt to integrate academic instruction with workplace skills development.

Many students volunteer for community service roles, from candy stripers in hospitals to food dispensers at soup kitchens, often exploring career options. In some states, like Maryland, community service experience is a high school graduation requirement. Those supervising student workers in community services may themselves be volunteers. Students often get a real feeling of accomplishment from helping others. Turning these volunteer activities into experiences that yield certifiable skills, however, is another matter and another challenge.

"Summer time and the living is easy" goes the old Gershwin refrain. But for millions of students, it is time to make a little money and, quite typically, their first introduction to the real world of work. Most summer job holders are hired without any government assistance. But for many others, the government may find and/or finance their summer job. Every summer for the last 25 years, hundreds of thousands of youngsters (almost 700,000 in 1994) worked in the federally financed Summer Youth Employment Program (SYEP). The federal government pays the salaries for SYEP youngsters, along

---

[9] Thomas Bailey and Donna Merritt, *School-to-Work Transition and Youth Apprenticeship in the United States*, New York: Manpower Demonstration Research Corporation, 1993.

[10] *Ibid.*

with administrative and other expenses for the city, county, and state agencies which run the program. Generally, SYEP youngsters work for not-for-profit organizations and public agencies. Besides the federally supported efforts, many cities and counties make special efforts to have both public agencies and private firms hire youngsters in the summer. The quality of these experiences are, to say the least, highly varied, which is one reason why SYEP is targeted for extinction in 1996, in the guise of budget balancing. Ironically, the Department of Labor had just begun to use SYEP as an educational experience that prevented disadvantaged youngsters from losing ground over their summer vacation, and communities were just beginning to recognize the potential opportunity for work-based learning for 700,000 students. (*See* Chapter 6 for descriptions of learning-rich summer youth employment programs.)

YOUTH APPRENTICESHIP

Although millions of students are employed, few have the kind of experiences that would stand out on a résumé. Recognition of the missed opportunity has led many labor market experts to champion youth apprenticeship.

European, especially German, youth apprenticeship systems caught the attention of U.S. policymakers in the 1980s. At the time (although not in more recent years), the European and Japanese economies seemed to be clearly outcompeting the United States. In Germany, 70% of 16- to 18-year-olds are enrolled as apprentices to some employer. These apprenticeships last 2–4 years and three-fourths of the student's training takes place at work. Certified trainers supervise this on-the-job training. The training is controlled, in great part, by employer-dominated local chambers of commerce, with participation from unions and schools.

As the 1990s unfolded, some of the admiration for European labor market practices started to wane. Economists noticed that unemployment rates in Europe were much higher than in the United States. Moreover, while their unemployment was going up, ours was coming down. During 1995, the unemployment rate in Germany was over 8% compared to less than 6% in the United States. Even the Germans were losing their enthusiasm for their own system. Apprenticeships in Europe were based on stable economies, in which a young person could expect to spend his whole life in a designated occupation, often in the same firm. Employers expected loyalty and low turnover. As long as stable conditions held sway, the rigid system seemed to produce great benefits. Those who were employed in the 1970s and 1980s enjoyed good wage gains.

But rougher, more changeable economic winds blew in by the 1990s. These conditions put premium value on flexibility and adaptation. Workers, in the U.S. at least, could be expected to change their careers multiple times. Indeed, as the *Wall Street Journal* reported, the European and U.S. situations reflected virtually mirror images.[11] While the number employed in the U.S. increased by 52% between 1970 and 1990, inflation-adjusted wages (and benefits) only went up by 10%. During the same 20-year period, European inflation-adjusted wages and benefits increased by 60% while employment increased by only 10%.

Although the apprenticeship system has been a long-standing tradition in Germany, it would prove problematic to replicate this approach in the U.S. Relationships between workers and their employers are much more tenuous here. Hiring and firing are easy and occur every day. Given a better opportunity, American workers quit easily. Compared to Europeans or the Japanese they are highly mobile, ready to change jobs and locations if the grass looks greener elsewhere. Apprenticeship is not an American tradition except in construction and a few manufacturing trades, and unions rather than employers are the organizing entities. For these reasons it is difficult to find employers who will participate.

In their informative report on America's experience with youth apprenticeship, Thomas Bailey and Donna Merritt offer this observation regarding German-like apprenticeship programs in the United States: "The problems of employer participation probably explain why, after two years of very enthusiastic advocacy for apprenticeship by the U.S. Department of Labor and many of the country's most influential foundations, there are still only a handful of apprenticeships pilot projects, which probably enroll a total of fewer than 1,000 students."[12]

The most striking problem with employer participation is that the usual participants are precisely those venerable old industrial

---

[11] Front page story in the *Wall Street Journal*, 12/9/93.

[12] Bailey and Merritt, *op. cit.*

giants which are in the throes of downsizing. It is very difficult to ask them to accept new youngsters when these very firms are laying off their parents. If it takes a week of meetings to convince an employer to take on five students, the effort to sign up thousands of youngsters is beyond the capacity of most programs. Consider the burden on a high school system with a thousand juniors and a thousand seniors. If half (the forgotten half?) are to engage in work-based learning, then counselors would have to line up 200 employers at five students per site. And let us remember, school-to-work is *not* just for the forgotten half; it is for *all* students.

Thus, we have the apparent paradox that millions of youngsters are employed but only a small percentage are enrolled in cooperative programs and only a handful of students are in apprenticeship pilots. While thousands of employers depend on youngsters to operate their facilities, many thousand others are uneasy about operating with them. The problem, of course, is that youth are mainly employed in so-called secondary labor markets — where earnings are low, learning is modest, and advancement is rare.

The issue of employer participation is one of numbers, of tradition, of lack of "bottom line" conviction and know-how in absorbing and training new young potential workers without threatening existing workers. There are almost 3 million high school juniors and seniors. How will we find employers for most of them? One employer participation strategy is developing apprenticeships in manufacturing and construction, two sectors which, combined, only employ about 23 million persons in total. However, the total potential apprentice rolls in these sectors would be only a fraction of that number. Another strategy is to begin where the youngsters are already employed: in the secondary labor market, in summer jobs, as volunteers, as well as in cooperative education and apprentice pilots. Clearly, resources will need to be allocated to help small and mid-sized firms take on this important new function of providing meaningful work-based learning opportunities.

Reportedly, one in 12 youngsters will work for McDonald's. This figure is virtually identical to the total number of U.S. high school juniors enrolled in cooperative education (8%), and more than twice the nationwide number of cooperative education high school seniors (less than 4%). Obviously, a strategy which goes where the jobs already are is more likely to cover a substantial fraction of the youngsters. However, this strategy makes the on-the-job pedagogy more difficult. Many are skeptical about the real learning possible at a fast food operation where one makes change with a picture cash register. On the face of it, manufacturing and construction are more desirable apprenticeships; in them, the application of hard-won academic skills like mathematics is evident.

So, if the second strategy to employer participation is chosen as the only feasible way to reach a large fraction of high school students, a major challenge presents itself: convincing these employers to transform and enrich the jobs they offer youngsters. Is there a way to show employers that such a transformation is in their own long-run best interest? A manager of a restaurant or retail store, worried about competition from down the block, unhappy about the tax and regulatory burden she already carries, may not be eager to take on educational tasks because the tax-supported school cannot do the job alone. She must be sold on the idea that learning-rich work is valuable to her bottom line. She also must be shown how to make the retooling easy to do, yet well-tailored to the needs of her operation. The employer (and supervisors) must be motivated, along with the teachers and the students, to make work-based learning effective. Two of the case studies provided in Part II, *WorkPlus* and *McDonald's*, take on these challenges.

MOTIVATING THE ACTORS

Teddy and Eric were, in the summer of 1993, 15- and 16-year-old residents of downtown Baltimore. They were enrolled in a dropout prevention program for at-risk students called Maryland's Tomorrow. They were also eligible to be hired for the city's Summer Youth (SYEP) program and were assigned to work at the Johns Hopkins University. During the 6 weeks that they were on the Hopkins campus, the two young men learned how to use a state-of-the-art wordprocessing program (WordPerfect 6.0); installed the program at a number of offices around the campus and provided technical backup to its users; and developed a newsletter, using the computer to fax it to offices where other young persons were employed.

They became the communication link between the city and the 42 other SYEP youngsters also working at the Hopkins complex. The newsletter and faxes told the youngsters about paydays and special events. They were the means for informing the administration of problems in the field. When a problem arose between one youngster and her Hopkins supervisor, Teddy found out about it and brought in the SYEP site supervisor to straighten it out.

Teddy and Eric were not involved in "make work;" instead, they performed a valuable service for Johns Hopkins, for the city, and for the other summer employees. They did not stand at the copying machine all day, refile old documents, or do other tasks the regular staff wanted to avoid. Instead, the two young men did jobs that few others were capable of performing. Their summer jobs were not boring, but *learning-rich*.

Teddy and Eric also practiced some high school math when they worked on a survey of their colleagues. They improved their writing skills by preparing memos and the newsletter. They brought some of this experience back to their schools because their Maryland's Tomorrow "Advocates," who were assigned to their schools, knew about their work at Hopkins. The two high school principals (Teddy and Eric go to different schools) allowed them to travel to Washington, DC, later in the year to attend a meeting and speak to senior policymakers at a Department of Labor conference. The experience had many valuable impacts for all involved. Initially, Teddy and Eric were not able to fully realize a connection between their summer experience and the academic subjects they studied in school. After several phone calls and letters between their summer worksite supervisor and school personnel, they received elective credit for what they learned at work.

As can be seen from this real-world example (*see* Chapter 6), three important groups are involved in work-based learning: employers, educators, and students. Work-based learning will succeed as a school-to-work transition strategy only if it really helps each party in this three-way effort achieve their own goals (*see* Fig. 2.4). What will motivate employers? Higher profits, a better image in the community, and a chance to make a social contribution are all possible inducements. Employers want performance that is genuinely useful to the enterprise.

Policymakers devote much of their attention to those at the top of organizations — the business owner or executive. Good workplace learning, however, requires participation from line supervisors. One size will not fit all. The people in everyday contact with young workers are the most instrumental players in determining if the youngsters are going to have a positive, learning-rich work experience. Each workplace must invent — or reinvent — its own set of tasks. For

---

FIG. 2.4. MOTIVATING THE THREE ACTORS IN THE WORK-BASED LEARNING DRAMA

Supervisors: The effort they put into supervising the youngsters should be worth it, in terms of both the useful work the students perform and the benefits that the youngsters gain.

Teachers: The youngsters should acquire skills that are valued in academic circles and the program should give the teacher or coordinator as little hassle as possible.

Students: The work should be interesting, useful, and leave them with skills that are valued by potential future employers (all of this, ·of course, in addition to being paid and/or receiving the school credit).

---

example, a hospital administrator may take lead responsibility for the inception, perhaps the design, of a health-related youth work program using either volunteers or paid employees. But it is the nursing supervisor who will have to choose the actual tasks assigned young workers, provide them support at work, and assess their performance. It is his responsibility to assure that the work assignment meshes smoothly with ongoing activities and is not "make-work."

Each school also must make its own arrangements. Leadership from the superintendent and the principal is crucial. But, again, it is a serious mistake to forget about the person who sees the student daily, the classroom teacher. Successful programs motivate teachers to change their curriculum and influence their school district so that students receive academic credit for workplace learning.

The intent of the SCANS effort was to provide a common language which both workplaces and schools can use. A checklist of competencies teachers and employers mutually agree on would make granting academic credit for learning workplace skills easier. Indeed, it would probably be impossible to do this without such a language. Figure 2.5 shows some instances of the way this kind of school-work linkage might work in practice.

Consider a situation in which the student learns the algebra of scheduling while also learning to use either a general-purpose spreadsheet or scheduling software. Each "variable" is a vector of hours for every one of a restaurant's workers. The work-based problem and the school-based problem are actually the same: How can we

---

FIG. 2.5. EXAMPLES OF SCANS AT SCHOOL AND WORK

Learning planning and scheduling in mathematics;
And scheduling a workshift at a restaurant.

Using information by analyzing data in a geography class;
And collecting and analyzing data on customer preferences.

Learning interpersonal skills by reading about cultural diversity in
English;
And working on a multicultural team.

Understanding systems by studying social change in history;
And monitoring error rates in food shipments and finding the source
of the problem.

Applying technology by using test instruments in science;
And using test instruments to maintain equipment.

---

assure coverage without exceeding 20 hours of work for all those
who are still in school?

Compared to the "canoe algebra" referred to in the last chapter,
this is a win-win-win situation. All three actors benefit. The work
supervisor benefits because his worker understands the math behind
a schedule or budget and, better yet, has applied the skill to help
solve a real problem. The teacher wins because, while still teaching
rigorous algebra, his students now better understand the connection
between algebra and their lives beyond school. Perhaps most importantly, the student is served because the transition — better, the
relevance — between school and work has been made.

If this integration is properly done, Teddy and Eric would see
that the workplace know-how they acquired at Johns Hopkins relates
both to their academic work and to other jobs they may aspire to
(writer of music software for Eric, law enforcement for Teddy). They
would have an opportunity to reflect on what they learned and how
its relevance extends to other academic and nonacademic areas. Fully
realized school-work integration means that relevant problems are
assigned at school and learning-rich tasks are performed at work.

ON-THE-JOB PEDAGOGY:
INVENTING LEARNING-RICH TASKS

It is no simple thing to devise meaningful tasks which serve the requirements of supervisors, teachers, and students. Both teacher and supervisor may well need to change their view of what youngsters can and should know and be able to do. They will have to speak the same language, one that can bridge their two worlds. One such language is the workplace know-how as defined by the SCANS competencies.

But even with a common language and set of goals the project is still not easy. What worthwhile scheduling assignment can a supervisor in a nursing home, or office, or construction site give a student-worker? What assignment to collect data or operate equipment will be productive? Are there interpersonal skills, such as providing customer service on the telephone, that can be learned in a work assignment without lowering the quality offered to the public? Can a student help the supervisor analyze the budget for a project and make useful suggestions for cost savings?

A procedure for inventing learning-rich tasks is outlined in Figure 2.6. This procedure was developed from the *Lessons Learned* by the *Summer Beginnings* experience documented in the promising practices section (Chapter 6) of this book. The inventors have to be the work supervisors just as the inventors of the classroom teaching strategies have to be the teachers. Educators want the work experience to confer genuinely valuable and measurable skills. They will have to live with the results of the process. No work supervisor can be expected to compromise her goal of customer satisfaction. On the other hand, young workers who sharpen and expand their abilities quickly become more useful, versatile, and valuable workers.

"Honor the youngster, honor the work" is a guiding phrase for this facilitation process. No one will give a high school junior responsibility — at school, work, or home — if they think of 16-year olds as irresponsible children without much to offer. Of course, the youngster has to honor the work too; mutual respect is needed. Only through this route can the student acquire the personal qualities noted by the SCANS commission — "individual responsibility, self-esteem, sociability, self-management, and integrity."

FIG. 2.6. PREMISES OF LEARNING-RICH WORK

As with most successful programs, the learning-rich work programs we have witnessed began with two guiding premises, namely:

1. **Honor the Youngsters**: Youngsters in work programs are capable of responsibly performing complex tasks if their supervisors are properly supportive. For our purposes, the "supervisors" are the front line staff who deal with the youngsters on a daily basis.

2. **Honor the Work**: With encouragement and guidance, supervisors can invent learning-rich tasks that are useful to the employing organization and instructive to the youngsters. That is, supervisors can design projects that are simultaneously useful to the workplace and provide the youngsters opportunities to learn the SCANS competencies.

It helps to bring supervisors together in discussion groups so that they can vent their bad experiences and hear from their peers about success. The group has to hear that "respect must be earned, not granted," "when I was their age I learned the value of a dollar," "the only scheduling skill I want is for them to come on time and ready to work," "they don't even call when they decide to skip work," and about two dozen other homilies and criticisms, most of which are not completely fabricated. The group also has to hear about how mutual respect can be built, to recall what it was really like to be a 16-year-old entering the unfamiliar workplace, and to learn that the corporate lectures on "total customer satisfaction" can translate into "learning-rich tasks" for young persons.

Figures 2.6 and 2.7 detail the premises and steps to creating learning-rich work experiences which were used in one set of case studies. Most of these, in some form, will be an integral part of program designs that are able to make workplace learning more than a slogan.

FIG. 2.7. STEPS TO A LEARNING-RICH WORK EXPERIENCE

In the course of bearing out the premises, the learning-rich work programs demonstrated the importance of the following eight steps in creating a learning-rich work experience.

1. **Management Buy-in**: The process of making youth employment learning-rich begins with buy-in from the management of the employing organization. Supervisors will not feel free to invent learning-rich work if their managers do not champion the effort.

2. **Time to Prepare**: The process, from buy-in through training the supervisors, takes considerable time. For summer programs, the process should begin at least 3 months before the program starts and should be tied to a year-round program where possible.

3. **Training the Supervisors**: Inventing learning-rich tasks requires some effort on the part of the supervisors, and usually outside support from creative facilitators who are familiar with learning-rich work. Often, supervisors need the perspective of an outsider to see the opportunities to create learning rich work within their organizations. There must be an opportunity early in the planning period for supervisors to work in teams with these facilitators to develop learning-rich tasks. A sample outline for supervisor training is provided in the first case study in the section on Learning-Rich Summer Employment Programs (Chapter 6).

4. **The Matching Process**: Once supervisors and work responsibilities have been identified, it is important to consider what criteria will be used to match youngsters with work assignments. Considerations include youngsters' vocational preferences, compatibility between supervisor and youngster, and among youngsters if more than one share a work assignment, and transportation to and from work.

5. **Reflection**: The youngsters need to understand why what they are doing is important, both to the organization and to their own development. This reflection can take the form of three questions:

A. What are you doing? What is the work that you are engaged in at the moment, during that week, and over the course of the project?

B. What are you learning? What skills and competencies are you learning (or have you learned) in order to do this work?

C. Where else can you apply what you have learned? How can you put these skills to use in projects at home, at school, and in future jobs?

6. **Documentation:** It is important to document the work and learning that youngsters accomplish. In creating a format for this documentation, one must consider its many purposes: connecting the work experience with other experiences, supporting future employment applications, gaining academic credit, and evaluating the employment program.

7. **Exploiting the Unexpected:** Unforeseen opportunities will present themselves both for the youngsters and the employing organization. These may be opportunities for learning rich tasks, or for teachable moments. Planning should provide the flexibility to make the most of these opportunities. Examples range from an opportunity to field test new products (*see* the first summer employment case study in Chapter 6) to mistakes or unforeseen challenges that provide opportunities for youngsters to reinvent their task.

8. **Continuous Improvement:** Quality requires continuously monitoring and improving the system. Assessment must be made of each year's program, and this assessment must be considered in planning for the following year. There are many things that must be considered. Did you carry out your planning and implementation in a timely fashion? How effective were the various worksites? How can you increase the quality of learning at worksites that did not meet your expectations? Should you use the same worksites again? These questions can be addressed through surveys and focus groups with employers and participating youngsters as well as by assessment of the learning that took place at each worksite.

3

MAKING INFORMED DECISIONS

He who knows others is learned;
He who knows himself is wise.

Lao-tse[1]

"Who are you?" said the Caterpillar. . . . "I-I hardly know, Sir,
just at present," Alice replied rather shyly, "at least I know who
I was when I got up this morning, but I think I must have changed
several times since then."

Lewis Carroll[2]

Johnny was in the "general" track at the local high school. He did not take the college track because his teachers told him that he wasn't college material. He didn't choose the vocational track because he wasn't interested in any of the vocational programs. Anyway, he wanted school to interfere as little as possible in his life. The general track led nowhere in particular. Johnny kept the job at the fast food store that supported his car during high school and for 6 months after graduation. Then he "retired" for a while, pumped gas, and hung out a lot until he was almost 30. By the age of 30, he had finally found a permanent factory job that paid him an annual salary of $18,000.

Permanence proved illusory; the factory closed, and Johnny is now in a training program to become a computer technician. The

---

[1] Lin Yutang, *The Wisdom of Lao-tse*, New York: The Modern Library, [year].

[2] Lewis Carroll, *Alice in Wonderland*, New York: W.W. Norton, 1971.

training isn't going well because Johnny's basic skills are a tad weak. Besides, he's not sure there are any computer technician jobs out there.

Barbara was a little smarter than Johnny. When she started high school she wanted to be an engineer, but her parents thought that it would be better for her to study something more traditional like nursing or cosmetology. She liked "working with people" and was "good with her hands," so either of these fields would serve. Her parents were also eager that she go to college. Her counselor told them, and her, that she could study either career in the vocational track and go on to the local community college. She took a mix of academic and vocational courses in high school, and a few in community college, but quit before getting a degree or qualifying for a license in either field. She got a job in a supermarket for a few years, then took a course in wordprocessing and worked in an office. Finally, in her late 20s, she decided that she really wanted to be a nurse and entered an accredited training program to prepare for a career.

These are the "pictures" that led to the current effort to change the current bumpy school-to-work transition path. The data show that, even at 30, scarcely more than one in three workers have held their jobs for more than a year. For these young people, the school-to-work transition is full of gaps or disconnects between the classroom and the workplace. Whatever is learned in one class or worksite is self-contained and isolated from the requirements of the other classes or other jobs. One purpose of the new school-to-work legislation is to improve the connections, making the transition to adulthood a "seamless" fabric rather than a crazy quilt rent with holes at each stage.

The disconnects arise because the majority of students are not well-served by today's comprehensive high school. "All too often a school's energies are focused primarily on the minority of youngsters who will go to and complete a 4-year college," said Mike Smith, Deputy Secretary of Education, in an interview. Mike sees all the Clinton administration's legislative accomplishments — School-to-Work Opportunities, Goals 2000, reauthorization of the Elementary and Secondary Education Act, and reforming direct loans for postsecondary education — as parts of comprehensive education reform. According to Smith, reform requires:

- Introducing *standards* in academic subjects for schools, and industry-recognized skills standards for entry level jobs;
- *Certificates* of mastery to document the attainment of the requisite competencies; and
- Eliminating academic, vocational, and general tracks and replacing them with *career majors* for all students, based on broad occupational clusters.

These standards, certificates, and career majors are intended to facilitate a young person's transition from student to worker. Whether they will effectively close the gaps that now exist depends on how well they are designed, and on how they are implemented at the local level.

PORTABLE STANDARDS

If the reforms succeed, Barbara's and Johnny's younger brothers and sisters will have a very different start to their working lives. Up until the 11th grade, they will follow a single curriculum of rigorous school work. This curriculum will be designed to meet new academic standards. The administration hopes that these academic standards will be in place as a result of the *Goals 2000: Educate America* Act, the centerpiece of its drive for education reform. "We need high standards," said Secretary Riley in introducing the legislation in the Spring of 1993.

This still controversial legislation seeks "standards that define what all students should know and be able to do in each subject area" along with "opportunity-to-learn standards" and "assessments."[3] Standards will come at two levels of specificity: content standards which broadly define the skills and knowledge in each subject area, and performance standards which explicitly delineate and describe what each skill entails. An example often given to illustrate the distinction between content and performance standards comes from the sport of diving. "Must do a full gainer" would be a content stand-

---

[3] At this writing, the future of NESIC is up in the air and the entire issue of academic standards is being rethought. Part of the problem is the hostile reaction to the history standards and the inclusion of the opportunity-to-learn standards.

ard; the performance standard would specify what the dive must look like. The opportunity-to-learn standard would tell the school that it must have a trained diving coach and a pool that is deep enough to use a diving board if students are going to be held to the content and performance standards.

The standards are designed to assure that Barbara and Johnnie are not a "tad weak" in basic skills. Meeting the standards assures that they will be able to pursue college-level academic work and/or training for an occupation. The goal is standards that facilitate, not frustrate, Barbara's and Johnnie's connections on the path between school and work. Standards make connections possible, as anyone who has traveled to Europe with an electrical adapter knows. Without an adapter it is a mistake to plug a "standard" 110-volt electrical appliance into a "standard" 220-volt outlet.

Academic standards should permit students to make a smooth connection between different stages of education, for instance between a high school tech prep program and certified technician training at a community college and between the community college and the state university. Proof that one has mastered the material covered by the standards should also be a valid passport into the world of work.

To return to the mathematics sequence discussed earlier, consider math standards based on current college requirements for calculus. What if the standards are: "the student must know enough trigonometry and precalculus to take the integral of $\sin(x) \cdot \cos(y)/\cotangent(x)$?" If these bits of trigonometry and precalculus are rarely needed, the youngster who asks "why do I need to study this junk?" will remain unsatisfied. Answers such as "that is the standard" or "so that someone who wants to be an engineer can get into college" will not suffice. These answers will especially fall short if Johnny knows he doesn't want to be an engineer and Barbara knows that few practicing engineers use calculus to solve real engineering problems. Academic standards that institutionalize ossified teaching practices will be worthless. They must be connectors to adult life and to real adult work.

If academic standards are like the plugs on the educational appliance, then skills standards are the receptacle into which they should fit. Aspiring lawyers know they must finish law school and be admitted to the bar, aspiring doctors must finish medical school and pass their boards. The law bar and the medical boards set the academic standards one must meet before practicing these two professions. Students choosing to study law or medicine know the system has these prerequisites; they spend years earning the credentials that will allow them to plug in. But the majority of students lack such clear-cut career goals and have no such clear standards, especially for careers that do not require a 4-year college degree.

The apparatus established by the *Goals 2000* legislation is designed to remedy this situation. The new law established a National Skills Standards Board (NSSB) to help industries develop their own standards for entry into careers. Like academic standards, skill standards can either facilitate or frustrate the school-to-work transition. Indeed, some would say that most standards — including those for lawyers and doctors — are conscious ploys to frustrate those outside the charmed circle and benefit those already inside.[4] Using occupational standards to restrict entrants from entering an occupation has a long history, at least back to the guilds of the Middle Ages.

The administration does not want the new skill standards to restrict access arbitrarily. The intent of the new legislation is to facilitate effective transition into the workforce by making connections easier. If the competencies taught and acquired in school match those needed by employers, then connections can be made. Thus, it is important to "crosswalk" between the academic standards and the skills standards. A group of business organizations, led by the National Alliance of Business, has recommended to the Goals Commission that SCANS be the basis for this crosswalk.

The National Skills Standards Board (NSSB), established by Title V of the Goals 2000 Act, has 28 members appointed by the President and the Congressional leadership. The responsibilities of the NSSB (which held its first meeting in the Spring of 1995) are to:

♦ Identify broad clusters of major occupations, and for each of these clusters establish partnerships to develop standards. The standard-setting consortia mentioned in Chapter 2, such as those for the hospitality, health, and electronics industries, are precursors for these partnerships. The board will assist the partners by disseminating information, providing technical assistance, and formulating

---

[4] James M. Fallows, *More Like Us: Making America Great Again*, Boston, MA: Houghton Mifflin, 1989.

long-term plans for crafting and applying the standards.

+ Endorse *systems* that include both the standards themselves and a means to assess individuals and certify that
they meet the standards.

+ Coordinate the skill standards and the academic content
and performance standards.

Each of these three broad areas of responsibility constitutes an
enormous challenge. Such a comprehensive system of standards,
and the mechanisms to update and enforce them, are unprecedented.
Completing the plan as envisioned and having it in place by the end
of the century will be very ambitious achievements, given the challenge and the current level of Congressional hostility. Yet, the result
will qualify as a success if the new system actually makes the connections between school and adult life significantly more effective. On
the work end, connections may only be possible if the standards
are consistently gauged in terms of a generic set of workplace competencies such as the workplace know-how developed by the SCANS
commission.

There is another set of connections that call for generic workplace
know-how. Americans are likely to change jobs a half-dozen times
or more during their work lives. It is important, therefore, for skill
standards to be as "portable" as possible. Returning to the electrical
appliance simile, it would be tough for manufacturers if every state
and every business had its own "standard" voltage. Analogously,
educators will be faced with an impossible challenge if every industry
has its own unique twist on what its own skill standards should be.
Of course, all careers do not require identical versions of the same
skills — but skills do have a consistent generic typology.

Similarly, the utility company (read employer) would be challenged if every state that manufactured appliances (read educators)
designed their own plug. It is much better if everyone could agree
on a common design. Again, schools could differ in what they
emphasize, but they should use a common language where possible.
Career academies, or magnet high schools that emphasize the arts
or sciences, need not all turn out the same student, but there should
be sufficient agreement on standards for employers to know what
to expect.

Generic workplace skills, such as those developed by SCANS,
can be a universal adapter that will connect school to work or, better

yet, students to careers. Time will tell if generic "workplace know-how" can bridge the differences between the various academic standards and industry skill standards. In the meantime, efforts continue on a number of fronts to develop tests and assessments for the workplace know-how as defined by SCANS. It is encouraging that efforts are being made to use a common set of definitions in both the manufacturing and service sectors (*see*, for example, Chapters 5 and 6).

TESTS, ASSESSMENT, AND CERTIFICATION

Some wag has said there will always be prayer in school as long as students pray to avoid failing their finals. Too often, tests are used to track students, eliminating the mathematically challenged from engineering or the academically challenged from the college track. Starting in World War I, psychometric, multiple choice testing has been a procedure for differentiating or sorting individuals to screen out the less desirable. Today's Scholastic Aptitude Tests (SAT) are a direct descendent of these *sorting tests*. The premise is that intelligence is inborn and independent of schooling. These tests are a device for disconnecting.

But, increasingly, many now question the educational paradigm when tests evoke fear. Medical practice suggests a better model. Physicians use tests diagnostically to prescribe remedies for a dysfunction. While patients may "pray" for a good test result, most will not cheat on a physical exam. We think finding out what is wrong will, in the long run, be helpful to us. Coaching for sports or teaching the arts are similar; the coach/teacher is seeking ways to improve her students' performance in an activity both value. *Assessment* is a better word than tests for this model. Assessment then connects the student to a corrective action.

Finally, there is *certification*. Certificates are devices designed to make connections. One institution certifies to another that a standard has been attained. The American Red Cross certifies to the beach patrol or swimming pool management that the student is able to save people from drowning; the welding school certifies that their graduates can produce a good weld. Obviously, testing is part of the certification process, but there are important differences between a final exam or SAT test and a certification process.

Both student and teacher know what will be on the certification test. Teaching is directed to passing the test and it would be considered improper for there to be any "trick" questions. There is no need for the test-maker to keep the questions in a safe; everyone knows what has to be learned. The test is established by a valid third party, such as the Motor Vehicle Administration. Both teacher and student are motivated to see the student pass. There is a *standard* of competency that every student is expected to attain, rather than a *sorting* to determine who wins and who loses. The motivated student will take the test multiple times if needed to obtain the certificate.

A certification process might require high schools to certify that the graduate is ready for college or responsible work. Unfortunately, too few high school diplomas carry that meaning today. John Bishop made the point that few employers ask for high school transcripts, with the result that American high school students put in considerably less effort than their Japanese counterparts. Indeed, American students put in 30 hours weekly, while the Japanese are occupied twice as many hours in school and homework.[5] One might think this was all a function of culture except for the fact that once in a postsecondary status, American college students work harder at their studies than their Japanese counterparts. In Japan, high school is the career-maker (because performance there gains entry to the right college); in the U.S. it is college performance that counts.

Thus, one reason for establishing certificates of mastery is motivating students who now feel that their high school performance has little to do with success at the next step, unless they are seeking entry into an elite college. A related goal is to hold schools accountable for having their students reach a level of mastery.

Certificates, based on standards, serve two purposes. First, they systematize the connections between school and work, providing the specs for the plug and the receptacle. Second, they motivate the workers in the system — most importantly the students, but also the educators in the schools and those who supervise the learning at work.

---

[5] John Bishop, "What's Wrong with American Secondary Schools? Can State Governments Fix It?" in *Economic Consequences of American Education*, edited by Robert Thornton and Anthony O'Brien, Greenwich, CT: JAI Press, 1993.

The promising practices described in the next section illustrate some approaches to the problem of assessment and certification. A "portfolio of authentic performance" is described for youngsters employed in the Summer Youth Employment Program (SYEP). Asking the supervisors to create learning-rich work experiences is a challenge. Asking them to make out report cards for their young charges requires even more. Yet, it is characteristic that real supervisors evaluate their workers and are a source of recommendations, a connection to the next job on the career ladder. Moreover, if the supervisor evaluates a young worker's learning it is more likely that learning will take place. In school and at work, people pay attention to what is assessed or measured.

CHOICES, NOT TRACKS

A different kind of assessment can help students choose a career major. A good school-to-work program will give students a chance to assess their own capacities and match them to the requirements of particular occupations. Holland's *Self-Directed Search*, for example, assesses student characteristics and matches them to occupational characteristics. A close match promises job satisfaction, while a mismatch often leads to quick turnover.[6] American College Testing (ACT) has a comparable product. Students who have chosen a career major like health, retailing, engineering, and so on, will begin to build the connections they need. If the student understands the requirements for her chosen field, she — like those with ambitions for law or medicine — will begin to take the steps needed to meet them. Her selection of school courses, part-time jobs and other experiences will reflect her choice.

Choices today, as illustrated by Barbara and Johnny, are usually made among two or three tracks on the basis of very sketchy information. "School today has a 'good' track leading to a 4-year college and, all too often, another track that leads to nowhere special," said Ricky Takai at the U.S. Department of Education. Even where states have presumably eliminated general tracks, he noted, student transcripts disclose that no cohesive course of study has been followed.

---

[6] *See* John L. Holland, et al., "Validity of vocational aspirations and interest inventories," *Journal of Counseling Psychology*, July, 1990;37:337–42.

This pattern is also followed by the majority of community college enrollees. Most take a smattering of courses which clearly do not constitute a cohesive program, and too many do not graduate.

As Mike Smith, at the Department of Education, and others, such as the State of Oregon, interpret current policy, all existing tracks will be eliminated, to be replaced by a single track leading to a career path initially started in the 11th grade. These paths will presumably be between health and banking careers, or between construction and hospitality or other career clusters in which the initial choice does not imply either going to, or foregoing, a baccalaureate degree. Later, well after the 11th grade, further choices can be made between being a paralegal or lawyer, a lab technician or a surgeon. The idea is not to burn any bridges early. Eleventh grade is too soon to make any kind of irreversible commitment. The new connections between school and work should not come at the expense of the connection between high school and college.

Implementing a process whereby students make their initial choices in an intelligent fashion is not easy. Psychological reality is that most young people (and even those who are not so young) find a decision on what to do with one's life extremely elusive. Ask any successful adult over the age of 40 whether she had planned her life to bring her to this point in her career. Typically, she will relate to you a series of fortuitous accidents and coincidences. "Perhaps looking back," she will say, "I can make sense of my life and the success I have had. But there is no way I could have foretold it, especially when I was in high school."

Choosing among career clusters in high school should also reflect the realities of today's economy. Workers can generally expect to change jobs often; they must avoid being trained for narrow specialties that may be eliminated by technological advances or the vagaries of international trade. What's most important is to learn a set of workplace competencies that can be adapted and utilized in alternate career settings.

Learning how to decide among career fields may be more important than the "career choice" made in 11th grade. The first step in the process is getting the right information to make an intelligent decision. A student probably has some idea what kind of activity and work setting appeals to him, and a pretty good idea of his strongest abilities. But he may not have access to a sophisticated assessment process that can help him put these aptitudes and affinities in the proper context — what careers make the most of the skills he has to offer, what those careers involve, and their potential rewards. Nor have most students had the opportunity to test their interests or inclinations in a real-world environment, either through job-shadowing, site visits or work experience. Unfortunately, many students will find it difficult to get that information. Moreover, those they might turn to — school counselors, parents, mentors, or others in the community — are not often well-equipped to help. Sometimes students are even subjected to downright misleading, misguided, or irresponsible pressures. The decision is too big and complicated to reach alone, but open channels of sound guidance are not always available either.

COUNSEL FOR THE BIG DECISION, AND FOR THE LITTLE ONES

School counselors are a group under challenge. Their case loads are very high: 200 students is common, many more than that not uncommon. Additionally, the need for emotional counseling is on the increase. Besides, school principals often use their counselors as special assistants to handle the multitude of crises that too frequently intrude on the school day.

Many changes will have to take place for career major destinations to be more than a bureaucratic charade. Principal and school administrators must be convinced that career counseling is as important for the noncollege-bound student as the college choice is for the baccalaureate candidate, if not more important. The entire in-school and outside-school mentoring and guidance infrastructure needs to be expanded and reshaped to accommodate the needs and interests of the "forgotten half."

Parents are inevitably part of the process, at a time when for various reasons parenting has become more difficult. Single parents and parents who both work full-time to maintain an adequate standard of living, often cannot help their offspring reach a wise career decision. Perhaps many parents as well as many schools overemphasize college as the only avenue to career success because of their inability to pick a winning occupation. The community as a whole must look to its youth as an important resource. Informal — and some formal — mentoring goes on in most communities; at its best it can be very effective. Many young people find making a successful school-to-work transition difficult because the adult world of work is too much like a "black box." Interested citizens could find personal and civic fulfillment by opening that box, giving students and novice workers a clearer view of the responsibilities and rewards they can expect as they claim their maturity.

4

THE FUTURE: A VISION OF SCHOOL-TO-WORK ON THE INFORMATION HIGHWAY

Most of what follows is about programs that have worked or are being tried. We look to the past so as to deal wisely with the future. One thing we have not examined is the use of technology in school-to-work (STW). Yet, technology surely is a cause for the widening gap between those with and without education and skills. Can it be used to help STW? The following scenario outlines one possibility for its use.

A POSSIBLE STW WORLD IN 2005

Imagine the year 2005. Successful school reforms are achieving the National Education Goals. Every state has implemented its own successful STW program. Skills standards have been adopted by industry clusters working with the National Skills Standards Board (NSSB). Youngsters transit from (reformed) schools to (transformed) workplaces through a seamless system. Most adults are life-long learners. All states are using the nation's information highway to help young students make the transition from adolescence to productive adulthood and to help adults make the transition from welfare, unemployment or underemployment to a promising future.

The information highway carries one-way television on demand, two-way (teleconference) video, and data. High-quality education is available on broadcast TV, interactive seminars on two-way video, and labor market information, and other relevant data are available via electronic mail, electronic bulletin boards, and other media. Millions of students, teachers, employers, parents, counselors, and others use the highway to facilitate the transition from school to work.

Figure 4.1 summarizes this litany of possibilities for each of five groups — students, parents, teachers, work supervisors, and counselors, as described below. The students and their parents are shown in the top two rows of the table. Students participate in three elements shown in the three columns: school-based learning, work-based learning, and the counseling that connects the two worlds.

STUDENTS

Students, the most important group, receive information at their homes, in schools, at their jobs, in the counselor's office, and at the one-stop employment office. Students view videos about the requirements for entry-level jobs, for career ladders, and for colleges. They use tools such as wordprocessing and scheduling software, tapping into databases for school assignments and to complete tasks at work, taking tests to determine their career aptitudes and interests, entering their réumés and transcripts and filling out job and college applications. Students' educational plans are available along with these assessments (with appropriate codes to protect confidentiality). Teachers can and do customize instruction to meet the needs of individual students.

By the year 2005, the following milestones had been passed:

1995 – The NSSB began operation.

1996 – American College Testing (ACT) completed National Jobs Task Analysis.[1]

---

[1] ACT now has a contract for the task analysis. See *Performing a National Job Analysis Study: Overview of Methodology and Procedures,* ACT, 1993. ETS is developing an electronic system, **WorkLink** to maintain and transmit high school transcripts.

FIG. 4.1. USING THE INFORMATION HIGHWAY FOR THE SCHOOL-TO-WORK POTENTIAL APPLICATIONS

	SCHOOL-BASED (Teachers)	WORK-BASED (Supervisors)	CONNECTION (Counselors)
Students	Class Projects, Homework	Work Assignments	Career Choice Job Search
Parents	Assessment Conference with the Children's Teacher	Evaluation Conference with their Children's Supervisors	Career Choice
CURRICULA	Projects: Fort Worth, New Standards Project, Associate Degree, Arts Projects	Learning-rich: Summer Youth Employment Program, Apprentice, Work-PLUS	Career Exploration: Requirements and Opportunities
ASSESSMENT	Portfolio	Resume	Interests and Aptitudes
TOOLS	Academic and Business Software	Business Software	Matching Jobs and Job Seekers
DATA	Library and Case-study Data	Business and Industry Data	Labor Market Projections

1997 – Industry began to adopt national standards.[2]

1998 – ACT, the Educational Testing Service (ETS), and others developed instruments to assess generic workplace know-how.

1999 – Industry and cross-industry skill certificates began to be widely used by employers.

2000 – Full-scale assessment of workplace know-how began.

2005 – Most job applications call for skill certificates and assessments of workplace know-how.

PARENTS

Parents, too, use the highway to see how their children are doing and what their homework assignments look like. They engage in two-way video conferences with their children's teachers, counselors, and work supervisors. Parents help their children choose colleges and careers. Some parents use the same services for their own career planning. They, and their children, have access to labor market information provided by national, state, and local organizations, both public and private.[3]

CLASSROOM TEACHERS

Classroom Teachers share good projects, curriculum, and materials among themselves. There is an extensive database of curriculum

---

[2] The National Skills Standards Board started working with industry groups during 1995. Some of these industry groups are among the 22 that began working on industry standards in 1993 and 1994 and published results in 1994 and 1995. See *Setting the Standard — A Handbook on Skill Standards for the High-Tech Industry*, Washington, DC: American Electronics Association Workforce Skills Project, 1994, and *The National CADD Skill Standards*, Washington, DC: Foundation for Industrial Modernization, 1994.

[3] At present, such information is provided electronically by the National Occupational Information Coordinating Committee (NOICC) and its state counterparts (SOICC). The *New York Times* has also computerized its classified section. *See also* T. Plewes, "The LMI Bridge on the Information Highway," *Workforce*, Spring, 1994.

and project ideas that have been tried and evaluated.[4] Many of these integrate school and work and teach academics in the context of "workplace know-how." Some of these projects were developed in the 1990s at Fort Worth or in the New Standards Projects and by innovative classroom teachers all over the nation.[5] In addition to these services that teachers can call upon on their own schedule (asynchronous services), they use two-way video to have teleconferences with peers and experts (synchronous interactive services).

Middle and high school teachers also assign work that can be done with the help of services available on the information highway. *"Read this book, watch that TV show that is available in the electronic library, take this computer course, study datasets A and B that are available on the Internet,"* are the normal stuff of homework assignments. Community colleges use courses offered on the highway by other community colleges, by 4-year colleges, and by others who develop and market courses for credit.[6]

Work Supervisors share good "learning-rich" tasks among themselves in both an asynchronous (using databases,[7] including video, that had been previously stored) and synchronous interactive (using two-way video) fashion. They also assign tasks to their workers in a manner that resembles the way teachers give assignments to their students. *"Read this manual, learn how to do this task, take this computer course, study that data."* Again, a database of successful learning-rich tasks has been developed and documented in the work-based

---

[4] The Education Department in the state of Delaware is planning to develop such a service. Also, there are electronic bulletin boards already in operation which offer this information in a less comprehensive fashion. These include HandsNet, Scholastic, and others.

[5] The workplace know-how may be the SCANS competencies. The New Standards Project (NSP), established by Marc Tucker and Lauren Resnick, is developing and testing school-based projects. Project C3 at the Fort Worth Independent School District (FWISD) is part of NSP and is also independently developing classroom projects. Also *see* Chapter 5.

[6] *See* Arnold Packer, *An Associate Degree in High-Performance Manufacturing,* unpublished paper, Johns Hopkins University, 1994.

[7] HandsNet's Youth Development Forum already includes many sample learning-rich tasks and support materials for supervisors. HandsNet is operated by the HandsNet Organization, Cupertino, CA.

and apprenticeship programs that sprung up around the country during the last decade of the 20th century. The learning-rich tasks appear in both primary and secondary labor markets; they range from tasks performed in Siemens electronics factory to work done at the Marriott hotel and McDonalds.[8]

WORK SUPERVISORS AND HUMAN RESOURCES DEPARTMENTS

Work supervisors and Human Resource Departments access on-line résumés of youngsters who want jobs. They conduct interviews via two-way video. They also assess the work-based learning that takes place at the job and enter their evaluations into the database. These data entries update the students' résumés and are used by the school system to strengthen their curriculum and develop customized courses.

COUNSELORS OF STUDENTS

Those Who Counsel Students find out about job and college requirements and opportunities. They advise youngsters about courses to take, lectures to listen to, and career paths to explore. They can access video created by industry groups who developed standards during the last 5 years of the 20th century. They also receive data about labor markets, employer requirements, and training and education opportunities. Counselors have access to student assessments, worker résumés, and job openings.

WILL THE INFORMATION HIGHWAY BE READY?

How likely is it that the technology will be able to support these possibilities (and many others) in the next 10 years? According to one survey, in December of 1983, 2 million microcomputers were

---

[8] P/PV's Work-PLUS project began in the spring of 1994 and is directed to the secondary labor market. Even earlier, McDonald's began their **National Youth Apprenticeship Model.** Also see T. Bailey and D. Merritt, *"The School-to-Work Transition and Youth Apprenticeship: Lessons from the U.S. Experience,"* MDRC, 1993; A. Packer and F. Stluka, *"Developing Learning-Rich Tasks for Summer Youth Employment Programs,"* Johns Hopkins University, 1994; Ed. Pauly, H. Kopp, and J. Haimson, *"Home-Grown Lessons: Innovative Programs Linking Work and High School,"* MDRC, 1994.

in place in education settings of all types: schools, colleges, and private and public training sites. By December, 1993, 16.2 million were in place (all exclusive of student-purchased machines).[9] Even if the growth rate slows, most students will have access to computers by the end of the next decade. These machines are valuable in their own right. Many have the capacity for multimedia. With the appropriate accessories, computers can already hook into information highway services such as Internet.

Will the highway technology be able to carry out the vision described above a decade from now? Progress, although uneven, is being made. The Iowa Communication Network (ICN) fiberoptic system supplies data, voice, and interactive video from 128 classrooms to all of the state's 99 counties. A linkup of 662 sites is planned by 1999. The *New York Times* reported that Southern New England Telecommunications (SNET) announced that it would "... completely rewire Connecticut over the next decade with $4.5 billion of fiberoptic cable. That will allow video, voice, and data. . . ."[10] By 1996, West Hartford should have access to 300 or more television channels. Bell Atlantic has installed an innovative system in Union, New Jersey, which provides many of these capabilities (including parent-teacher conferences).[11] Bell Atlantic is also moving forward in Maryland with two systems: one to provide two-way video and another to provide dial-tone video. Bell Atlantic offered to make this technology available for educational purposes. The company also offered up to $50,000 in equipment to link each of the state's public high schools, colleges, and universities in a statewide network. Schools, however, will be charged about $1,350 per month for the service. Meanwhile, in July of 1995, the Federal Communications Commission approved Pacific Bell's plan for its Video Dialtone service, which includes high-speed Internet access. The company announced it would start installing the video portion of its service in areas of California covering 1.3 million homes.

---

[9] W. Bozeman and D. Baumbach *Educational Technology, Best Practices from America's Schools*, Princeton, NJ: Eye on Education, 1995:3.

[10] The first page of the *New York Times*, April 17, 1994.

[11] *Washington Post* Education Section, April 3, 1994, p. 25.

Back on the East Coast, Bell Atlantic ultimately hopes to offer dial-tone video in the home. Under one option being considered, the service will provide an image of a shopping mall on the user's television set or computer monitor. Customers are envisioned as cruising the mall and entering the movie house or dress shop or library. It takes little to imagine schools, libraries, and employment offices sharing space on the mall. Clearly, progress will come in fits and starts; *The Wall Street Journal* headline for July 24, 1995, was "Phone Giants Discover the Interactive Path is Full of Obstacles." These obstacles include "Headaches of the Hardware," "soaring costs, regulatory hurdles, and uncertain markets for interactive services." Still, even the pessimists expect one-fourth of U.S. households to have such services by 2005.

The hardware will progress. Software and content are the real issues. These are some reasons for optimism. The Public Broadcasting System (PBS) recently announced *Ready to Earn*. This program will use broadcast video classes leading to an associate degree. Other activities might include "work-centered curriculum, professional development, career education, [and] industry profiles. . . . " PBS is considering strategies other than broadcast, such as "video-conferencing, interactive online networking, CD-ROM. . . . "[12] August of 1994 saw the debut of the *Colorado Workforce Channel*. Deputy Secretary of Labor Glynn was involved in the PBS announcement and the effort was supported by Department of Labor.

Is this enough? Today, technology is not widely used to inform and give students practice in the generic skills needed in the workplace.[13] What sort of software or content will be developed? The case study described in Chapter 5 (Community Colleges) provides a hint of what may come. A similar project, linking middle schools, high schools, employers, parents, and community centers in Baltimore to each other and to curriculum and employment databases just received funding under a U.S. Department of Education "Technology Learning Challenge Grant." More importantly, as the technology begins to reach a market in the next few years, SNET, Bell Atlantic, and other telephone and cable companies will look for vendors (e.g.,

---

[12] Personal Letter (sent to the *Ready to Earn* Advisory Group) from PBS, dated 3/9/95.

[13] Elizabeth Mathias.

those selling movies, ties, or books) who want space on the highway. Authors will sell their products through entrepreneurs who will perform the way publishers of textbooks do today. However, tomorrow's publishers will market and deliver the products electronically. ACT, ETS, and others will be offering their tests on the highway. Other newspapers will follow the *New York Times'* lead and make their classified help-wanted section electronic and put it on-line. Industries that are developing standards will advertise for help or will sell the rights to their standards to electronic publishers. (The CADD standards are now on sale for $22.50 a copy!) Myriad other opportunities will be seen and exploited by the market.

At issue is whether the information highway will serve public interests, or only be used for commercial purposes.[14] Specifically, will this emerging new information resource help in achieving the STW goals? Will the vision sketched above be realized? The answer will depend, in great measure, on whether the nation continues to pursue STW. That answer will determine whether the projects described in the following pages are precursors to a fully functioning system that will emerge over the next decade.

---

[14] After all, the original electronic networks and much of the current infrastructure were developed with public money.

PART II:
PROMISING PRACTICES

Promising Practices:
Introduction

The School to Work Opportunities Act was signed into law in May, 1994 and the first state implementation grants awarded shortly thereafter. But interesting and innovative classroom/workplace connections have been enriching the learning experience for kids in many parts of the country for several years. They have grown out of local ingenuity or local economic development needs. They have received financial support from state legislatures, foundations and the federal government. They are not yet systemic in vision or reach, but in toto, the 23 examples cited in this Part represent rich and varied approaches to making the path from schooling to careers more thoughtfully focused and ultimately more successful.

In reviewing these case studies, several points should be kept in mind. First, there is no single "right" model, no one size fits all, no catalog number to order. Hard work at the local school and community level is needed to craft the components that will spell success. Second, as can be gleaned from the stories that follow, there is no single point of origin as the base for program activities. Middle schools, high schools, community colleges, workplaces, large and small, national and local . . . each and all have spawned innovations worthy of study and emulation.

The school to work movement is still in its fledgling state. But there is much to learn from the pioneers whose stories are told in this section.

5

SCHOOL-BASED PRACTICES

INTRODUCTION

Chapter 1 of this book addresses what schools must do if they want to prepare their students for the world of work. The "promising practices" you are about to read describe 10 ways that educators have attempted to reshape schooling so that it achieves this goal. They range from middle school projects that mostly only affect one class or grade, to a national program that attempts to create a community college curriculum, test it in several sites, and make it available nationally. They include programs that have been in practice for over 20 years, and plans that have not yet been implemented.

These school-based practices attempt to engage their students in learning projects that are authentic — their content and/or structure reflects the world of work — yet they are programs and projects that have been achieved primarily by the efforts of schools.

The elementary and middle school practices were submitted by teachers who conducted them to a contest sponsored by Scholastic's *Instructor* magazine. The contest asked them to describe projects they were using to integrate subject areas and teach the SCANS skills and competencies. Projects described range from media projects conducted entirely at the school to entrepreneurial projects that worked extensively with business partners.

The high schools practices include the complete revamping of a high school curriculum for all students at the school (Roosevelt), implementation of programs that create "schools within schools" for a group of students within the school (Philadelphia High School

Academies), and a program that leaves the school building behind and educates youngsters in the natural context of agricultural, environmental and related work (Smokey House Project).

Finally, the community college section includes two projects. The first is a national attempt by educators and manufacturers to revamp the community college curriculum so that graduates with an "Associate Degree in High-Performance Manufacturing " will have a balance of general and specific knowledge and skills, and a portable credential that attests to their mastery of the standards established by their industry. The second is a local effort in the suburbs of Washington, DC. The strong-point of this Montgomery College Tech Prep program is its articulation with high schools.

ELEMENTARY AND MIDDLE SCHOOLS

Imagine a group of 10-year-olds incorporating, developing a business plan, and running a profitable restaurant, then using their profits to support a nonprofit that provides food to the needy. Then imagine 10- and 11-year-olds conducting market research, and developing, manufacturing, and marketing products. Or, imagine several 13- and 14-year-olds designing and building all the machines in a working assembly line. Finally, imagine seventh and eighth grade students taking ownership of their school and cooperating with the faculty to redesign and implement the school's curriculum, grading, and student management systems. These are only a few of the projects that pioneering teachers around the United States have used to motivate their students by integrating the middle school curriculum and facilitating students' acquisition of workplace know-how.

The examples just cited suggest that youngsters are ready to start thinking about and acting upon school-to-work issues well before they reach high school. Indeed, one of the goals of most preschool and kindergarten curricula is that students develop the skills needed to "work and play well with others."

Many schools hold "career days" throughout the elementary and middle school years. Usually, these are designed to introduce students to the characteristics and responsibilities of various professions. Rarely, however, are these responsibilities linked to or backed up by a curriculum explicitly connecting work and school-based learning. Thus, an opportunity is missed to build these connections into student's earliest understandings of the role and value of education in their lives. Cognitive and developmental psychologists, however, advocate the "spiral curriculum," in which youngsters learn the rudiments of complex concepts and skills early, then refine and complete this knowledge through increasingly complex activities as mental capacities mature.[1]

The project descriptions that follow demonstrate how imaginative teachers merge the realms of school and work as early as fourth and fifth grade. These projects were culled from a pool of 54 entries to a contest sponsored by The Scholastic Corporation's *Instructor* magazine and the SCANS/2000 Program at the Johns Hopkins University.[2]

The entries fell into five categories: microsocieties, entrepreneurial projects, media publications, construction and manufacturing enterprises, and workplace-based activities.

Properly planned and executed, projects such as those described in this section can expose students to various career options and increase their potential for success. The projects cross the borders of traditional curricula, integrating and applying mathematics, science, art, social studies and language arts. They develop work skills and provide an authentic context for academic learning.

MICROSOCIETIES

Microsocieties integrate work and learning by transforming the classroom (or other environment) to model the real world. Each student has a job to perform, for which he earns a paycheck. This paycheck is then used to purchase needed goods or services from other students, faculty, or school staff. Microsocieties provide a strategy for managing one classroom, a whole school, or an academy within a school.

Approximately 160 seventh and eighth grade students at **Mohave Middle School in Scottsdale, Arizona**, function within such a microsociety. The faculty, staff, and students of House Four reorganized themselves to increase student responsibility for their own education. The whole faculty team, including five teachers, a media specialist,

---

[1] Jerome S. Bruner, *The Process of Education,* Cambridge, MA: Harvard University Press, 1960.

[2] *See* Arnold Packer, "Building Workplace Know-How," *Instructor,* September, 1993.

the school nurse, and a special education teacher, designed and implemented the project. They began by organizing the school into several "houses," or academies, each with its own team of teachers.

First, the team eliminated the artificial distinctions among traditional disciplines, and integrated them into five themes, each of which draws on all of the academic disciplines. These themes are academic skills, environment, community, cultural diversity, and the future. These themes underlie all school activities and experiences in the new curriculum.

Then the faculty and students identified "jobs" that students could perform, with titles like homework hotline coordinator, computer specialist, security specialist, and healthcare assistant. Students applied for and were hired into specific positions. Students also served on student government, leadership academy, and technology, custodial, and disciplinary task forces. Students completed job descriptions which incorporated their job requirements with learning objectives. For their work, students received paychecks, which they used to purchase school services and rewards, such as exemption from homework, or telephone use.

WHAT IS LEARNED?

The redesigned curriculum included all of the school's traditional subject matter. Additionally, students learned the skills needed in the workplace: **systems** and human **resource** skills by identifying the tasks needed to support their community, aggregating these tasks into discernible "jobs," and applying for these jobs. They learned the **interpersonal** skills needed in the workplace while carrying out their jobs, relying on others who were performing jobs that aided them, serving each other as clients, and working together on committees. By identifying, obtaining and using the various resources needed to carry out the responsibilities of their jobs, and by using their "paychecks" to purchase the goods, services, and privileges provided by other students and school staff, students learned to manage **resources**. They acquired **information** skills by studying curricular requirements and school system regulations, consulting with school staff to get the information they needed to carry out their jobs and committee assignments, and communicating this information via presentations and written reports to each other. Finally, they learned various **technology** skills by determining what tools they needed to perform their jobs, and by using and caring for these tools.

ADDITIONAL MICROSOCIETIES

The faculty of the Blue Wolves Core (academy) at **Desert Sky Middle School, in Glendale, Arizona,** created another middle school microsociety. Under the direction of the core's faculty, and with the assistance of several local businesspeople who served as consultants to the students, 120 seventh-grade students set up their own simulated town. Each student held a job in the "town's" post office, bank, court, or healthcare systems. They got fictional paychecks for their work in these jobs, as well as for time spent at school. They received bonuses for extraordinary work, and were fined when they were not prepared for class, or when they violated school rules. They spent their money for school supplies, services, and privileges. At the end of the project, they spent the balance of their account at an auction, where they bid on items donated by the community.

In Debra Toomey's self-contained fifth-grade homeroom at **Washington Elementary School in Independence, Kansas,** students received salaries for their academic work. They earned overtime when they put in extra effort on academic work, and their pay was docked when they arrived at school late. Students spent money on school services and privileges, including desk rental, school supplies, and free-time. After they got used to the payroll and banking system, some of the students took "jobs" to help support it, or started up their own businesses to provide services that were not already available, such as carrying books or tutoring.

ENTREPRENEURIAL PROJECTS

In entrepreneurial projects, students combine work and learning by researching, developing, and selling goods and services for a profit. They can be led by one teacher or more, but they usually benefit by drawing in the outside community as both clients and consultants.

In a project called *Mind Your Own Business,* 100 sixth-, seventh-, and eighth-grade students at **Smitha Middle School in Marietta, Georgia,** were assisted by consultants who came into the school, representing a variety of professions, including bankers, attorneys, and insurance agents. After describing the roles they play in the larger business community, they helped the students develop their business plan. The students produced marketing plans to determine product potential and launched advertising campaigns. They built prototypes of their products, refined them, and produced them in quantity. They produced audio and video commercials, business cards, and their own booths to house their business on Market Day, when the goods were offered to the community. After Market Day, students prepared a profit/loss statement and a business analysis.

This project is a 12-week component of a larger *Kids Business Academy* economics curriculum, developed by Glenda Wills, a master teacher of economics education at Smitha Middle School. She developed the curriculum while at Mabry Middle School in Cobb County, Georgia, and has since moved it to Smitha. It has been replicated by other teachers throughout Cobb County.

WHAT IS LEARNED?

This project emphasized the principles of market economics. To prepare for developing their own businesses, students studied biographies of successful entrepreneurs, economic trends, and such concepts as supply and demand. In followup to Market Day, the class discussed which businesses sold out, who priced themselves out of the market, who held a monopoly, and other underlying business principles. Students also applied skills they learned in other academic disciplines, especially mathematics and writing, as they developed their business plans and followup analysis, advertising, and accounting procedures.

In addition to learning much that is in the traditional school curriculum, students increased their SCANS competencies. They learned **information** skills by researching markets, production procedures and costs, and by keeping and analyzing records of their own expenses and sales. They learned about **systems** by developing, executing, analyzing, and refining their business and advertising plans, as well as by building prototypes of their products and improving them. They learned **resource** skills by identifying, obtaining, organizing, and using the materials, funds, space, and human resources they needed to develop and market their products. They learned and practiced **technology** skills by using computers to design business cards, posters and flyers, and by selecting and using various tools to design and manufacture their products, to create their audio and video advertising campaigns, and to build their sales booths. They learned **interpersonal** skills by working on teams to identify, design, and manufacture a product that would appeal to clients.

Additional Entrepreneurial Projects

At **Lippman Day School, in Akron, Ohio,** Mike Currey and Rebecca Tolson are the fifth and sixth grade math and social studies teachers. Together, they supervised students in developing and running four companies. One prepared and sold popcorn at recess. Another sold school supplies from a cart that they took to each classroom. A third prepared and sold sandwiches for lunch. The last sold a variety of snacks during recess. Students invested in stock for the company of their choice, and ran the company throughout the school year. At the end of the year, all companies were liquidated, and dividends distributed to stockholders.

Laurie Harling and Rhea Oberholtzer of **Lilburn Elementary School, in Lilburn, Georgia,** organized their fourth grade students to take over a floundering school store which had previously been managed by school staff. Students surveyed clients to determine their needs, analyzed the existing business structure and identified areas for improvement. Then they divided themselves into business departments, such as accounting, advertising, personnel, and purchasing. Students rotated departments every 6 weeks so that they would have experience in all departments. They increased store profits from $200 to $1,600 in the first year!

Media Publications

Media publication projects combine work and learning by involving students in writing stories, creating a newspaper, or developing a multimedia publication. Projects can range from a classroom newsletter or class presentations which require little cooperation from anyone outside of the classroom, to more sophisticated multimedia productions which may rely on teachers from various disciplines and consultants and clients from the outside community.

Multimedia Technology is a 10-week curriculum devised and implemented by Patrick Kern for his seventh grade social studies class at **Bulkeley Middle School in Rhinebeck, New York.** Under Mr. Kern's supervision, teams of three to five students research and develop multimedia educational units for topics such as the Holocaust, the Gold Rush, and the Women's Suffrage Movement. Students then make their presentations to the rest of the class, and lead discussions about the topic with their classmates. In addition to working on their media projects, students discuss the topics of the presentations, the processes and skills associated with multimedia production, and read and discuss articles about careers in multimedia production.

WHAT IS LEARNED?

This curriculum addresses several areas of the traditional school curriculum. While learning in-depth about a social studies topic of their choosing, students integrated the writing, mathematics, and art aspects of the school curriculum as they wrote and rewrote storylines, developed budgets, determined how much time to allocate to each section of their presentation, and chose an aesthetically appealing format.

Students gained exposure to a burgeoning industry and acquired generic workplace know-how. They learned **information** skills as they analyzed the topic of their presentation and decided appropriate formats to present this information to their classmates. They learned **interpersonal** skills by working with a team to conduct all aspects of the project, and by considering the learning styles of their classmates when developing their presentations. They learned **systems** skills by developing, implementing, and revising their production plan, and by participating in the evaluation of their own and their classmates' productions. They acquired **resource** skills by setting and modifying timelines for production and by allocating tasks to various team members. Additionally, they learned how to use and maintain the various wordprocessing, filing, taping, and other **technology** that they needed for their projects.

ADDITIONAL MEDIA PROJECTS

S.E.A. Peterson led a staff of ten 9- to 13-year-old students at **Pacific Island School in Avalon, California**, in writing, illustrating, and selling a newspaper. *The Isthmus Bee: The News* addresses issues of concern to the students and their community. It was produced solely by students, and distributed by a combination of door-to-door delivery and sales through a newspaper vending machine and at a local bookstore. Proceeds from the project supported school field trips.

Kids Learning and Teaching Zone (KLTZ) Media Services produced educational products for teachers and students at **Knowlton Elementary School in Farmington, Utah**. KLTZ was staffed by James Harris and his 44 fifth grade students, who produced weekly radio and television shows and a monthly newspaper. KLTZ also produced bulletin boards, audio tapes, and other educational products on a contractual basis. Students applied for specific jobs, such as general manager, public relations manager, equipment manager, and head editor or sports writer for the newspaper. Professionals from the community served as consultants on some of KLTZ's projects. Students also visited several media companies to learn about production processes and explore careers in this field.

CONSTRUCTION AND MANUFACTURING ENTERPRISES

In construction and manufacturing enterprises, students learn academic subject matter and work skills in the context of designing and assembling a product. The need for outside resources and cooperation among teachers will vary with the complexity of the product manufactured and whether and to whom it is sold.

For the past several years, Rodney Wheeler and Craig Uline's seventh and eighth grade classes at **Shaker Junior High School in Latham, New York,** designed and manufactured products using the *Lego Technic* modeling system. The *Lego Technic* modeling system integrates traditional *Lego* building blocks with mechanical parts so youngsters can assemble them into movable figures, such as automobiles or robots.

In seventh grade, students individually designed, constructed, and raced four-wheeled vehicles. The students' goal was to have their vehicle pull a predetermined weight across a given distance in the shortest amount of time. They used computers to monitor and control the entire race event.

In eighth grade, students worked together to develop an assembly line with eight or nine stations. Teams of two or three students designed and created the machines needed at each assembly station. Teachers predetermined the purpose of the machine (for example, to paint the assembled product) but gave the students no plan or description of how the machine should look or function. Students then set out to analyze, design, and construct the machine, while making sure that it remained compatible with the other machines being developed by other groups in the class. When they completed their individual machines, students put the assembly line together, tested and refined it.

WHAT IS LEARNED?

Over the course of these two projects, students learned to conduct their own experiments in product design and applied physics. As they faced problems with their designs, they consulted with their teachers and peers, and researched alternate solutions. The organization and sequencing of the projects were key to success. In the seventh grade project, students learned how best to invent their own technology (the vehicle) using the **technology** and **resources** available in the *Lego Technic* system and the computer system which monitored and controlled the race. With reflection, they learned to generalize these resource and technology skills to other applications. In the eighth grade, the project assumed these skills, and focused on the more elaborate **interpersonal** and **systems** skills needed to work on a team to develop and refine a manufacturing system (assembly line). The assembly line project also reinforced the **technology** and **resource** skills developed in the seventh grade by requiring students to apply them to a much more elaborate product. Throughout both projects, students learned **information** skills as they read and applied the specifications that came with the equipment, studying and comparing designs for their particular station and assembly lines generally, and communicating this information to their classmates and teachers.

ADDITIONAL CONSTRUCTION AND MANUFACTURING PROJECTS

After studying Thomas Jefferson's design of the University of Virginia, Winnifred Bolinsky led 20 fifth graders at **Fogelsville Elementary School in Allentown, Pennsylvania,** in designing their own university. After consulting with architects and surveying various colleges and universities, they broke themselves into teams to address the spatial needs of each department within the university. They consulted a real estate agent to find a site for their university, and surveyed that site. They toured a college to gather more information about considerations for layout. Then they began designing. They worked with their small groups to design areas for each department. The groups came together to make decisions that affected the whole class. They used building blocks, paper cut-outs, and computer assisted design programs to develop their designs. They used each other and their contacts at universities to decide what programs the university would offer, and the spatial requirements of these programs.

Representatives from each small group formed a landscape architecture group to design walkways, parking lots, and locate the buildings on the campus. The students worked with an architectural firm to translate their drawings into blueprints. They wrote a campus guide and designed university T-shirts. Finally, the students constructed a scale model of their university and held a ribbon-cutting ceremony to share the project with the academic community, parents, and external community who supported them.

WORKPLACE-BASED ACTIVITIES

In workplace-based activities, middle school students can learn academic and job skills in a real world-of-work setting. Coordination between the school and the place of business is crucial. The successful project requires a true partnership between school faculty and employers at the workplace. Both parties must understand each other's goals, policies, and procedures. And both must be committed to making the project a success.

Hatton's Hangout is illustrative of how such a partnership can work. Bonnie Hatton, a fifth grade teacher at **Gleason Lake Elementary School in Wayzata, Minnesota**, met Peggy Rasmussen at a *Business/Education Partnership* meeting. Peggy Rasmussen owns and operates a local restaurant. The two women hatched a plan whereby Mrs. Hatton's class rented and operated Mrs. Rasmussen's restaurant for a weekend. Mrs. Hatton served as the expert on the children's behavior management and learning, while Mrs. Rasmussen provided material resources and business information. Additionally, several other area businesspeople were invited into the classroom. They served as consultants on various aspects of the project and told the students how their careers draw on the skills and knowledge that they learned in school.

Under the two women's guidance, the students incorporated and took out a loan at a local bank to start the business. Then they studied legal concerns, such as employees' rights and health department requirements. They developed a menu, ran an advertising campaign, and did all that was necessary to serve customers, from taking orders and serving food, to running the cash register and cleaning up at the end of the night. They also kept meticulous financial records. Finally, they prepared a grocery list for a family of four, purchased the groceries with the profits from the restaurant business, and donated it to a local food bank.

What is Learned?

The 4-week curriculum addressed many areas of the school curriculum, with emphasis on writing (a business plan and publicity) and mathematics (mostly accounting). Students also learned about nutrition in preparation for menu planning and compiling the shopping list for the donation to the food bank. And they came to understand the wide variety of occupations directly involved with the operation of a restaurant, including bankers, nutritionists, and even social workers at the food bank.

Additionally, the project offered the students an opportunity to develop the SCANS competencies. They learned about **systems** by developing and implementing their business plan, and by dealing with the various bankers, suppliers, advertisers, and other professionals on whom they had to rely to run their restaurant. They developed **interpersonal** skills by working as a team to serve clients, and by consulting with many different professionals who helped them. They learned to manage **resources** by developing their budget, getting a loan, assigning people to different tasks, and doing this all in a timely fashion. They developed **information** skills by researching the many board of health requirements of a restaurant, as well as by comparing prices for the items they purchased and consulting with various experts in developing their business plan. Finally, they learned about the proper use and maintenance of restaurant **technology**, from food preparation tools to cleaning equipment to cash registers.

Additional Workplace-Based Activities

Kandie Barber and her colleagues at **Mandalay Middle School in Broomfield, Colorado,** wanted to involve their students in active citizenship, so they arranged for 140 seventh grade students, in groups of five, to spend a week serving lunch to the homeless. Each group was excused from school for 2 hours per day for this purpose. They also invited guest speakers into the school to discuss the services available to homeless people. Then the whole group toured a homeless shelter to see the facilities and learn about the services firsthand. Students also visited local libraries, where they used computerized networks to further study the needs and services provided to the homeless.

After they educated themselves on issues of the homeless, the students wanted to do more. In their teams of five students, they put together presentations on the needs of the homeless and services available to them. After rehearsing the presentations in class, they made their presentations at 20 local businesses and solicited donations to support services for the homeless. They also toured the businesses they visited to develop career awareness. They raised over $1,300. Finally, they held a board meeting, where they decided how to distribute the money they collected.

GUIDING PRINCIPLES

All of the innovative projects described in this section share common, but critical themes.

♦ **Cooperation among teachers:** Most of the projects described in this chapter are the product of two or more teachers working together. Students can then work on their projects during more than one class period per day. It also expands the knowledge base from which the teachers draw, allowing them to show students how lessons from at least two academic disciplines apply to their work.

♦ **Resourcefulness:** Teachers must take stock of the resources available to them in designing these projects. What other adults can they recruit to cooperate with them: teachers, staff, parents, community businesspeople, others? Where can they find the material or physical resources they need for the project? Or, how can they design a project to best use the resources they already have?

♦ **Flexibility:** No project goes exactly as planned. Teachers build in as much flexibility as possible to take advantage of unexpected resources or opportunities that become available or challenges that students will face.

♦ **Value the work:** As discussed in Chapter 2, it is important that projects have intrinsic value, other than the lessons that they teach. They should provide goods or services that are of value. They can provide services that help to run the school or classroom, or improve its information flow, as illustrated by the case studies of microsocieties and media publications. Or they can provide a salable product, or one that is of value beyond the school, as is the case with the entrepreneurial, workplace-based, and construction and manufacturing projects. This value helps students take pride in what they are doing, and provides motivation to do the project well.

♦ **Value the youngster:** Projects must start with the skills that students already have. Teachers and other adults involved in these projects must believe that students are able to perform at a high level. As the old saying goes, students will rise to your expectations. Teachers must be comfortable coaching students, while allowing them to design and manage their own projects.

♦ **Connections with the community:** Many of the case studies in this chapter build connections with the community by drawing in local businesspeople as consultants, employers, or resource providers. Some of the projects involve their students in work at a community organization outside of the school. Others draw on the community for clients.

There are many benefits to such connections. They make the project possible. They get the community more involved with the school. And they expose the students to aspects of their community with which they might not have been familiar prior to the project.

♦ **Reflection:** It is not enough for students to engage in these projects. Time must be set aside for them to think about what they did, why it did or did not work, what they learned from the activity, and where else they can apply what they have learned. This puts the learning in context, increases its meaning to students, and increases the likelihood that the lessons learned will be transferred to other situations.

The arts are a sixth category of projects that can be used for these purposes at any level of K–12 schooling.[3] They, too, require adherence to these principles if the projects are to succeed. Teachers have to cooperate and be resourceful and flexible. They have to value the

---

[3] See Arnold Packer, "Meeting the Arts Standards and Preparing for Work in the 21st Century," a preconference paper prepared for *Arts Education for the 21st Century American Economy* — a conference arranged by the American Council for the Arts, Louisville, KY, September 1994.

work and the youngsters, letting them make many of the judgements usually reserved to staff. (How do we choose and plan the play and use rehearsals to improve the performance?) The activity must connect to the community and students given the opportunity to reflect on the experiences.

Figure 5.1 illustrates the relationship among the five domains of SCANS competencies and four artistic disciplines. Figure 5.2 shows how this relationship can be applied in a practical way in the production of a school play. This approach has been used, in a somewhat context, in schools that have adopted the IMAGINITIS program. This program, a form of media publication, has students developing a class book (jointly) and individual books (by themselves). The effort begins with a story shell provided by the program and culminates in a "book party" when the class product is delivered to the school library.

A recent application in Los Angeles tested the ability of the IMAGINITIS program to convey the SCANS competencies. The results were most impressive. All (100%) of the teachers reported covering more than half of the competencies. Over 90% reported covering the remaining competencies. On this basis, early and middle school grade teachers believe that their students are learning the SCANS workplace know-how through the program.

FIG. 5.1. RELATIONSHIPS BETWEEN THE ARTS STANDARDS AND WORKPLACE KNOW-HOW

	ARTISTIC EXPERIENCES			CONTENT	MIND-SET
	Resources	Technology	Interpersonal	Information	Systems
Dance	Allocate stage space	Design lighting and sets	Work in ensemble, teach	Communicate via body movements	Know how finished work develops
Music	Decide the time frame of a composition	Choose instruments: acoustic vs. electronic	Negotiate, work in ensemble, conduct	Communicate via sound and notation	Know how various parts fit together
Theater	Allocate time, money, and staff for production	Design lighting effects, staging, and sets	Work in an ensemble to create scripts and production, direct, teach	Communicate via dialogue and gesture	Move from creation to rehearsal to performance
Visual Arts	Allocate space on a canvas, in graphic design, or in a gallery	Select medium and, in some cases, technology	In some forms it requires collaboration, ability to teach	Communicate through visual symbols	Put together a multimedia presentation

FIG. 5.2. SCANS SKILLS LEARNED DURING AN ARTS PROJECT
(PRODUCING A THEATER WORK OVER 8 WEEKS)

The discipline of theater was selected for the purposes of illustration since it is inclusive of all art forms and clearly demonstrates the transfer of skills and knowledge gained from study in the arts to the work place. Similar tables could be developed for other art forms.

Week #1:   The executive group (director, producer, set designer, and costume designer) select three or four plays from which they will choose one in week #2.

Information	Acquire and evaluate	Organize and maintain	Interpret and maintain	Use computer
	Evaluate 20 possible plays in terms of requirements for set, costumes, number and capacity of actors, recent performances in the community, popularity {w/computer entered data in data base}.			

Week #2:   Brainstorming: group decision-making to select play and consider treatment (e.g., will it be Hamlet in modern dress?)

Interpersonal	Team partici- pation	Teach	Lead	Negotiate	Work with other cultures
	Explain position, persuade, negotiate compromises, all with a culturally diverse team (repeats in different form during following weeks of project).				

Week #3: Develop schedule and budget, select actors and support staff, block stage.

Allocates Resources	Time	Money	Space	Staff
	Plan the tasks that need to accomplished to put the performance on in week #8. Establish rehearsal schedule and the things that go with it (sets, make-up, and costumes for dress rehearsal) Develop budget. {W/computer use scheduling/ budgeting software}. Run tryouts for actors, review resumes for support staff (who will do make-up, paint sets, publicity, etc.).			

Week #4: Set, lighting, and costume design.

Technology	Select	Use	Maintain	Troubleshoot
	Determine technology for each of the three elements. Acquire and/or start building/making each {w/computer consider graphics software}. Use technology. Develop way to maintain equipment, set, and costumes.			

Week #5: Team Decision-making and Guidance after First Rehearsal

Interpersonal	Team participation	Teach	Lead	Negotiate	Work with Other Cultures
	Communicate vision to actors and support staff. Come to agreement about the ways the characters will be realized. Come to agreement about set, lighting, costumes and make-up.				

Week #6: Review rehearsals and make improvements

	Understand	Monitor	Correct	Design
Systems	Understand and communicate what represents a quality performance. Develop process for review and critique (note changes, check that changes have been incorporated into work). See to it that process is working. Change process to make it more effective.			

Week #7: Publicity

	Acquire and evaluate	Organize and maintain	Interpret and maintain	Use computer
Information	Examine past publicity campaigns at this school and campaigns for this play when it was on Broadway. Organize message. Design posters, letters, media presentation. Determine coverage needed and implement publicity campaign.			

Week #8: Performances

	Understand	Monitor	Correct	Design
Systems	Make a quality performance, review for possible improvements after each performance, make improvements for next performance.			

HIGH SCHOOLS

PHILADELPHIA HIGH SCHOOL ACADEMIES, INC.
PHILADELPHIA, PENNSYLVANIA

BACKGROUND – A LARGE URBAN SCHOOL SYSTEM

A sadly familiar urban landscape characterized by widespread social problems and chronic fiscal distress complicate the mission of Philadelphia's public schools. Deficient educational performance is the not unanticipated outcome. Only two of the city's 34 high schools turn in schoolwide average SAT scores at or above the national average. From each citywide group of incoming ninth graders, three out of 10 will leave without graduating.[4] The poorest performing schools turn out more dropouts than graduates. Students whose academic performance falls far short of their expected grade level are passed to maintain classroom groups of age peers, a dropout deterrent tactic that vitiates the atmosphere and challenge of learning.

This unrelenting need to improve often promotes a greater willingness to experiment and embrace change. Despite cost and institutional constraints, troubled school systems often offer a congenial setting for implementing innovations. The Philadelphia district as a whole, led by new superintendent David Hornbeck, recently committed to a large-scale restructuring based on decentralized management and ambitious performance goals.

Philadelphia's High School Academies, located in selected public schools, launched their model of cohesive instruction centered around a career theme long before the current reform discussion. During an era in which urban school shortcomings grew starker, the academy approach provided a promising alternative. The Philadelphia academies take the form of a public-private educational partnership in which an independently supported nonprofit corporation oversees and develops programs which are taught by regular city teachers. The academy program is no longer the only restructured, work-oriented schooling venture ongoing within the city system, but it represents one of the largest coordinated efforts of its type in the entire nation. Some 4,300 youngsters in Philadelphia public schools

---

[4] *Philadelphia Inquirer* (special supplement), October 28, 1994.

enrolled under the academy aegis during the 1994–95 school year. Administrators project 5,000 participants by 1996.

Philadelphia's academy program also claims the distinction of being the nation's longest-running school-to-work transition project outside of traditional vocational education. Originating as an electrical trades instruction program in one school in 1969, it now encompasses 11 different career focus areas with sites in 19 schools. Most importantly, and in dramatic contrast with aggregate citywide statistics, the academies consistently demonstrate lower dropout rates, more successful job placements, and increasing postsecondary enrollments of academy graduates. This quarter-century record of growth, continuity, and performance can serve as a benchmark for more recently initiated school-to-work programs.

Philadelphia's academy movement was begun by the Urban Coalition, a civic-business consortium, in response to civil unrest during the 1960s. The aim was to motivate young people to stay in school, while upgrading the linkage between high school programs and workplace requirements. Business that became actively engaged with schools could serve their need for better prepared entry-level workers while reaping the general benefits of good community relations.

GOALS — EFFECTIVE, CAREER-ORIENTED, SELF-SUSTAINING LEARNING PROGRAMS

Academies typically attract moderately underachieving to average students seeking career-relevant instruction, work experience, and the support and camaraderie of a cohesive group. As economic pressures intensified over the last decade, emphasis shifted toward more postsecondary placement, redefining what was originally conceived as a high school completion mechanism for entry-level workers. The Philadelphia academies have evolved to accommodate a gamut of academic achievement levels. While participating students are at the lower-middle achievement level, enrollees range from some who aspire to attend top colleges to a small number of special education students. This inclusiveness is possible because each academy group is small enough to permit individualized instruction, and because the broad career fields offered encompass multiple education, training, and placement possibilities.

Philadelphia's earliest academy programs were the Electrical Academy (initiated in 1969), Business Academy (1972), and Automotive Academy (1974). A Health Academy was added in 1982. As emphasis on improving the school-to-work transition heightened through the late 1980s into the 1990s, diversified options augmented the program: Environmental Technology, Horticulture, Fitness, Hotel-Restaurant-Tourism, Law, Aviation, Communications. Impetus for inaugurating academy projects and locating them in a growing array of schools has usually come from business or labor groups, but has on occasion originated within the schools. At first, each academy had its own independent administrative entity. Without altering the *modus vivendi* of the separate governing boards, these were consolidated under one organization in 1988.

Academies have a unique cooperative arrangement with the schools. While maintaining independent management and program autonomy, academy programs conform with school district and state stipulations for credit hours and course distribution. Regular public school teachers are the instructors. But the academy board — the umbrella administration over the 11 career programs — is an independent nonprofit organization, primarily accountable to meet the performance standards set by sponsoring businesses and other private donors. Each of the 11 career programs has an active board of governors composed of interested representatives from the relevant industry. These directors come from locally, and often nationally, prominent firms in their field. The governing boards have a strong hand not just in overseeing, but in shaping the programs. In a very few cases, they have even terminated academy pilots in schools where they deemed participants' levels of interest or competence inadequate.

Johannes Ponsen, program director for the academies, stressed that independent sponsorship and oversight is vital to the project's identity and progress. Regularly soliciting corporations and foundations for support tends to produce a truly performance-driven operation. The process entails some degree of financial insecurity, which certainly made itself felt during the early 1990s recession. But reliance on the outside community accentuates the need to deliver a high quality program, and curbs tendencies toward humdrum routinization. Independent sponsorship also provides flexibility to the process of organizing and managing an academy program. Coordinators at each school site have latitude for experimentation and adjustment.

The academies seek effective career-oriented learning for the students they serve. Their academic success also influences the tenor of education in the city. It was a major factor in the school district's decision to beef up its Office of Education for Employment. The district has also expressed commitments to outcome-based learning and eliminating the general track in favor of charter or magnet schools programs. Even without a direct hand in these reforms, the academies are seeing a change of direction that meets their approval. As early exemplars of a sharpened focus on the school-to-work transition, the academies opened the way for other projects, which fall outside the academies' administrative domain but share similar goals. Workforce preparation programs, some initiated within the school district and some arising through outside impetus, have been appearing in city schools with increasing frequency. The now officially sanctioned pressure for change will likely accelerate this trend.

Testifying to the format's attractive features, academy-type projects are now proliferating across the nation. Another organization, the New York-based National Academy Foundation (NAF), coordinates academy programs in over 100 high schools across the nation, and has steadily extended its reach since the mid-1980s. The NAF formula, like the Philadelphia program, marshals corporate and nonprofit support for independently administered academies cooperatively integrated with local schools. The largest number of NAF-sponsored academy students are in the fields of finance and travel/tourism. NAF also collaborates with the Ford Motor Co. in a manufacturing sciences academy program, and has recently launched a public service curriculum.

In a departure from the voluntarist private sector grounding which has characterized much of the youth academy movement, California has officially recognized academy programs as a component of its public education mix. Such a step introduces an element of mandated public support, along with the perhaps ambiguous benefit of more centralized state administrative control.

PROGRAM MODEL — WORKPLACE-ORIENTED SCHOOLS WITHIN SCHOOLS

The youth academy embodies a "school within a school" design. The Philadelphia academies maintain complete block scheduling during ninth and tenth grades. Students gain a strong sense of group cohesion and rapport through being together in all their classes. Teachers are able to relate the material they are presenting to the academy's career field, not just in classes specific to the academy program but also in required core academic courses.

In their junior and senior years, students pursue personally selected schedules. Some prepare for admission to baccalaureate programs, some for other postsecondary education or training, and some — a declining percentage — for entering the workforce immediately after high school.

Each high school academy site has one teacher designated as the academy program coordinator. The coordinator handles administrative duties, minimizing the academy-related workload for the regular school administration, and facilitates supervision and guidance of students. Program coordinators annually receive an additional stipend of about $5,300 from the private academy organization as compensation for their added responsibilities. The organization would also like to provide supplemental stipends for all teachers working in the program, but funds to achieve this goal have been limited.

The academy combines required high school courses with an introduction to a specific career field. About 75–80% of academy enrollees also receive paid work-based learning, either after school or during the summer. The proportion of students placed in jobs varies greatly by career program. Business academy students find clerical positions rather easily, whereas trainee positions in the skilled crafts are scarce. In some cases, academy students in college preparatory programs forego work to concentrate on their studies. Job experience is a recommended, but not compulsory, part of the Philadelphia academy program. The academy directors stress that they want qualified students to perform responsible work related to their chosen field. The academies do not seek to promote fast-food jobs and other unskilled work as part-time placements (although these are a realistically available earning and learning opportunity and students frequently do take such jobs). Nor are the academies interested in contriving make-work positions for students, even if getting employers or organizations to pay for unproductive training slots were feasible. The academy students who get jobs are meeting genuine demand on the labor market. By the same token, academy teachers and counselors only refer students for work when they determine that the students are truly job-ready.

Philadelphia's academy program features numerous other support, incentive, and workplace familiarization components which help shape its distinctive identity. Many of the juniors and all the seniors take part in mock interviews, with followup feedback from the businesses and agencies involved. Working students have an organization, the Gold Star Club, where they can discuss job-related issues and difficulties in a supportive atmosphere. Trips to participating businesses or other places of interest, as well as school visits by professionals in the targeted career field, pique the curiosity and develop motivation of the students. Award ceremonies at the end of each grading period recognize the top achievers at each academy site. The academies also hold a citywide speech competition which has elicited favorable notice from the press and public officials.

Placement in academy programs reflect both competition and self-selection. Students are considered for an academy if they have passing grades and 90% attendance, but the most popular programs have waiting lists. At the other extreme, some schools have assigned students to available academy slots in lieu of the disbanded general track. Philadelphia's high school assignment process is quite complex. A number of schools serve as both neighborhood schools for youngsters in the local area and as providers of specialized programs which attract students from other parts of the city. All eighth grade pupils attending city public schools are asked to list, in order of preference, their preferred high schools and programs. Not everyone gets his first choice, and competition for the city's two elite college-preparatory schools is particularly intense. The academies admit a significant number of students whose top preference would have been the baccalaureate-geared programs at Central or Girls' High. Many students prefer the academies, and administrators seek to accommodate them if at all possible.

CHALLENGES

The organization running Philadelphia's high school academies has an administrative staff of about 15 and an annual operating budget of $1.5 million — relatively modest numbers. The undertaking is large enough to have significant impact, yet small enough to permit close direction and followup. The academies exemplify the challenges and promises tied to implementing a significant innovation in the context of a large urban school district beset with academic, social, and financial difficulties. Both the size and longevity of this effort provide perspective for newer programs.

The academies have had to adapt to changing times and trends. High school completion is not the ticket to job security that it was decades ago. Philadelphia's industrial base has contracted drastically since the 1960s. A new array of enterprises — communications, pharmaceuticals, finance, and insurance — have supplanted traditional "smokestack" manufacturing. The skills to earn a good living in these rising sectors require education beyond high school. Responding to this trend, the academies increasingly emphasize that students should seriously plan some kind of postsecondary program, leading to a baccalaureate or associate degree, or other recognized certification.

While learning challenges have escalated, schools have also had to cope with mounting social changes and problems. More of the population is not native English-speaking, necessitating additional language programs. More teenage girls are having babies; some schools have opened nurseries to care for infants and toddlers while their mothers attend classes. Many schools are located where a high percentage of local residents live on public assistance. Some youngsters lack positive parental guidance. All these developments directly or indirectly influence educational practices.

Each academy career focus program is available at a limited number of sites (some at just a single site), so the time and expense of transportation can be an obstacle. Students in city schools are responsible for their own transportation, and daily bus or subway fare to an academy or magnet school poses a significant burden on those with low incomes. Some academy coordinators attempt to maintain a discretionary fund for emergency transportation assistance and other needs. But there is no policy guaranteeing transportation, and ad hoc disbursement of limited funds may raise an equity question.

With the academy movement's recent thrust toward more college-preparatory emphasis, there are signs that the student population being served is changing. As Basil Whiting observed in a paper for Public/Private Ventures, "While the academies may be recruiting a better grade of skim milk, they are a long way from 'creaming.'"[5] Nevertheless, more selective admission standards correlate with disadvantaged or at-risk students having a more difficult time making their way into the program. Tension between the goals of a sufficiently rigorous program and that of maximizing the achievement of all willing students is inherent in this kind of project. Numerous academy personnel, including executive director Natalie Allen, have expressed a commitment not to abandon what they consider the academies' seminal task — providing a boost for average or marginal students. If the program turns into a vehicle for students who would probably succeed anyway, a segment of the student population that will benefit most from its services would be denied access.

The challenges are different for each particular academy. Programs unambiguously pointed toward college-level career skills, such as the health and law-public administration curricula, appear to have valid grounds for more selective admission policies. Newer programs are just finding their niche, and if a popular academy attracts more prospective enrollees than it can admit, administrators will have to choose which students would most benefit in keeping with the program's stated goals. Personalized scale is an important ingredient of the academies' success; effective models can better extend their influence by being "cloned" at other sites than by growing to an unwieldy size. But garnering sufficient private support and coordinating the project with school officials is never a simple process.

Program director Ponsen noted that expansion of academy programs into new fields makes curriculum development more of a priority. Automotive technology follows a fairly set routine, but endeavors in areas like hospitality or fitness are still formulating much of their methodology. Philadelphia business academy students learn a package of clerical skills — wordprocessing, spreadsheets, and database management. With these they will have a foothold in the job market; those who are able can separately pursue college preparatory courses. By contrast, the National Academy Foundation's finance academy program — which has a more generally college

---

[5] Basil Whiting, "Developmental Education and Work in the Secondary Labor Market," *Public/Private Ventures*, November 1991. *See also* Peter Kilborn, "Job Training Program Seen as U.S. Model," *New York Times*, December 27, 1993.

preparatory slant — integrates an ostensibly more highly conceptual-
ized approach, offering courses on economics, banking and credit,
and securities operations, among others. The populations in different
programs vary, but all students can best stimulate their interest and
sense of career potential if they are able to get both a theoretical and
hands-on grasp of the field being presented. As an example, consider
a classroom full of tenth-graders in Philadelphia's hotel-restaurant-
tourism academy. None of these youngsters had chosen the program;
they were reassigned from the abolished general track. They had
gone on a couple of field trips to hotels and restaurants, but had
little visualization of any potential role beyond housekeeping or
food service. The academy they attend plans to start up an actual
working travel agency at the school next year. One can hope their
horizons will expand as they get a chance to perform the range of
operations such an enterprise entails.

Academy teachers must keep current with ongoing changes in
the workplace. Traditionally, the classroom has been cloistered, and
teachers' professional development outside the world of formal
education continues to lag. Fostering better information exchange
between educators and the larger economy will be a key to devising
more effective school-to-work transition programs. The Philadelphia
academies' governing boards have latched onto this issue, but much
progress remains to be made.

After lining up overall sponsorship for the program, connecting
students with employers is the biggest challenge. Arranging mock
interviews for several thousand students is a formidable project in
itself. Getting job-ready students into suitable employment is a constant scramble. While results have fallen short of ideal, the success
achieved has been quite creditable. Even through the early 1990s
economic downturn, the percentage of academy students able to
find jobs remained close to its historic level of about 75%. During
those lean times, academy students were competing for positions
with experienced adults and even college graduates. Their employment record reflects the quality of the academies' educational program, as well as assiduous effort by the administrative staff.

Seventy-five to 80% employment is the aggregate average for
all 11 career programs. It is bolstered by historically very high employment rates for business academy students. The business academy
is the largest single program, accounting for nine of the total 28 school
sites. Some other programs find jobs for students at a much lower

rate. For instance, employment of electrical academy students runs only about 30%.

There is a widespread perception that union work rules discourage hiring student workers. Restrictions of this type are a factor, but academy administrators have discovered that the terms of employers' liability insurance can be an even bigger obstacle. Many policies virtually preclude the presence of anyone under 18 at sites with heavy or potentially hazardous machinery.

The philosophy of the Philadelphia academy program is grounded on a belief in the private sector's efficacy in making the right choices. The academies' primary mission is to inculcate students with appropriate skills and motivation. Once students are so equipped, they should be able to secure work on the open market. With this outlook, academy board members tend toward ambivalence about the desirability of subsidized work slots. Nonetheless, in at least one instance public funds have helped support jobs held by academy students. This was a project under state legislation, termed the *Health Tech 2000 Initiative,* in which health academy students worked during the summer at doctors' offices and other facilities. The grant was for only 1 year, and administrators hoped it would function as seed money for an ultimately self-sustaining venture.

Lessons Learned

Philadelphia's high school academies have operated over a 25-year span. The passage of time brings the need to rethink and adjust approaches, but it also generates positive momentum. A successful record boosts support for and confidence in the program. Securing corporate and other private backing takes sustained effort, but long-term sponsors come to realize that the reservoir of good will in the community built by their participation becomes an asset in itself. They usually stay on board.

Teachers and school district administrators strongly support the academy project. If the relationship were not so amicable, it is doubtful whether the endeavor could have lasted. Monetary rewards for teacher participation are modest, and some dedicated academy teachers have even spent their own money for special supplies or activities. Academy scheduling does provide teachers an additional release (nonclass) period, which serves as an incentive. But the major attraction of the program is that it works. Both the school district and the outside consortium running the academies express proprietary sentiment about them, reflecting the adage that success has many parents while failure is an orphan. The independent academy staff like to describe the academies as "in the schools, but not of the schools" — a characterization which rankles school district personnel. In fairness, the complicated disbursement formula for school monies and the fact that academy class size is usually smaller than most regular classes legitimizes the district claim that the academies actually do receive public support. The extra cost per pupil is not borne entirely by the private sector.

The investment in academy students, whatever its origin, has paid off with impressive results. High school graduation rates from the program have edged steadily upward. Less than 3% of academy enrollees are currently dropping out, an extraordinary contrast with the district as a whole. Individual students have achieved some distinguished recognition. For example, the horticulture academy's 1994 exhibit at the world-famous Philadelphia Flower Show, competing in a collegiate-level category, won best in show. The same year, two graduates of the fitness academy at Benjamin Franklin High School were awarded full 4-year scholarships to Ithaca College in New York.

Aggregate measures bear out the success of the program. Accurate recordkeeping and followup surveys are given high priority on the academy administrative agenda. Academy graduates are contacted at 6 months and again at 18 months after finishing high school, with an almost universal response rate. Compiling data on participants after they complete a program is not a common practice; many other programs base outcome projections on respondents' reported plans at the time of graduation. The academy surveys show 50% of alumni attending college, and 30% working in the private sector. Defined "positive outcomes," which also include graduates in the military or in trade school, come to 85% of the followup group. Of the remaining 15%, 8% were unemployed and looking for work; 7% were not currently in the labor force. These numbers would be satisfactory for any group of 18- and 19-year-olds; they are strikingly good for a group with a high proportion of students from modest achievement backgrounds.

The Philadelphia academy program is nearing its fundraising limit. The current scale makes a difference for thousands of students each year, but the schoolwide student workforce transition problem is far bigger than that. The Academy directors are committed to maintaining an independent program, and hope to wield much of their influence through agenda-setting and example.

An expanding array of schools, representing a wide range of social and educational contexts are replicating the academy model. Its success should be encouraging to those seeking to inaugurate new, similar programs.

ROOSEVELT RENAISSANCE 2000
PORTLAND, OREGON

BACKGROUND — AN URBAN HIGH SCHOOL WITH AN
UNENVIABLE PAST TRACK RECORD

Roosevelt High School serves a working class, ethnically and culturally diverse area of North Portland. When plans for its restructuring came to the fore in the late 1980s, Roosevelt had long been one of the city's most troubled schools. It had the highest absenteeism, suspension, and expulsion rates in the district. Its dropout rate was also the worst. Half the young people coming in as freshmen never received a high school diploma. Today, these bleak baseline indicators serve as reference points for a dramatic turnaround still in progress. Roosevelt has become nationally noted for its thoroughly redesigned curriculum, which aims to provide a more cohesive and relevant school experience while strengthening connections between education and the workplace.

The community provided the impetus for Roosevelt's rebirth as a radically restructured, career-focused, comprehensive high school. Forces for change arose around, rather than within, the school. Business and labor groups, concerned about workforce needs and the negative social repercussions of failing schools, were the driving force. Education administrators and other state officials played a collaborative role. Many members of the business community expressed the resolve to become active players in educational initiatives.

Roosevelt Renaissance centers around a career pathway selected by the student from six choices. All classroom material is related to the pathways; newly implemented introductions to the worksite extend the integrated approach. The redesigned curriculum was unveiled in the fall of 1991 for that year's ninth grade class. A 4-year phase in incorporated successively higher grades: ninth and tenth grades in 1992–93, and so forth. The reshaped Roosevelt Renaissance learning plan is now truly schoolwide, distinguishing it from almost all other school-to-work transition projects.

GOALS — A FULLY REDESIGNED HIGH SCHOOL PROGRAM

Serious discussions about reforming Roosevelt's curriculum started in 1989. A 2-year planning period preceded the introduction of Roosevelt's redesigned curriculum. Over many rounds of discussion, the business community kept the emphasis on enhanced job readiness as the desired outcome of secondary education. In the vision that emerged, high school would be a place where students begin preparing for specific skilled careers. Employers and educators would become partners who together develop curricula and standards which facilitate that preparation.

During the second year of planning, a series of retreats brought together educators, employers, and parents. Disparate viewpoints gradually coalesced into a practical agenda for change. The reform plan had to be coordinated with the school faculty, who had developed their own ideas of how to address Roosevelt's deficiencies. Oregon's Bureau of Labor and Industry helped shape the terms of debate by advocating a revitalized occupational focus in the schools.

Roosevelt's school-wide program intends that each student not only graduate, but graduate prepared to pursue a positive career option. The reconfigured curriculum had to be flexible enough to provide all members of a diverse 1,100-member student body with a valuable personal learning experience, yet rigorous enough to meet high academic standards. Roosevelt students explore a range of career possibilities, choosing a particular focus area for more substantive preparation. But the program aims to avoid tracking students into traditional vocational education. Eighty percent of Roosevelt students do not go on to 4-year colleges. The reform collaborators were particularly concerned with upgrading the career prospects for this nonbaccalaureate majority.

PROGRAM MODEL — SIX CAREER PATHWAYS

Roosevelt bases its restructured curriculum on exploration of six "career pathways:" arts and communication, business and management, manufacturing and engineering technology, health services, human resources, and natural resource systems. Each represents a field projected for high quality job growth in the early 21st century, and each area covers a wide range of career possibilities. The business and management path, for instance, includes trade and tourism. Human resources is an umbrella category for an array of skilled service careers, from law enforcement to education.

The centerpiece of the ninth grade program is a class called Freshman Focus. It introduces Roosevelt's unique instruction format based on learning clusters grouped around the six career pathways. Students are exposed to each pathway in successive 3-week units. Freshman Focus also helps youngsters understand, develop, and apply "skills for success" such as critical thinking, goal setting, self-assessment, and teamwork.

Freshman Focus, which students frequently cite as their favorite class, occupies a daily 1-hour period. Ninth graders spend the rest of their schedule on familiar academic subjects, modified to emphasize applied context and job readiness. A math project might deal with allocating materials for a construction project. Science and geography concepts are related to the local environment. An applied academic focus is sustained in math, English, and science courses through all 4 years of the high school program.

At the end of their freshman year, Roosevelt students select one of the six pathways. Many will remain in that pathway until graduation, but it is not a rigid career choice. The paths are very general; each path contains many career fields, and each career field accommodates multiple positions demanding different levels of education and training. Moreover, students are free to switch if another pathway fits their aptitude and interests better.

Freshman Focus is a key class because the subsequent 3-year program clusters around their pathway decision. If students understand their strengths and desires, if they effectively survey different fields and find the one which best matches their talents and characteristics, there will be fewer midcourse corrections.

In tenth grade, students explore their chosen pathway through a core class which presents basic concepts and terminology specific to that career field. For example, students in the technology concentration take an introductory computer course, and those interested in business study principles of marketing. From tenth grade on, to the extent feasible, students take required academic classes clustered by pathway groups. This enables teachers to tailor assignments according to the students' chosen areas. In social studies, an arts group may research the biographies of important writers or performers, while students with a medical focus trace the origins of mass vaccination and other public health measures.

The Roosevelt Renaissance program is consistent with Oregon's 1993 Educational Act for the 21st Century, which it antedates by 2 years. (*See* Oregon's plan in Chapter 8.) Mandated statewide reforms will institute a system of performance measures, with students required to demonstrate satisfactory command of reasoning, calculating, and communication skills in order to graduate from high school. Plans call for students to earn a Certificate of Initial Mastery (CIM) at the end of tenth grade, and a Certificate of Advanced Mastery (CAM), showing grasp of core material related to a chosen career path, in twelfth grade. The CIM/CAM process will be outcome-based rather than schedule-based. As a Roosevelt information sheet notes, "The goal of this program is to educate students, not merely test them." Some students will meet initial mastery qualifications during ninth grade, some not until their junior year.

Along with the career-focused curriculum, Roosevelt Renaissance emphasizes job shadowing. Freshmen shadow at least one job; sophomores, at least two. The school staff have been refining the methodology for planning, securing, and following up the job shadows, and the procedure has become impressively smooth and effective. School administrators recruit employers. Community involvement helped conceive the school's entire restructuring experiment, and employers are generally glad to participate. About 100 different employers — mostly private businesses with a sprinkling of nonprofit organizations — now support job shadowing. Nearly 100% of employers who sign on agree to continue it annually, so the process of setting up job shadowing sessions has become more routinized and institutionalized. Employers receive followup questionnaires, usually faxed immediately after a job shadowing session, which ask for impressions of the student's interest, acuity, and demeanor, and for general comments about the experience. Roosevelt staff are delighted that many employers (or their workers who actually show students around the jobsite) find the chance to share a slice of working life one-on-one with a young person gratifying for themselves as well as for the student.

The job shadow format comprises a 3-hour worksite visit by an individual student, who gets a firsthand look at skilled craft or professional work and an opportunity to talk with the people doing it. "That doesn't sound like much," notes Rene Leger, Roosevelt's coordinator for the job shadowing program, but he goes on to explain how the worksite session itself is only the highlight of a larger process. The students are responsible for contacting an employer and making the job shadow appointment, and for acknowledging the visit with a letter of thanks. They must also produce an essay discussing why they decided to shadow a particular job, and how the experience affected them. Interested students may be able to arrange extended job shadowing beyond the minimum single session. In their sophomore year and beyond, all students are expected to conduct job shadows related to their personally chosen career pathway.

Challenges

The Roosevelt program tries to integrate academic and career-oriented elements by scheduling together each career pathway group in a cluster for all their courses. Scheduling complications, however, make fully clustered class arrangements difficult to attain, so that they remain more of an ongoing ideal than a norm. Roosevelt's ninth and tenth grade program is easier to schedule, and constitutes the curriculum segment which has been in place for the longest time. For these grades, the restructured plan has reached a stable, functional level of implementation. The eleventh and twelfth grade curriculum, which includes structured work experience, is in a state of greater fluctuation and experimentation.

The original Roosevelt Renaissance prospectus stated an intention to place large numbers of students in paid part-time "youth apprentice" jobs. This proved too ambitious a goal for the number of students. With no equitable means of allocating scarce positions readily apparent, program administrators have dropped plans for schoolwide paid placements. They are now concentrating on developing a comprehensive system of intensive unpaid rotations — job shadowing writ large — for each career pathway. The health occupations focus has the most fully operational structured work observation sequence at the present time. Various area hospitals and laboratories have agreed to open their facilities to the Roosevelt program. Juniors receive a minimum 20 hours of worksite exposure over the school year; seniors go on a 3–4 hour worksite visit every week.

In the other pathways, structured worksite experiences have not yet been comprehensively introduced, but pilot programs are running. One of the newest and most exciting stems from an agreement between the natural resource focus group and Oregon's state environmental agency. About 15 students accompany technicians on regularly scheduled monitoring of water quality of area rivers and streams. School staff expect that structured work experience sessions of this type will become a standard feature of the eleventh and twelfth grade curriculum for all six pathways.

On an individual basis, some students have obtained paying jobs, and those experiences have proved valuable in preparing classroom projects. Also valuable are a limited number of officially designated unpaid internships, including nine with the *Oregonian*, Portland's daily newspaper. Interns devote half a day per week to their positions. Some students have also received grants to attend conferences or other events.

Initially, teachers did not embrace Roosevelt's restructuring with enthusiasm. The curricular changes proposed were unusually sweeping, particularly since they would affect the entire school, not just a selected pilot group. Unsurprisingly, teachers worried about disrupted routines and loss of turf. The teacher's union raised issues of work rules. Proposals to replace schoolroom time with workplace orientation sessions loomed as a possible financial threat in a compensation system based on class hours. The difficulties were eventually worked out, but only through protracted and delicate negotiations.

Similar adjustment and coordination problems await Oregon schools as a whole, during the phase-in of legislatively mandated performance standards. At present, the state teachers' association has expressed a rather skeptical position on Oregon's reform agenda, believing schools have been asked to meet extensive new demands with insufficient resources.

If the Roosevelt experience can be seen as a bellwether, teachers will gradually warm to projects that generate positive student outcomes. That student success has converted many Roosevelt teachers who now strongly endorse their school's reform effort. Students' interest in school has increased dramatically since the program's inception. Teachers note that freshmen now take part in class discussions with a seriousness and maturity that used to be rare among seniors.

LESSONS LEARNED

It is too soon to evaluate the project, since the first class of seniors who took part in the program through all 4 high school years only graduated in 1994. Program administrators anticipate great improvements in attendance and completion rates, and other measures of scholastic performance. Teachers, administrators, and the many interested community members who put so much effort into launching Roosevelt's revitalization eagerly await an outcome that should mark a welcome break from the school's lackluster past.

Although the planning process was quite lengthy, including 2 full years of formal meetings and discussion, the program design has undergone substantial modification in use. Perhaps, there is no way to iron out the kinks except through practical experience. Conversely, the politics and intergroup dynamics of school restructuring arguably require extended preliminary negotiations.

Strengthened ties between the business community and education are a tangible and gratifying result of the initiative. School administrators, students, and involved companies and organizations express nearly universal approval of a process that brings the working world and high school closer together. Employers who sign on for job shadowing or other forms of participation retain their commitment year after year. However, paid work experience for the students was not a feasible commitment on a schoolwide basis, and Roosevelt is determined that Renaissance be a schoolwide program.

THE SMOKEY HOUSE PROJECT
DANBY, VERMONT

We decided to bushwack down from the peak on the 30th. The terrain turned out to be steep, slippery, full of holes, and generally hazardous. The crew really pulled together to accomplish the descent. Ed, Don, Darcy, and Christine formed chains to get themselves down safely. This required teamwork, clear communication, understanding of personal and group limitations, sacrificing personal progress in favor of the group, and positive attitude. Jim, Chad, and Tom volunteered to scout ahead to find the safest routes — this was Jim's suggestion. This required initiative, communication, planning, and patience. The crew as a whole were very good at balancing their need to stop and rest with the need to make good time; they had to understand personal limitations and the urgency of time and effectiveness.

— P.J. Jonesku, Smokey House Crew Leader

BACKGROUND — A 20-YEAR TRADITION OF
LEARNING THROUGH WORK

What would you do if you were interested in education for at-risk youths and you had 4,825 acres of forest and farmland to maintain? In the early 1970's, the Catoctin Foundation faced this question. Its solution: set up a work-based learning program where students who are not succeeding in traditional high schools can succeed and learn through real work.

Smokey House Project is an alternative high school serving the youths of Rutland and Bennington Counties in southwest Vermont. Having established itself early as a model for work-based learning, it recently received statewide and national attention for its programs. It has groomed many Rutland area youths to go on to careers in forestry or agriculture, or to develop the skills, discipline, and self-esteem needed for training and successful careers in other professions.

It has also given many professional educators hands-on experience with work-based learning. (Susan Curnan, Director of Brandeis University's Center for Human Resources, started her career at Smokey House.) Capitalizing on its reputation for hard work and serious learning, and its idyllic surroundings, Smokey House constructed a conference building in which it hosts professional development and in-service workshops for teachers, school administrators, and employment and training personnel. The conference center was mostly designed and constructed by Smokey House students. One of the authors of this book received his first exposure to learning-rich work while attending a workshop at Smokey House. He quickly realized that the real learning, not just for the youths, but also for the workshop attendees, was in the fields, working side-by-side with the youths as they harvested herbs and vegetables.

The staff and administration would contest this description of Smokey House. It does not talk enough about work — the backbone of the Smokey House philosophy. In discussions about their work, Lynn Bondurant, Smokey House's Executive Director, her staff, and even Jane Lee Eddy, the Chair of Smokey House's Board of Directors, seem to be apologetic about the learning they facilitate. They emphasize the work. When pressed on the issue, Lynn Bondurant will explain that the learning comes out of the work naturally. If young people do real work, not watered down tasks nor make-work, they will inevitably learn from it. If they plant a crop, they must plan it

out. In the planning (the work, Smokey House staff would emphasize), they learn. If they blaze a trail down the side of Dorset Moun-
tain, they are going to learn and practice teamwork skills, surveying
skills (including applications of math, geography, and other science
skills), and proper use of their tools. They almost seem to laugh at
the rest of the country's efforts to figure out how to combine work
and learning. As one of Smokey House's flyers reads, "We know
that young people are motivated to learn complex academic material
when these concepts are applied to the solution of interesting
problems and the challenge of producing concrete results."

GOALS — BUILDING A BASE FOR FUTURE SUCCESS

The Smokey House Project has simple goals: motivate high school
students from Rutland and Bennington Counties to stay in school
and provide them with the skills and personal qualities they will
need to succeed in school and at work. At Smokey House, this means
that the immediate goal at any given time may be "get these trees
planted," or "clear this trail without hurting anyone."

PROGRAM MODEL — LEARNING BY DOING

Smokey House collaborates with area high schools to improve
the academic trajectories of its student-workers. Youths come to
Smokey House because they are attracted by its reputation and apply,
or they are referred there by guidance counselors who sense that
they need a more engaged experience than traditional schooling.
Smokey House and each of its cooperating high schools negotiate
separate arrangements. During the school year, students are typically
employed at Smokey House for half of the day and at their regular
high school for half of the day. Their tuition is paid by the school
district and their wages are paid from the profits they make on what
they produce, as well as funding through state, federal, and private
grants. During the summer, Smokey House operates the JTPA Summer Youth Employment Program in which youths work at Smokey
House for up to 7 hours per day.

Crews of five or six young people and one experienced crew
leader plan and carry out the work. For the most part, the supervisors
do not come to Smokey House trained in education or youth development. Smokey House prefers that they know their craft, have natural
people skills, and a concern for youth. Then, Smokey House takes

on the task of training the crew leaders to supervise the youth and capitalize on the learning experiences provided by the real work.

Learning emerges from the work naturally. Crew leaders coach their crew members to design their own plans and solve their own problems as a team, not to just do the job to the boss' specifications. When crew members are uncertain about how to proceed, the crew leader may capitalize on this "teachable moment" by directing them to resources they can use to solve their problems themselves. Additional time is taken for crew members to evaluate their work and document their learning. This is usually done by combining daily group discussions about the work and learning with individual meetings between the crew leader and each crew member.

Methods of documenting work and learning accomplishments have evolved over the years at Smokey House, but invariably include crew members' self-assessments, crew leaders' assessments of the crew members, and peer assessments. Smokey House and its cooperating schools developed a detailed benchmarking system which resembles the "standards" that are now becoming widespread. Evaluating against these benchmarks, cooperating schools award academic credit for what students learn at Smokey House.

More recently, Smokey House has been developing a portfolio approach to documentation and evaluation. Students are encouraged to collect evidence of their learning, such as a paper on which they have diagrammed a plan for constructing a barn or calculated how much timber the barn would require; the survey they developed to assess client satisfaction and demand for new products in their stand at the farmers' market; or "before" and "after" photographs of the trail they restored. Students also keep a journal in which they reflect on the challenges and accomplishments in their work and learning. This portfolio supports the claims to learning that are made in their benchmarking system.

In partnership with Bennington and Middlebury Colleges, Smokey House recently expanded its programs to include a middle and high school environmental field studies program. Based on the same "learn by doing" philosophy, the environmental field studies program brings groups of students to Smokey House for 1–2 week projects that complement, apply, and extend the academics they learn at school while creating a real product through real work.

CHALLENGES

Smokey House has faced many challenges over the years. They have had to prove to several schools that their crew members are learning. Frequently, with a change in school or school system administration, they have to revise and reinforce their documentation of that learning.

Often, youths come to Smokey House with a long history of failure and disillusionment with school. They may see Smokey House as a freer environment than their old school, permitting them to act less responsibly. Although this illusion is usually quickly eliminated by the demands of real work, the coaching of the crew leaders, and peer pressure from their crew members, it sometimes results in fights between crew members or hazardous misuse of tools. Crew leaders must be vigilant about conduct and safety requirements.

Smokey House's broad rural catchment area means that many crew members must commute an hour or more to get to work. Breakdowns in transportation arrangements mean that someone else has to pick up the slack in the work. Crops and livestock cannot be neglected simply because someone could not get to work.

LESSONS LEARNED

Smokey House offers two major lessons to people grappling with work-based learning:

♦   Given proper support, youths who are not succeeding at school are usually capable of planning and executing real work. Perhaps the more concrete demands of work appeal to them in a way that the more abstract learning of traditional schooling does not.

♦   Learning is a natural consequence of real work. If the work is not watered down, students will learn complex academic material. Smokey House's "just-in-time" approach to learning means that subject matter is learned when it is needed. For example, a student who may otherwise have lacked motivation or context for learning geometry will take to it much more enthusiastically when planning the location of support beams for a barn in which he or she will work.

COMMUNITY COLLEGES

AN ASSOCIATE DEGREE IN HIGH-PERFORMANCE MANUFACTURING NATIONAL PROJECT

BACKGROUND — MANUFACTURERS AND COMMUNITY COLLEGES SET THE STANDARDS

Can community colleges prepare their graduates for the 21st century? Can they help students learn competencies that will be of use as technology changes and graduates change jobs and employers? Can they provide students with a degree that is "portable," one that is recognized by employers hundreds or even thousands of miles away from the granting institution? The Johns Hopkins University, Hagerstown Junior College, and four other "lead" community colleges are engaged in an National Science Foundation (NSF)-funded project to "test a concept" for answering these questions affirmatively.

Harry Featherstone, President of the Will-Burt Corporation in Orville, Ohio, suggested such a project a few years ago. Harry demonstrated, to a national audience, that training, education, and a commitment to high performance can move even a small firm like Will-Burt from imminent failure to long-term viability. His goal was a portable associate degree that workers in firms such as his could acquire, knowing that it would be valued by many employers. A second motivation came from a report issued by the Competitiveness Policy Council in March of 1993, which included recommendations for an improved system for school-to-work transition. They urged developing a portable associate degree in manufacturing as one means to this end.

With the support of the Sloan Foundation, a panel of employers from the manufacturing sector met three times with a panel of educators between the Fall of 1993 and the Spring of 1994 to address this issue. The National Association of Manufacturers hosted the Employer Panel of 17 individuals representing small and large manufacturing firms, unions, and trade associations. The Employer Panel included representatives from four groups that developed pilot standards for four subsectors of the manufacturing industry: the metalworking industries, the printing industry, the electronics industry, and computer-assisted drafting and design (CADD). The American Association of Community Colleges hosted the Educator Panel composed of 16 educators from the nation's community colleges, including presidents and administrators of colleges and college systems.

These two panels defined and agreed upon standards for a portable 2-year *Associate Degree in High-Performance Manufacturing* (*see* Fig. 5.3). It was envisioned that this single degree, with industry-specific areas of concentration, would serve the entire manufacturing sector from aircraft to electronics to printing. The panels also agreed on criteria for the curricula needed to meet these standards.

Subsequent to this initial planning effort some of the panel members joined together to find a way to implement the plan. The result was a successful proposal to the National Science Foundation (NSF). The "proof-of-concept" grant enabled faculty from the Johns Hopkins University and five community colleges to begin work. The colleges included South Seattle, associated with Boeing in the state of Washington; Northern Essex (Haverhill, Massachusetts), associated with the Alliance formed by AT&T and its constituent unions; Modesto, part of the California system; New Hampshire Technical Institute, part of that state's system; and Hagerstown, Maryland, part of the Consortium for Manufacturing Competitiveness. These "lead" colleges represent five college groups which, together, include over 100 community colleges.

This is a three-phased project: a completed, Sloan-financed planning phase, a proof-of-concept phase that began in 1995, and a full implementation phase scheduled to begin in 1998. The planning phase provided a way for employers, coming from various manufacturing industries, to agree on a single set of "standards." Unlike standards that are job-based, these standards are to be met by all those graduating with an associate degree in manufacturing. Educators from diverse institutions also agreed on a way to provide the instruction to grant the degree. They found a way to reconcile the needs of students whose formal education will end with the associate degree with the graduates who will continue on to a baccalaureate degree.

GOALS — PREPARING STUDENTS FOR HIGH-PERFORMANCE MANUFACTURING

Preparation for "high-performance manufacturing" must be broad enough to give employers and employees the flexibility to adapt to a changing workplace. Yet it has to be specific enough that

FIG. 5.3. HIGH PERFORMANCE MANUFACTURING:
22 COMPETENCIES[6] AND RELATED COURSEWORK

Discipline	Competencies	Module
Mathematics	Allocate Time	1
	Allocate Money	2
	Select Technology	2
	Allocate Material and Facility Resources	3
	Allocate Human Resources	4
Information Science	Acquire and Evaluate Information	5
	Organize and Maintain Information	6
	Use Computers to Process Information	7
Technical Communication	Interpret and Communicate Information	8
	Participate as a Member of a Team	9
	Negotiate to Arrive at a Decision	9
	Teach Others	10
Science	Identify, Understand, Work with Systems	11
	Understand Environmental, Social, Political, Economic, and Business Systems	11
	Monitor and Correct System Performance	12
	Improve and Design Systems	13
Business of Technology	Serve Clients/Customers	14
	Work with Diversity	
	Understand/Comply with Legal Requirements	15
	Exercise Leadership	16
Work-Based Module Manufacturing Technology	Apply Technology to Task	17
	Maintain and Troubleshoot Technology	17

[6] For a description of the competency specified by this number, *see* Arnold Packer, *Associate Degree in High-Performance Manufacturing*, Johns Hopkins University Institute for Policy Studies, 11/1/94.

the graduates can quickly become productive workers. Meeting these goals should both increase the earnings of the graduates and the competitiveness of American manufacturing. A recent NSF survey disclosed almost 700 2-year colleges awarding an associate degree in at least one field of engineering technology.[7] The ultimate goal is to improve the preparation of students in a majority of these institutions.

PROGRAM MODEL — BALANCING A BROAD EDUCATION WITH SPECIFIC TRAINING

The full curriculum intends to bring students to 22 generic SCANS-based standards (see Fig. 5.3) for an associate degree in High-Performance Manufacturing. The graduates' needs for a broad education are to be reconciled with the training they require for specific jobs. The SCANS workplace know-how provides a means for the reconciliation. While there will be room to specialize in electronics, or steel fabrication, or printing, or chemical processing, the core of the degree will be constant across all of the community colleges offering the degree.

Employers throughout the manufacturing sector (and other sectors as well) need these generic competencies. **Working in teams and other interpersonal skills** are universally required; these skills are easily transferred among manufacturing industries. **Scheduling and other planning skills** are quasiuniversal; they take one form in manufacturing discrete products, such as autos, and another in continuous manufacturing processes, such as chemical production. **Technology skills**, in contrast, are industry-specific. Printing technology is too different from metalworking technology to be included in a single course, although there are principles of technology that are common among these industries. The Educator Panel recommended imbedding (or infusing) the common competencies into the basic academic, or general education, courses. The infusion strategy insures that the degree is not terminal. The Associate Degree will prepare students to continue to a 4-year degree.

---

[7] Lawrence Burton and Carin Celebuski, *Technical Education in 2-Year Colleges*, HES Survey Number 17, Washington, DC: National Science Foundation, Division of Science Resource Studies, 1995.

NSF funded a project to test the concept model curriculum, by working on nine of the 22 standards specified as needed for a portable associate degree in manufacturing (*see* Fig. 5.4). The mathematics, science, and communications faculty at the five lead colleges will design a series of CD-ROM and print media instructional modules. The Educational Film Center will produce the instructional materials. The lead colleges will then integrate these modules into general education courses in math, science, and communications. The American Institutes for Research will evaluate the project to capture "lessons learned."

FIG. 5.4. PROOF OF CONCEPT
HIGH PERFORMANCE MANUFACTURING —
NINE COMPETENCIES AND RELATED COURSEWORK

Discipline	*Competencies*	*Module*
Mathematics	Allocate Money (#2)	2
	Select Technology (#18)	2
Technical Communication	Interpret and Communicate Information (#7)	8
Science	Identify, Understand, and Work with Systems (#15)	11
	Understand Environmental, Social, Political, Economic, and Business Systems (#15a)	11
	Monitor and Correct System Performance (#16)	12
	Improve and Design Systems (#17)	13
Work-Based Module Manufacturing Technology	Apply Technology to Task (#19)	17
	Maintain and Troubleshoot Technology (#20)	17

The project will accomplish the following over a 3-year period:

♦ **Design and Produce Five Modules of Instructional Material.** Each module will provide 9 hours of instruction for one (or in some cases, two) of the 9 standards shown in Figure 5.4. The modules will use CD-ROM and print media to deliver instruction.

♦ **Design an 8-Week Work-Based Module.** Colleges will use this work-based learning to provide students with practical experience and develop knowledge and skills using the technology found in real workplaces.

♦ **Design a School-based and a Work-based Curricular Strategy.** The strategy will integrate the 5+1 modules into a standard 60-credit Associate Degree program.

♦ **Implement the School-based Curriculum.** Five lead colleges will design, field-test, and implement the 6 modules. These lead colleges represent technician education programs across the nation. Each lead college will provide a discipline expert, a coordinator, and four discipline associates. These faculty members will design and implement the modules and curriculum strategy. A Board of Directors and Steering Committee will guide the work of the local Working Groups in carrying out the tasks. *See* Figures 5.5 and 5.6.

♦ **Evaluate the Modules, Strategy, and Implementation.** In addition to a formative evaluation of each product and its implementation, the project will also evaluate the employment prospects of the first graduating class (in year 3 of the project) and compare them to a control group, as a summative evaluation.

♦ **Write and Disseminate the Final Report.** The National Association of Manufacturers and the American Association of Community Colleges will participate in disseminating the results.

♦ **Develop Faculty.** The Johns Hopkins University will provide continuing education support for the community college faculty members involved in designing, implementing, and evaluating the curriculum.

CHALLENGES

This will be a difficult project to manage. Success requires motivating faculty to integrate the new program into the fabric at the five lead colleges. College faculty, especially those who teach general education, are notoriously difficult to manage. Phyllis Eisen, of NAM, remarked that business executives are accustomed to having their employees follow their lead. This is a far cry from college presidents

FIG. 5.5. NATIONAL ORGANIZATION STRUCTURE

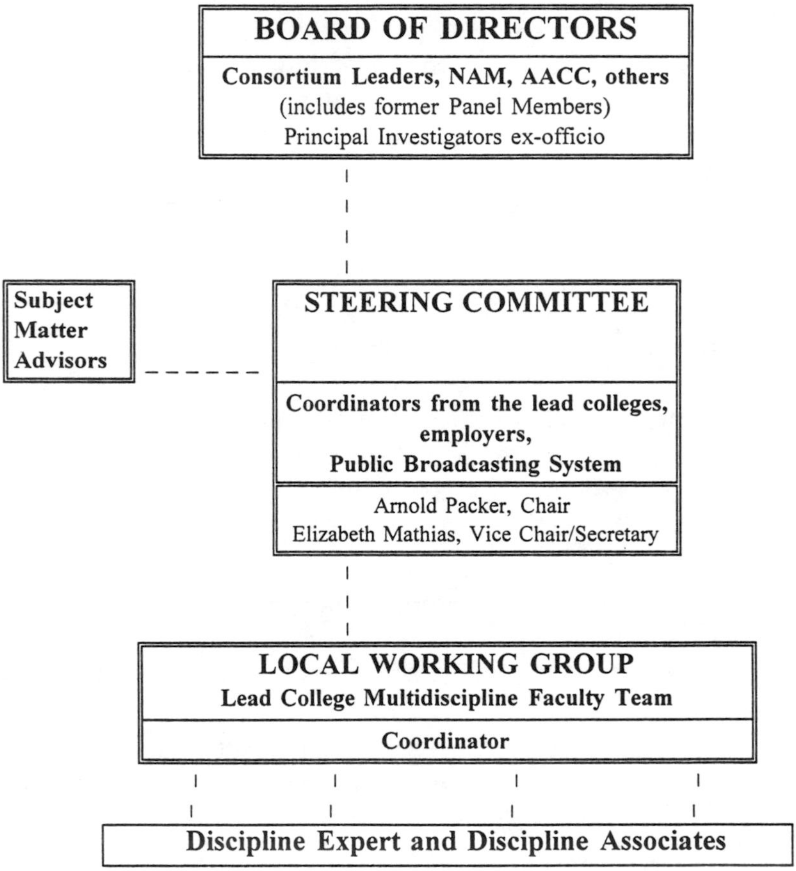

BOARD OF DIRECTORS

Consortium Leaders, NAM, AACC, others
(includes former Panel Members)
Principal Investigators ex-officio

| Subject Matter Advisors |

STEERING COMMITTEE

Coordinators from the lead colleges,
employers,
Public Broadcasting System

Arnold Packer, Chair
Elizabeth Mathias, Vice Chair/Secretary

LOCAL WORKING GROUP
Lead College Multidiscipline Faculty Team

Coordinator

Discipline Expert and Discipline Associates

FIG. 5.6. COMMUNICATION WITHIN THE WORKING GROUP

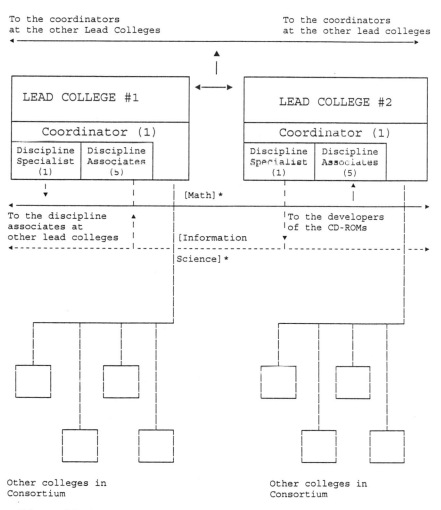

* Only two of the six discipline areas are shown.

who have to plead with faculty to acquiesce to the direction they set out.

Faculty will not acquiesce if they believe that the changes proposed will "water down" their courses. The acid test will be the willingness of 4-year colleges to accept their students. Three steps were taken to deal with this challenge. First, the project contains a professional development component for the involved faculty. Second, the overall project has two prestigious advisors representing math and engineering education at the baccalaureate and graduate school levels. Finally, the project requires that each lead college work with a local 4-year college on this effort.

The project will also have to develop adequate assessment tools. These will have to bear the responsibility of being valid and replicable across sites. The ultimate validity will be success on the job, which will, hopefully, be correlated with assessment results. Responsibility for evaluation rests with the American Institute for Research.

Coordinating the work of faculty at five colleges located on both sides of the country will not be easy. The Internet will augment old-fashioned telephones and face-to-face meetings to build a coordinated team out of the participating faculty at the five lead colleges. Video conferencing with AT&T donated equipment is being explored.

Few have successfully met the challenge of developing good instructional software. Developers typically fall down in instructional design. Part of the difficulty is the artificial nature of many of the problems that are portrayed. By grounding the context in manufacturing and the SCANS know-how, this project should avoid that failing. Adequate production values for the video and unimaginative computer programming are other obstacles. The project seeks to overcome them by using the highly-experienced Educational Film Center to produce all the materials based on the faculty's design.

Complete success will require that each lead college export the results to other schools in their consortium. Imbedding the course materials in easily adopted CD-ROM technology will facilitate transfer without compromising the design principles. Academic papers, conferences, and other ways to get the message out, should also be helpful. Most reliance, however, will be placed on the affiliate colleges who will attend meetings, receive pilot versions of the software, and receive assistance as they attempt to adopt the curricula.

LESSONS LEARNED

The planning project imparted one very important lesson. Employers in manufacturing, a broad industrial sector that includes a number of subsectors that are pursing their own standard-setting exercise, can agree on standards based on the SCANS framework. Developing the NSF proposal imparted a second lesson. Major firms such as Boeing and IBM, labor/management groups, such as the Alliance, and community college systems, such as the Consortium for Manufacturing Competitiveness, California, and New Hampshire, are eager to work together to bring students to these standards.

As is usually the case with school-to-work projects, the major lessons will come during the implementation experience. Design will take place during the 1995–96 school year and test modules during the 1996–97 year. By September of 1997, the project expects to begin implement all five CD-ROM modules, and the work-based module, at each of the five lead colleges. If that implementation succeeds, the participants will seek additional support to develop and implement the remaining 10 modules required to meet the entire set of standards listed in Figure 5.3.

MONTGOMERY COLLEGE TECH PREP
MONTGOMERY COUNTY, MARYLAND

BACKGROUND — A SUBURBAN COMMUNITY COLLEGE

Montgomery College, the community college for Montgomery County, Maryland, has three campuses in the communities of Rockville, Germantown, and Takoma Park. Montgomery County ranks near the top in per capita income in the United States. The economy of this suburban Washington, DC, area benefits from government facilities, biomedical research, and technology development. The population and tax base assure a good labor market for skilled technical and professional jobseekers.

Montgomery County's public education system, including the community college, has the fiscal capacity to offer an array of services most districts would envy. The college guarantees entrance to any interested student with a high school diploma or GED, and can usually arrange financial aid for those who need it. The campuses sport an impressive range of state-of-the-art equipment and other amenities.

GOALS — IMPROVED ARTICULATION BETWEEN EDUCATION
OPTIONS AND THE JOB MARKET

In recent years, the college has taken a more active intermediary role in postsecondary education. The college reaches out to local high schools for students interested in its programs. Qualified high school students can take technical education courses for postsecondary credits. The college is also strengthening ties with industry organizations. Employer contacts and a practical job readiness context have taken on a more vibrant presence in its expanded tech-prep curriculum.

Montgomery College offers tech-prep programs in six disciplines, triple the options available in the early 1990s. The fields are building trades; landscaping; automotive technology; printing; biotechnology; and systems technology. Most programs yield a technical certificate after 1 year, with the option of earning an Associate of Arts degree in a second year. The tech-prep arrangements with county public schools permit high school students to accelerate completion of their chosen credential. Part-time enrollment allows working persons to complete the credential without interrupting their careers.

Montgomery College's tech-prep program prepares young people for skilled work that provides a decent and sustainable standard of living. The concentrations offered have been carefully matched with existing and projected employment opportunities in the area. For instance, the U.S. Office of Technology Assessment rated the county as a national "hot spot" for technology development. Montgomery County has 100 biomedical technology firms who estimate that they will employ an aggregate 15,000 people within several years. Another example is a traditional field — printing — which is undergoing an explosive technical transformation, with the rise of desktop publishing, laser scanners, and the like. Greater Washington, DC, is a leading producer and consumer of printed material. Additionally, as one of the nation's most populous metropolitan areas, the region sustains strong demand and good salaries for certified mechanics, electricians, and other skilled workers.

Choosing the tech-prep path entails a fairly firm career decision by relatively young students. The college heavily promotes its expanded tech-prep effort with speakers, brochures, and a video entitled "Imagine Your Tomorrow." Tech-prep can anchor a young person's commitment to education with a credible promise of an interesting, high-paying job. The Suburban Maryland Technology Council, an employer association, advises educators on development of the program and assists in marketing it. Especially in the medical and computer technology fields, recent hiring prospects for tech-prep graduates have been excellent.

Program Model — An Articulated 1+1 Certificate and Associate's Degree

Whether the tech-prep programs lead to a 2-year associate degree or 1-year certificate programs, they articulate with offerings in the county public high schools. High school students enter a tech-prep program in their junior year. The county public school system operates a separate technical education campus, the Edison Career Center, and provides transportation from local schools to Edison for courses not available at the regular high schools. They earn advanced placement college credit for applied science courses, such as Principles of Technology, if they make a grade of B or better. Frequently, high school students in tech-prep also take one or two community college classes each semester during their senior year. Career-minded students who vigorously pursue an accelerated option can knock off half a year from the time it takes to earn an associate's degree.

Many 4-year colleges accept these advanced placement credits as well. Articulation options in the systems and biotechnology programs can readily be coordinated into a 4-year baccalaureate course of study.

Industry sends speakers into the schools and provides more substantive support, such as internship and tuition reimbursement programs. The cooperative arrangements uniting community college, public schools, and employers around the Montgomery College programs provides mutual benefits that go beyond public relations. In this part of the country, at least in selected fast-growing fields, qualified workers are in genuine demand. In Montgomery County, recently, job slots for certain biomedical technicians were created so rapidly that an individual who met requirements could immediately secure a respectable income.

Community college continues to be a place where many adults select only courses directly related to personal or career interests. One nondegree alternative the college actively promotes is a short

5–11 credit hour horticulture sequence in landscape technology. This option can introduce high-school students to a career in landscaping, or provide valuable theoretical and practical skills for persons already working in the industry.

CHALLENGES

Educators actively involved in school-to-work transition realize that the volatility of both labor markets and technology poses a challenge. Modern technical education, exemplified by tech-prep programs like Montgomery College's, must keep abreast of current developments in equipment and processes. Employment-relevant schooling for today's and tomorrow's jobs requires ongoing investment in expensive technology. Information about business practices and market trends needs to be updated continually.

Educators confront two seemingly divergent goals. On one hand, employers highly value specific training which enables hirees to come on board and quickly become productive in a particular job. Conversely, broader conceptual competence is the key to self-directed problem solving and innovation, the most remunerative workplace skills. This kind of flexible cognitive facility increases economic security as prospective career changes and retraining becoming normal expectations for much of the workforce.

Balancing these considerations calls for creativity built on the recognition that no technical education program can remain fixed for long. A collaborative relationship with employers promotes access to equipment and know-how, and the interaction makes tech-prep more adaptive to leading-edge trends.

Counselors and school administrators who favor tech-prep must overcome the resistance engendered by Montgomery County parents' high expectations for their children. Although many of these parents dismiss any program below the baccalaureate level, tech-prep advocates point to the large number of college dropouts (as high as 50%), who often have difficulty finding nonmenial work. In contrast, tech-prep promises to teach tangible skills that will land good jobs. Nevertheless, tech-prep promoters also respond to the pro-baccalaureate degree argument by trying to close the perceived gap between the two levels of advanced education. The possibilities for transferring course credits from 2-year to 4-year institutions are expanding significantly. Montgomery College's pitch to parents whose kids are thinking about entering tech-prep, notes that classes for its biotechnology concentration can be part of a package which would ultimately qualify a student for admission into medical school.

LESSONS LEARNED

Montgomery College's tech-prep programs are regionally and nationally recognized for outstanding quality. A student team from the building trades division recently won first prize in a competition sponsored by the National Association of Home Builders. The students modified a set of architectural plans to meet client specifications, used computer-aided drafting, and compiled a comprehensive construction estimate and schedule.

The systems technology program — which deals with advanced applications of robotics, microelectronics, lasers, and other devices — was named the top high school-community college partnership by the Middle States Association. The biotechnology program has an evolving affiliation with the region's leading firms and research centers, including world-recognized innovators like Cellmark Diagnostics.

Awards help to confirm the worth of new programs, but the most significant measure of success is its students' career advancement. Montgomery County is auspiciously located for positive outcomes: diversified forces propel the area's economy, with an irremovable (albeit shrinking) large actor ensconced among them — the federal government. But Montgomery College's tech-prep proponents know success is not automatic. They will have to earn it by staying in close touch with changing workforce requirements and delivering students who have mastered them.

6

WORK-BASED PRACTICES

INTRODUCTION

Most youngsters work at some time while going to school. At any point during the school year over six million are employed and untold additional numbers are serving as volunteers in community service. During past summers, close to 700,000 were employed in the federally financed Summer Youth Employment Program and hundreds of thousands in other summer jobs. This section contains six case studies of attempts to make these jobs "learning rich" work experiences. Employers are the major players in each. However, the integration with the schools is less complete than it is in the programs described in the "Integrated Practices" section of this book.

The public sector section describes what has been the largest public employer of disadvantaged youth. In most summers over the last 25 years, up to 700,000 youngsters have been employed in the Summer Youth Employment Program (SYEP), which, at this writing, is threatened with extinction by the budget cutters en route to a balanced budget. Although the employment has been federally funded, the employers have been a mix of state and local government agencies and not-for-profit institutions. Unfortunately, despite attempts over the past 10 years to add educational components, Summer Youth has been labeled "make work." Indeed, the program started in the riotous 1960s as "fire insurance." Two paradigm shifts make it possible to change SYEP. First, the downsizing and reinventing of all institutions make public and private agencies more eager to use this free resource well. Second, the school-to-work movement gives more impetus to using SYEP as an available, paid, work-based learning experience for youngsters who may have few other opportunities. Making the experience worthwhile does, however, require a changed mind set on the part of the supervisors of agencies in which the youngsters work. One of the two case studies describes what happened when these ideas were applied to Maryland's SYEP program. The other describes Summer Beginnings, a national demonstration of a similar type.

Two groups of private sector employers are described in the private sector section. One is the group associated with Public Private Venture's (P/PV) WorkPlus project. The other is McDonald's and other customer service firms that have joined their Apprenticeship program. In the former, community organizations have to enroll companies in the retail, food, lodging, tourism, and supermarket businesses. In the latter, McDonald's has to convince schools and community organizations that the project serves their needs. Both projects use SCANS and the industry standards to create a certificate of competency. Both seek to help youngsters turn the jobs they are likely to have in these industries (over three million youngsters work in them) into career ladders. The McDonald's Apprenticeship program seeks to involve traditional high schools and community colleges. WorkPlus emphasizes community-based organizations and alternative education. Both are in the early stages of implementation but, together, they can have an important influence on so-called "secondary labor market" that characterizes most jobs for youth. Both projects share an important characteristic often missing in other projects. To be successful, these program not only need to help youngsters, but must also payoff for the private employers. If that payoff can be demonstrated, the idea will spread.

The final two case studies describe a third venue, service learning. This category has both a long tradition and a recent paradigm shift. Youngsters have volunteered to work in the Red Cross, as "Candy Stripers" in hospitals, and in similar situations for decades. Recently, school systems have begun to see community service as a way to learn citizenship skills. One of the case studies describes Maryland's Community Service Requirement. The other tells the story of one of Maryland's successes, *Magic Me*, which has become a national and internationally replicated model.

School-to-work is about systemic change, not a series of pilot programs. Reaching this goal means changing the workplaces where many millions of youngsters already work for pay, for credit, or for personal gratification. These case studies tell the story of successful attempts to make that work "learning-rich."

PUBLIC SECTOR SUMMER YOUTH EMPLOYMENT PROGRAMS

SUMMER BEGINNINGS NATIONAL DEMONSTRATION PROJECT

BACKGROUND — THE SUMMER CHALLENGE

In the spring of 1993, the Clinton Administration proposed to expand the Summer Youth Employment Program (SYEP) as part of its economic stimulus package. Both the size and purpose of this 25-year-old summer jobs program were to be enlarged. The number of slots was to be increased by 50%, from about 670,000 to 1,000,000. More importantly, the educational purposes of the program were to be greatly expanded even over the attempts of the past decade. First, the erosion in math and reading that many disadvantaged youngsters experience in the summer was to be arrested and, second, the range of educational experiences was to be broadened. Summer jobs were to become educationally enriched. The 1993 stimulus program was defeated by the "deficit hawks" in Congress. However, the Department of Labor financed a modest expansion of the Technical Assistance contract that Brandeis University's Center for Human Resources (CHR) had operated for many years. The aim of this sub-contract was to develop and field test an approach to running SYEPs which would meet these educational enrichment goals.

Susan Curnan, Director of CHR, called together practitioners from around the United States to advise her in developing a strategy. This team of practitioners developed working papers detailing a vision and providing a blueprint for enriching programs. Then, Curnan recruited 13 sites from around the United States to field test the new approach. These 13 sites formed the Summer Beginnings network. All were committed to academically enriching their summer programs. Some of them emphasized classroom learning, others were entirely worksite-based, and many combined the two.[1]

---

[1] For more detail on the Summer Beginnings findings, see *Field Kit For Communities Committed to Improving Academic Enrichment in Summer Youth Employment Programs*, Waltham, MA: Center for Human Resources, Brandeis University, 1994.

A subcontract was provided to the Johns Hopkins' Institute for Policy Studies (IPS) to provide assistance in developing work-based models, and to document their best practices (the campus of Johns Hopkins University was one of the Summer Beginnings sites). The following pages describe these best practices and the lessons learned from them.[2]

GOALS — ACADEMIC ENRICHMENT

The message from President Clinton and the United States Department of Labor was clear: summer youth employment programs must tackle the academic deficits of young people. They should break down the artificial barriers between school and work and provide academic enrichment which, at minimum, counteracts the erosion in basic academic skills which many youngsters experience over the summer.

PROGRAM MODELS — NATURAL VARIATION

Curnan quickly realized that the diversity of SYEP sites demanded the flexibility afforded by several program models. Supplying a vision and technical assistance and facilitating communication among the practitioners would permit a variety of models to emerge — each suited to the needs of their community. Curnan calls this a "natural variation" approach.

The vision started with four premises:

♦ Youngsters enrolled in SYEP are capable of responsibly performing complex tasks *if* their supervisors are properly supportive. In this case, the "supervisors" are those who are employed by the public agency or not-for-profit organization at the jobsite where the youngsters work. These adults supervise the youngsters on a daily basis.

♦ With encouragement and guidance, supervisors can *"invent"* learning-rich tasks that are useful to the employing organization and instructive to the youngsters.

---

[2] Arnold H. Packer and M. Frank Stluka, *Developing Learning-Rich Clerical Tasks: Value the Youngster, Value the Work,* and *Developing Learning-Rich Tasks for Parks Recreation and Natural Resources: Value the Youngster, Value the Work,* Baltimore: Institute for Policy Studies, Johns Hopkins University, 1994.

♦ The SCANS competencies can be learned while performing these tasks. Indeed, it is difficult to define responsible and useful tasks that do not teach one or more of the SCANS competencies. (*See* the descriptions of two tasks, on following pages.)

♦ Successful American workplaces will train their workers in the SCANS competencies as firms struggle to remain competitive and the public sector seeks to reinvent itself for the 21st century. Successful workplaces in both sectors will become learning organizations. Supervisors will become coaches and workers will be learners. Learning-rich tasks for summer youth workers can provide a model for employing organizations.

As stated above, each site developed its own model based on these premises. Two approaches can be generalized from these models: "internships," where one or two youngsters are placed in an existing worksite and supervised by a regular employee who may or may not have any teaching or supervisory experience, and "team projects," where approximately six youths are assigned to a project together with a supervisor whose primary responsibility is to supervise their work. One example of each follows.

Team Project: Taking an Inventory of Natural Resources

Delgado Community College occupies a heavily wooded campus of about 53 acres in New Orleans. They received a $16,000 federal grant for tree maintenance. Planning how to use the money, they needed an assessment of the number and condition of the trees on the campus. They wanted to know how many of each kind of tree they had, what pruning was needed, how many of the trees were wounded, and where vines had to be removed. A team of 42 youths and six supervisors supervisor conducted this tree inventory.

In a similar project, the same youths conducted a timber cruise on 8-acre Scout Island near New Orleans. They divided into six crews. Each crew charted the pine trees on a segment of the island and estimated their timber value. Then, they combined their findings and presented them to the Louisiana Department of Agriculture and Forestry. Projects like this — inventorying and assessing the maintenance needs of natural resources — are needed in a wide variety of settings, from waterfronts to flower beds. Similar tasks relate to purchased resources, ranging from cataloging office and medical equipment in a hospital to athletic equipment at recreation centers.

The team first developed a workplan, allocating time, people, and equipment needed to conduct the inventory. They prepared a map of the campus, and designed a data sheet to record the number, size, and condition of each tree. To count and rate the trees, they divided the map into several areas, and broke their team into several smaller teams. Each team inventoried one area. Then, they brought their data together, summarized it, and graphed the results. They formulated maintenance recommendations from the results of the inventory. Finally, they presented their findings and recommendations to the Delgado Beautification Committee.

In addition to the knowledge about trees, team members learned the SCANS competencies. They learned about **systems** by understanding how the trees would respond to alternative maintenance programs. They learned about **resources** by scheduling time and people to accomplish the inventory. They developed **interpersonal** skills by working as a team to develop and act on the workplan. They learned **information** skills by preparing a map, designing the data sheet, conducting the inventory, summarizing the data, drawing conclusions, and presenting them to the Delgado Beautification Committee. Finally, they learned about **technology** by selecting the tools they would need to accomplish the inventory and summarize the data.

Internship: Coordinating Communications

Johns Hopkins University's participation in Summer Beginnings was twofold: The University campus was a Summer Beginnings site that placed youngsters in jobs in offices throughout the university. Additionally, the Institute for Policy Studies at the University (IPS) was responsible for documenting the best practices in work-based learning throughout the Summer Beginnings network. The information-gathering at Hopkins required extensive communication with the 42 interns placed in 36 offices at two of Hopkins' campuses. IPS also monitored the work performed by youths in six of Baltimore City's recreation centers.

Communication has traditionally been a problem in SYEP programs. Participants (interns) do not know what is expected of them and site supervisors cannot maintain contact with the participants.

IPS used a field test of the then new WordPerfect 6.0 software and on-line curriculum as a model project for solving this problem. Several of the offices that hosted summer interns got copies of this software. The interns worked through the curriculum and reported back to IPS on its usefulness. Interns who completed the curriculum received a certificate from the WordPerfect Corporation. All of this required extensive communication via fax, telephone, and in-person, with people scattered across many locations.

SYEP interns in the Department of Human Resources at the Johns Hopkins Hospital performed a similar communications task. The work described below is easily applied to organizations that conduct operations in many locations. Possible settings include the headquarters of a company that communicates extensively with many branch offices, and an office that serves clients in many settings.

As described earlier, two interns developed, administered, summarized and reported on surveys and helped to schedule and conduct focus groups of the other interns at both Hopkins campuses. They wrote and distributed a newsletter with information about the SYEP, results of the surveys, and some suggestions for making the summer more meaningful. They installed the WordPerfect software on computers in several of the participating offices. They took turns answering the phones — and answering questions about the WordPerfect software, pay schedules, bus tokens, and other aspects of the SYEP. They also helped out with writing and faxing memos to other offices, as needed.

The two summer interns also accompanied other IPS staff members to the recreation centers. Often, the youths employed at these recreation centers spoke more openly with these interns than they would with adults. While the adult IPS staff were interviewing recreation center staff or observing recreation programs, the interns interviewed the youths at the recreation centers and observed their work. Back at IPS, the interns summarized their observations. The data from these observations and from the surveys and focus groups at the Hopkins campuses were used in developing the material for this publication.

As described, this was a learning-rich job for the interns. They learned about **technology** by working through the WordPerfect on-line curriculum, installing the software on computers (first with close supervision, then on their own), and using other office equipment. They learned about **systems** by designing and conducting surveys and focus groups. They learned **information** skills by gathering data from surveys, focus groups, interviews and observation. They also interpreted and reported on this information in the newsletter and summarized visits to recreation centers. They developed **interpersonal** skills by working together as a team in all aspects of their work, answering questions from other participants in the SYEP, and teaching each other what they knew about computers, other office equipment, and the SYEP program. They learned to manage **resources** by scheduling meetings and focus groups and by planning the labor-time needed to get each tasks accomplished.

In postscripts to the summer, the interns learned about larger systems. Eager to be reassigned to IPS the following summer, they wrote the Hopkins Vice President of Human Resources, requesting that he ask city officials to assign them to IPS. A draft letter to the city accompanied their letter to the Vice President. They learned how the "system" worked and learned how to make it work for them.

They also learned about leadership. After the summer was over, one intern ran for class president. Both boys made presentations at the Department of Labor's Summer Youth Conference in Washington.

CHALLENGES

♦ The biggest challenge to academically enriching summer jobs is to get people at all levels of program administration to **abandon their preconceptions about youths, work, and learning**. In the internship model, the supervisors often have no supervisory or teaching experience. And they often have very low expectations of what SYEP participants are able to do. Or supervisors may have supervised youngsters in the past and been expected only to keep them busy and out of trouble. Convincing these supervisors that youngsters should and are able to perform complex tasks is difficult.

♦ **Getting management buy-in** is also difficult. Once managers at the worksite realize that learning-rich work requires more preparation, supervisor training, and upfront supervisor time than merely putting kids to busy work, they may balk at the prospect. Usually (but not always) there are benefits to the worksite that outweigh this investment of employee time. For example, at Hopkins, the Vice President of Human Resources was championing a total quality management

(TQM) approach. He had sponsored training on TQM with department heads and other administrators, but did not feel that the message was getting through. He saw the summer program as an opportunity for staff at all levels to gain experience and training in TQM.

◆ **Connections.** All too frequently, summer programs are separated from what goes on during the rest of the year. Program managers must provide continuity with year-round programs. How can the summer build on the skills and knowledge learned during the school year? How can the administrators of summer programs inform and encourage schools and other year-round programs to recognize and build on the learning that takes place during the summer? Program managers must create channels of communication between summer and year-round programs.

◆ **Team projects or individual internships?** These two approaches provide very different managerial considerations and learning experiences. Team projects involve fewer supervisors. Usually, the managing agency is able to hire people specifically for this job. Teachers or other youth-serving professionals usually have expertise in managing youngsters. This simplifies the job of the managing agency. Team projects also offer the youngster a natural opportunity to consult with each other as equals, to share common challenges, and to develop teamwork skills.

Internships require more supervisors. Usually these supervisors are the frontline staff of the employing agency, and may have no experience either in teaching or supervision. This makes program management more difficult. On the other hand, this model allows for a more intimate mentoring relationship that is more likely to last beyond the employment period. Internships are also more likely to lead to future unsubsidized employment at the host agency.

The director of one of the Summer Beginnings sites recommends a team project assignment for youngsters who have little or no previous employment experience, and internships for more experienced workers. This arrangement allows youngsters to develop initial work maturity skills with peer support, then glean the benefits of internships later.

LESSONS LEARNED

The Summer Beginnings field test tended to bear out the premises identified at the start and to provide the following six lessons:

+ **Management Buy-in:** The process of making SYEP a "learning rich" experience begins with a "buy-in" from the managers of the employing organization. Those who manage the supervisors have to champion the approach.

+ **Creative facilitators:** Inventing "learning-rich" tasks requires outsiders who can creatively facilitate the process. The facilitators have to understand the specific workplace. "You have to walk in our shoes," as one recreation department manager said.

+ **Reflection:** The youngsters need to understand why what they are doing is important and, later, reflect on what they have learned and why those skills are important in many jobs.

+ **Time to Prepare:** The process, from buy-in through training the supervisors, takes considerable time. The process should begin at least 3 months before the SYEP program starts and should be tied to a year-round program if possible. During this period, there must be an opportunity for the supervisors to work in teams, with facilitators, to invent tasks that are both useful and "learning rich." Given this opportunity, most supervisors will rise to the challenge.

+ **Exploiting the Unexpected:** Unforeseen possibilities, such as the availability of WordPerfect 6.0 in the summer of 1993, will present themselves both for the youngsters and the employing organization. Planning should provide the flexibility to exploit these opportunities.

+ **Value the Youngsters, Value the Work:** Management and the frontline supervisors have to make it clear that they value the youngsters and what they can do. Supervisors must see to it that the tasks the youngsters perform are perceived as valuable to their organization.

MARYLAND'S SUMMER YOUTH EMPLOYMENT AND TRAINING PROGRAM

BACKGROUND — INTERAGENCY COOPERATION

Maryland's Summer Youth Employment and Training Program is funded by the U.S. Department of Labor (USDOL) under Title II-B of the Job Training Partnership Act. In an average year, over 11,000 youths are employed by state and local government, schools, and not-for-profit organizations. This program is jeopardized by plans to eliminate funding for JTPA, II-B after the Summer of 1995.

Local Service Delivery Areas (SDAs) administer the 6-week summer program. While each SDA is relatively autonomous, they band together across the state through several alliances. The Governor's Workforce Investment Board (GWIB) coordinates the state's workforce development efforts. In the fall of 1993, the SDAs asked GWIB for assistance in academically enriching their summer programs. GWIB created a partnership with Maryland's Department of Economic and Employment Development, the Maryland State Department of Education, the Institute for Policy Studies at the Johns Hopkins University, and the SDAs. These "partners" then developed a strategy to address the challenges listed below.

GOALS — ACADEMIC ENHANCEMENT THROUGH REAL WORK

The Summer Youth Employment and Training Program (SYETP) seeks to:

♦ Provide structured, well-supervised work in order to promote good work habits and valued output;

♦ Provide income to economically disadvantaged youth who would otherwise not be able to find summer employment;

♦ Prepare for the workplace and enhance occupational skills by performing important tasks and assignments ("real work");

♦ Experience the connection between work and learning;

♦ Build basic and higher order thinking skills through work;

♦ Develop a portfolio which demonstrates the acquisition of academic and work-related skills; and

♦ Explore career options.

PROGRAM MODEL — SUPERVISOR TRAINING AND SUPPORT

The Maryland partners, having determined that supervisor training and support are the key ingredients to enriching summer jobs, began developing "learning-rich" tasks that would import the SCANS skills and competencies in the context of real work. Supervisors were trained and supported to become "coaches." Their responsibilities now included planning, regular meetings, and evaluation.

"**Planning,**" the partners agreed, "is the difference between learning-rich tasks and make work." Supervisors took the time to identify projects that youths could plan and implement relatively independently, and to make the necessary arrangements at the worksite for these projects. As a result, youths became competent and confident as they developed and executed their own work plans.

Regular meetings between the supervisor and the youth were held to review the work that had been accomplished and the quality of that work, the skills that were needed to accomplish the work (the learning), and where else these skills apply (generalizing the learning).

Evaluation and documentation will be an ongoing process that occurred at the regular meetings. Youths saved evidence of their work and learning, in the form of photographs of their work before and after completion, copies of documents they wrote, and sketches or calculations used to plan their work. Youths reviewed these with their supervisors to evaluate and revise their work, learning, and strategies for accomplishing both.

The partners' designed and implemented a plan for training and supporting the supervisors. They developed a four-pronged approach:

♦ A **training-of-trainers workshop** was held in February of 1994. Trainers learned about the SCANS skills and competencies and how to incorporate them in the tasks youngsters performed in summer jobs. They also learned to replicate the training with other worksite supervisors in their programs. This workshop was developed primarily by the Institute for Policy Studies (IPS), capitalizing on their participation in Summer Beginnings (*see* "Summer Beginnings," discussed earlier). All participants in the training-of-trainers received copies of *Developing Learning-Rich Tasks for Summer Youth Employment Programs: Value the Youngster, Value the Work*, a volume which combined the two reports developed by

IPS for the Summer Beginnings Demonstration Project. The workshop was attended by approximately 75 representatives of the partners and their cooperating worksites.

♦ The workshop was videotaped. A small contract between IPS and Maryland Public Television produced **a video to support local training** efforts.

♦ IPS, in consultation with the rest of the partners, developed a **WorkPlan and Competency Résumé** (WCR). The WCR is a form designed to help planning learning-rich tasks and document the learning that occurs in them. It is included in the appendix to this narrative.

♦ GWIB, in consultation with the other partners, produced a **Supervisors' Handbook** that defined learning-rich work in terms of the SCANS competencies, defined the supervisors role in inventing and overseeing learning-rich work, and included the WCR and instructions for its use. Many SDAs used it "as is." Others supplemented it with local guidelines and additional further documentation of work and learning.

After experience with this effort in the summer of 1994, the partners reconvened in the fall and determined to revise both the WCR and the Supervisor's Handbook. Several focus group meetings produced a revised WCR and Supervisor's Handbook. The revised WCR and directions for its use, and a sample completed WCR are attached at the end of this narrative (*see* Fig. 6.1 at the end of the Appendix to this section).

CHALLENGES

Maryland's GWIB partners had to overcome many challenges before they could satisfactorily enrich their summer jobs program. First, the partners, each with their own priorities, had to agree on the goals and methods for this reform. They had to develop a format for reform that applies to all communities — whether rural, urban, or suburban — regardless of their traditions in developing past SYETP programs. One thing was clear: no one agency or region of the state could dictate an approach to the others.

Second, the partners had to overcome a lot of preconceptions about the nature of youths, work, and learning. Many supervisors and staff members within the partner organizations had low expectations about what SYETP participants could achieve. Similarly, they were initially skeptical about what the supervisors could do, given that many of the supervisors have little or no experience in teaching or supervision.

LESSONS LEARNED

The first lessons learned are common to many reform efforts. To quote Jobs for the Future's Tech Prep Manual, "**start at the bottom**," and "**start at the top**." Although this reform was initiated at the top — several state and local agencies banding together to implement changes mandated at the federal level — the planners quickly realized that the key to change was to draw from the organizational bottom, the worksite supervisors. Buy-in had to be obtained from all levels of the organizations.

Start with a vision. The partners agreed early on that academic enrichment *could* happen in the context of work. SYETP participants' vision of work had to be changed to include more complex tasks than they were traditionally assigned. This vision then had to be sold to all levels of management and staff, and to the youths themselves.

Start early. Although planning for the reform started in December, the initial training-of-trainers was not able to be held until late February, and the handbooks and training video were not available until well after that. For many of the SDAs, this was too late. Some had to conduct their supervisor training before these materials were available, and were not able to implement the reform in its entirety. Having learned from this, the second year's planning and handbook revision started much earlier.

Develop a plan. Having realized that training and support for the supervisors were the key to success, the partners quickly developed a plan to provide this.

Continuous Improvement. After the first summer's experience implementing the "learning-rich work" approach, the partners reviewed their experience and revised the training and support materials to address the difficulties they encountered.

FIG. 6.1. THE WORKPLAN AND COMPETENCY RÉSUMÉ

DIRECTIONS FOR COMPLETING THE WCR FORM

1. **IDENTIFYING INFORMATION:** Complete the top part of the form.
2. **COLUMNS:** Use this section to plan a learning rich work experience for the youth. There are three columns.
   A. **COMPETENCY or SKILL COLUMN:** The SCANS skills or competencies and one or two example tasks that use them are shown in the first column, marked Competency or Skill.
   B. **OPPORTUNITY COLUMN:** The column marked Opportunity is designed to help you monitor the youth's work as well as to help the youth acquire the skill or competency. Mark the column Y if there was the opportunity to learn the competency or N if there was no opportunity to learn the skill. Although it is often not possible to cover every competency and skill, the supervisor should consider broadening the job responsibilities so that the youth can learn as much as possible while doing the work that needs to be done. See Sample Completed WCRs for ideas for broadening job responsibilities.
   C. **TASK COLUMN:** The supervisor should list the specific tasks assigned to the young person. Another approach would be to let the youth complete the specific tasks with the approval of the supervisor.
3. **REVIEW WITH THE YOUTH:** It is important that the supervisor and the youth review the WCR often. This will give the youths the opportunity to improve their performance at the assigned task while overcoming weaknesses and developing strengths. These conversations provide the youth with an opportunity to reflect on what is being learned and how the skills and competencies can be used after the summer is over.
4. **FORMAL ASSESSMENT**
   A. **THE PERFORMANCE COLUMN:** Complete the Performance column on the right- hand side of the form at the end of the summer and at other times requested by the SDA, School Board, or subcontractor. It will document the SCANS skills and competencies learned by the youth. Enter 1 in the box if the youth was exposed to the competency or skill and began to learn it. Enter 2 if the youth is becoming competent in the task. Enter 3 if the youth performs the task well with little supervision.
   B. **USING THE COMPLETED FORM:** The final WCR should be a clean, presentable copy that the youth can share with teachers, parents, and potential employers, to show what they are able to do. The final WCR will list what the youth did (rather than what the supervisor had planned to do). The supervisor and the youth should sign the WCR at the bottom of the second page. Any additional comments can be written there. The local SDA will collect these forms on a schedule which they will discuss with you.

FIG. 6.2. WORKPLAN AND COMPETENCY RÉSUMÉ (WCR)
SAMPLE COMPLETED WCR FOR ENVIRONMENTAL AND MAINTENANCE SERVICES

Name: *Ellen D. Mason*   Job Title: *Assistant Maintenance Technician*

Supervisor's Name: *Demetrius King*   Work Site: *Alvernia Middle School*

School: *Alvernia High School*   Date: *August 6, 1994*

Competency or Skill The know-how the worker should learn, followed by examples.	Opportunity Was the worker given a chance to learn this? (Y or N)	Tasks List specific tasks that the worker performed.	Performance How well did the worker perform? Enter 1=Beginning 2=Improving 3=Mastering
Personal Qualities/Work Habits: Responsibility EX: Complete assigned tasks	Y	*Saw entire project through from planning to completion.*	3
Self-Esteem EX: Take pride in work	Y	*Made sure that work was done well. Solicited feedback from clients (teachers).*	3
Appearance EX: Dress appropriately	Y	*Always dressed appropriately: jeans & t-shirt for painting, neater when with teachers.*	3
Social EX: Get along with coworkers	Y	*Enjoyed co-workers company and worked well with them.*	2
Self-Management EX: Work independently when needed	Y	*Continued to work quickly and carefully when no supervisor was present.*	2
Integrity/Honesty EX: Report work hours accurately	Y	*Kept careful records of hours worked. Did not steal or waste supplies.*	3
Basic Skills: EX: reading, writing, math, listening, speaking	Y	*Calculated surface area of walls & amount of paint needed. Wrote survey of teachers' needs.*	2

Skill		Example	Rating
Thinking Skills: EX: problem solving, creativity, reasoning	Y	*Developed workplan to prepare and paint classrooms. Identified and solved problems with this workplan.*	2
INFORMATION: Obtain & Assess EX: Read directions, ask questions, do research	Y	*Read paint and paint-sprayer directions. Surveyed teachers about how they wanted their classrooms to look.*	2
Organize & Maintain EX: File, update and retrieve records	Y	*Filed teachers' requests, price quotes from suppliers, and paint and equipment instructions.*	1
Communicate EX: Answer questions, write instructions	Y	*Drew floor plan, specifying amount & color of paint for each room. Answered co-workers' and teachers' questions.*	3
Use Computers EX: Create a database, enter and printout data	Y	*Used computer to estimate surface area of walls and amount of paint needed to cover them.*	2
SYSTEMS/OPERATING PROCEDURES: Understand EX: Make a flowchart	Y	*Understood steps to repair, clean, prime, and paint walls. Understood system to order supplies (get price quotes, select supplier, etc).*	2
Monitor & Correct EX: Find and correct error in instructions	Y	*Monitored team's work and corrected errors as they occurred. Followed-up on purchase orders and teachers' requests.*	3
Design or Improve EX: Streamline work plan for more efficiency	Y	*Developed system to prepare and paint classrooms. Checked after first room was done to improve system for remaining rooms.*	2

Competency or Skill	Oppor-tunity (Y/N)	Tasks	Performance (1, 2, or 3)
TECHNOLOGY: Select Tools EX: Choose equipment for a project	Y	*Chose equipment for spackling & painting (paint brush or sprayer, hand sander or power sander, ladder or scaffold).*	2
Use Tools Properly EX: Follow safety instructions	Y	*Avoided injuries, paint waste, & damage to machines when using paint sprayer and power sander.*	3
Maintain & Troubleshoot EX: Clean and fix equipment	Y	*Unclogged paint sprayer. Cleaned paint brushes. Cleaned and lubricated power sander.*	2
INTERPERSONAL: Work on Team EX: Cooperate with co-workers, provide help	Y	*Worked on team with three other summer youths & supervisor to repair and paint walls in 12 classrooms. Assisted with other projects as needed.*	2
Teach Others EX: Explain a task, demonstrate a skill	Y	*Taught co-workers how to use paint sprayer.*	1
Serve Customers EX: Greet clients, resolve complaints	Y	*Dealt with teachers to find out how they wanted their classrooms to look. Handled teachers' complaints when they were not satisfied.*	3
Lead Others EX: Make a presentation to motivate co-workers	Y	*Led work team, including three other summer youth workers, in planning and painting 12 classrooms.*	2

Competency	Y	Description	Score
Negotiate EX: Agree on activities, schedules, or prices	Y	*Negotiated paint prices with suppliers. Compromised on work assignments with other team members.*	3
Cultural Diversity EX: Work with people of other races or ages	Y	*Worked with co-workers of different cultural backgrounds (one spoke very little English).*	2
RESOURCES: Time EX: Schedule activities, use time effectively	Y	*Estimated amount of time needed for each step of workplan. Developed schedule to complete the job by end of employment period.*	2
Money EX: Collect coffee money, budget events	Y	*Estimated costs for wall repair and painting. Compared prices of several brands of paint and plaster.*	2
Materials EX: Determine supplies needed and order them	Y	*Determined supplies needed to spackle and paint 12 classrooms. Ordered these supplies.*	2
Space EX: Select meeting location, organize a room	Y	*Organized maintenance storage room.*	1
Staff EX: Decide who will do a task	Y	*Assigned duties to other summer workers to make sure that classrooms got painted.*	2

Please comment on worker's experience, skills, or competency below.

Ellen showed great maturity in her dealings with co-workers, and in her caution in using tools. She dealt with her team fairly, and made sure that all equipment was used safely. I would highly recommend her for any job that requires caution and uses heavy equipment. She would make a great supervisor someday.

Student's
Signature: __Ellen D. Mason__

Supervisor's
Signature: __Demetrius King__

PRIVATE SECTOR

WORKPLUS
NATIONAL PROGRAM

BACKGROUND — NONPROFIT AND FOR-PROFIT COOPERATION

In 1994, the DeWitt Wallace Foundation funded Public/Private Ventures (P/PV), a not-for-profit organization based in Philadelphia, to test the proposition that the jobs youngsters typically hold — at fast food restaurants and other retail establishments — can be made learning-rich. The resulting project is WorkPlus. P/PV then set about signing up communities and designing program operations. P/PV plans to engage seven sites. In each of these seven communities, Local Coordinating Agencies (LCAs) will implement the model.

Three LCAs will be operating in 1995: The Boston Private Industry Council and Action for Boston Community Development (ABCD), Cleveland Works, Inc., and New Ways Workers, in Sonoma, CA. Each organization is recruiting local employers and, through them, their employees. The employers are often part of a chain (for example, Bradlees and Au Bon Pain in Boston and Marriott and Wendy's in Cleveland). P/PV, the SCANS/2000 Program within the Institute for Policy Studies at the Johns Hopkins University, and other consultants are providing technical assistance to the LCAs.

As noted earlier, federal grants have supported national industry groups who developed and published standards for their industries in 1994 and 1995. Meanwhile, the 103rd Congress passed the *Goals 2000, Educate America Act* and established a National Skills Standards Board (NSSB) to create a national system out of these individual efforts. The creation of the NSSB and the maturing of the individual standards efforts led to a desire for cross-industry certification.

Three industry organizations are interested in piloting a common certificate and see WorkPlus as an opportunity to do so. These are the National Retail Federation (NRF), the National Grocers Association (NGA) and the Council for Hotel, Restaurant, and Institutional Education (CHRIE). These national organizations have developed skill standards for their industries and are participating in WorkPlus.

On Valentines Day of 1995, representatives from the three pilot sites met with P/PV staff and consultants and with staff from CHRIE, NGA, and the NRF. They sat down to thrash out the elements of the WorkPlus portfolio, to connect the local efforts in the three sites to the national standards efforts, and to agree on the guidelines for proceeding. In the Fall of 1995, a draft Service Certificate was developed. While useful products are likely in the short run (for example, a Service Certificate that industry finds acceptable) it will be a number of years before any definitive results are available.

GOALS — ENRICHING THE SECONDARY LABOR MARKET

WorkPlus will test the proposition that the typical jobs that youngsters hold can be made "learning rich." Enrollees will obtain certified skills and a start on a career path. Their 10-year process of "hopping from one lily pad to another" will be reduced. By their mid-twenties, enrollees in WorkPlus should be "graduated" from the secondary labor market and in a "good" job either in one of these service industries or elsewhere.

P/PVs larger purpose is to affect millions of young people. According to the Current Population Survey, 6,261,000 young people aged 16–19 were employed on average during 1990. About 1.35 million were working in eating and drinking establishments (including sit-down and fast food restaurants) and 1.8 million in other retail outlets, including stores in malls and supermarkets. The impact of enriching even only 10% of these 3.15 million jobs would be much more widespread than the most optimistic estimates of expanding traditional apprenticeship programs.

Changing the industry requires proving that job enrichment is profitable. P/PV believes that WorkPlus will reduce unwanted turnover and increase customer satisfaction and profits. This may be the only school-to-work effort that explicitly seeks to help employers become high-performance firms. Interestingly, the Hospitality and Tourism Skills Board pursued the same goals, along with the goal of increasing wages and job quality, as justification for adopting standards.

PROGRAM MODEL — CHANGING THE RELATIONSHIP BETWEEN WORKER AND SUPERVISOR

The program model, at the community level, begins with the Local Coordinating Agency or LCA. The LCA's first step establishes an employer consortium. The LCA then enrolls youngsters from these local employers. They offer training to the workplace supervisors and support both supervisors and enrollees as they change their relationship. The LCA will also provide case managers to guide the enrollee's experience on and off the job. The start-up stage at each site will last 3 years and be of modest size: 8–12 employers and 50–100 workers. Substantial expansion is expected in year 4.

Work-based learning, leading to a portfolio and a portable *Work-Plus Service Certificate*, is the centerpiece of WorkPlus. Youngsters will build a WorkPlus portfolio and work record that will be widely honored by retail stores, supermarkets, restaurants, and hotels. The development of national skills standards makes this possible.

The three national industry organizations (CHRIE, NRF, and NGA) are working with Johns Hopkins and P/PV to develop the *WorkPlus Service Certificate*. Each of these industries are developing a taxonomy of **tasks**. The ability to perform these tasks will signify that a worker has met the industry standard. That ability, in turn, requires a set of **competencies**.

Figure 6.3 lists the content of the *WorkPlus Service Certificate*. The Certificate is based on the five workplace competencies described by the Secretary's Commission on Achieving Necessary Skills (SCANS). This common language allows employers in these industries to describe, assess, and certify the competencies they value. The portfolio will help young workers describe and document what they know and can do. Using SCANS makes the certificate portable. Work-Plus employers will not be restricted to only hiring workers experienced in their own industry and community. WorkPlus workers will be able to apply their skills in other fields and other venues.

The WorkPlus portfolio contains work samples and four other documents:

♦ **Development plans** to guide the enrollee's acquisition of competencies.

♦ **Checklists** that work supervisors use to provide the **evidence** that tasks have been successfully accomplished.

♦ The Service Certificate relating competencies acquired or demonstrated as the tasks were performed at the workplace.

♦ **Résumés** that enrollees can use when they seek a new job.

FIG. 6.3. WORKPLUS SERVICE CERTIFICATE (DRAFT)

SCANS Competency and Subcompetency	Work Tasks Performed (The tasks listed below are taken from the NRF publication, *Raising Retail Standards.*)	Points*
Allocating Resources		
Time	R.6.1.5 Work out schedule conflict R.1.2.11 Schedule shopper appointment	
Money	R.3.2.4 Identify damaged items and handle	
Space	R.4.2.1 Arrange merchandise R.4.1.2 Organize stockroom	
Staff	none	
Managing Information		
Acquire/evaluate	R.1.1.1 Determined Customer Needs	
Organize/maintain	R.3.2.3 Respond to request for merchandise transfer	
Interpret/communicate	R.4.2.2 Relay customer feedback on effectiveness of displays	
Use computers	R.3.1.1 Check in merchandise against paperwork (using computer)	
Interpersonal Skills		
Team work	R.6.1.3 Assist/turnover sale to co-worker to provide better service	
Teach	R.6.1.4 Assist with training and orient new employees	
Serve customer	R.2.1.4 Handle customer objections	

Lead	NEW Was team leader for a week
Negotiate	R.2.2.5 Handle customer returns and transform into new sale
Work with diversity	NEW Served customers/worked on a team that included those of other backgrounds (age, sex, race, social class)

Technology
Select equipment/ tools

R.2.2.4 Test products to be displayed
R.4.2.4 Dismantle displays

Apply technology

R.5.1.2 Attach and remove security device

Maintain and troubleshoot

R.4.2.3 Maintain displays
R.4.1.4 Report need for repairs

Systems
Understand

R.3.1.3 Review stock and restock

Monitor and correct

R.6.2.3 Track sales vs established standards

Improve and design

R.6.1.1 Share ideas about selling, marketing products

The example below relates the competency to the work tasks and the evidence that the competency had been acquired.

SCANS Competency	Work Tasks	Evidence of Competency
Acquiring and Evaluating Information	Determine Customer's Needs By Listening and Asking Questions (retail task 1.1.1)	In an ABC Men's store, John dealt with customers at the door and directed them to proper department during the Christmas rush.
	Analyze Guest Needs (Hospitality Task)	At the Ritz, Mary found that the guest needed a nonsmoking room with a crib.

In addition to development plans for "on-the-job" activities, the case manager will assign "around-the-job" activities to each enrollee. These support service activities may include building basic skills, day care arrangements, and transportation arrangements. This external support should help enrollees overcome the special challenges that often hamper their success at the job.

The case managers, along with the work supervisors, will determine the success of WorkPlus. They are responsible for each enrollees' sequence of activities. Some enrollees may have to have their work responsibilities rotated in order to acquire the experiences needed to earn a Service Certificate. Others may have to change employers. The case manager will also connect the on-the-job and off-the-job responsibilities of the enrollees.

WorkPlus has a number of other components in addition to those that feed directly into developing the portfolio. The LCA must first create a consortium of employers who want to participate. Supervisors must be motivated and given the tools to enrich the jobs of their young workers. Case managers must be equipped to work with the employers for on-the-job activities and with other agencies for around-the-job activities. Finally, P/PV wants the LCA to offer each enrollee a developmental sequence of jobs.

At least initially, WorkPlus will not attempt to create formal connections with schools nor to affect school curricula. However, WorkPlus will encourage youngsters to continue their education and to take specific specialized courses where needed.

CHALLENGES

WorkPlus' ambitious goals will only be met if P/PV and their partners overcome a number of challenges. Their first challenge is enticing employers to participate. The second is changing the workplace culture. The work supervisors have to be motivated and trained to enrich the jobs and document the evidence of performance. These supervisors are often only a few years and one or two steps removed from many of the WorkPlus enrollees. Moreover, they have heavy workloads and limited time for outside training. Connecting WorkPlus to the national standards efforts and enlisting their corporate management may elicit their cooperation, but it is too early to tell. The job sequencing strategy poses special challenges if it means moving competent workers to jobs outside the firm.

The partners must also overcome the social support challenge. The LCAs and the case managers will have to buy into the WorkPlus goals which may be somewhat different than their own. The GED falls in importance while a supervisors' recommendation increases. Social service agencies, such as the three now involved in WorkPlus, will have to learn what makes it to the bottom line for the employers in their consortium.

The program must maintain the data needed for operation and research without putting an excessive burden on either the supervisor or case manager. P/PV will have to develop an efficient electronic system to maintain and generate the various portfolio documents. Their research design will have to be innovative to convince the three industries that WorkPlus improves profits while respecting firms' sense of security about proprietary data.

LESSONS LEARNED

Although P/PV was still in the planning and development stage for WorkPlus when this book was written, some lessons can be gleaned from the early experience.

- Developing collaboration and consensus within a business consortia is difficult, but necessary. Most large companies are aware of "high performance" concepts but may not have moved far in that direction. Social agencies that have employment as a goal should become familiar with the culture of the local workplace as well as the culture at the corporate level. These cultures may differ in their attitudes towards the concept of high performance.

- Developing collaboration and consensus among different service provider organizations around the country is difficult, but has a large potential payoff. As with any partnership, focusing on common objectives — in this case, developing the WorkPlus model — makes it easier to work together. Also, having a well-respected organization like P/PV manage the project and coordinate efforts of the partners facilitates cooperation. Cooperation pays off through the sharing of lessons learned by each organization. Some of the lessons are only in the accumulated wisdom of individuals, some are reflected in curricula and materials, and some in information systems.

- Contrary to popular opinion, many businesses that employ youngsters are interested in developing the skills of their employees. They are especially interested if the process leads to lower turnover and higher productivity.

- Pilot programs can change the school-to-work process for significant numbers of youngsters by changing large systems. The largest systems, by far, are the workplaces that already hire millions of youngsters.

MCDONALD'S YOUTH DEMONSTRATION PROJECT
NATIONAL PROGRAM

BACKGROUND — A MAJOR EMPLOYER OF YOUTHS
SEEKS TO EMPOWER EMPLOYEES

A sizeable fraction of America's youngsters are introduced to the world of work behind a counter at one of McDonald's 10,000 U.S. restaurants. One of every eight American workers have worked at some time for McDonald's. Students account for half of all the company's employees and the company recently surpassed the U.S.

Army as the nation's largest training organization. Yet, McDonald's is often synonymous with the kind of noncareer ladder job to be avoided. A decade ago, management gurus praised McDonald's for deskilling their jobs to the point were counterworkers were easily replaceable. Education gurus, however, criticized the firm for replacing the numbers on their cash registers with pictures to reduce their training costs.

Workforce 2000's warnings on demographics and the corporate movement to quality by some of their competitors changed the company's perspective. Additionally, McDonald's began hearing complaints about the quality of the work "crews" from their franchisees. As McDonald's sought to maintain market share in the competitive 1990s, they changed their previous strategy. They developed McDonald's Service Enhancement which: "1) recognizes that customers define what exceptional service is and 2) empowers the crew to do whatever it takes to satisfy customers." Thus, McDonald's decided to be the "Employer of Choice in the fast food industry." They are now praised for adopting a corporate strategy for upgrading their employees. Given that McDonald's is the largest employer of entry-level workers in the United States and that more than one-half of their frontline workers are minorities, this is a significant change.

In 1993, working with Bob Sheets at Northern Illinois University, McDonald's began to develop a National Youth Apprentice Demonstration Project. Building on their experience, first in Project Prepare in Chicago, and then in Denver McPride, and Philadelphia Freedom Theatre, they seek to change schools and change work for tens of thousands of American youngsters. Initially, they are seeking partnerships with noncompetitive firms in the retail trade and hospitality industries. McDonald's budgeted $1.6 million to the effort and sought another $1.8 million from other sources such as foundations and government. The U.S. Department of Labor has committed $234,000. Program operation will begin in the summer of 1995 in three cities: Portland, Chicago, and Baltimore. The Oregon Chain of Fred Mayer superstores will participate in Portland and Walgreens in Chicago.

GOALS — IMPROVING CUSTOMER SATISFACTION AND BUILDING A CAREER LADDER IN THE SERVICE INDUSTRY

McDonald's has at least three corporate goals: improving their reputation as a quality employer (the "Employer of Choice" in the fast food industry), increasing the flow of employees from the counter level to management, and improving customer-focused service or, as they call it, McDonald's Quality Management (MQM). The broader goals are to improve the quality of schools, to make students aware of the management opportunities in the hospitality and retail trade industries, and to test the concept of apprenticeship in the consumer service industry.

The program's "Partnership Guideline" seeks school partners whose school-to-work programs prepare students:

♦ To meet their state's academic standards and graduation requirements and to go to college.

♦ To enter hospitality and/or retail management through an integrated academic and vocational program.

These programs should have high entrance requirements but help at-risk students with preparatory programs. They should share the goal of certifying enrollees in four SCANS-like areas: allocating resources, systems, technology, and interpersonal skills, especially leadership.

PROGRAM MODEL — A PARTNERSHIP BETWEEN EMPLOYERS, SCHOOL, PARENTS, AND STUDENTS

Youngsters will enter this management trainee program in their sophomore or junior high school year. They should emerge, 4 years later, prepared for management careers in consumer service, hospitality, or retail trade firms. In the meantime, they will have taken 2,000 hours of training in McDonald's regional training centers and be prepared to attend McDonald's U. It should be noted that this program offers the first path to management careers for high school students that McDonald's has ever offered. Traditionally, they have recruited management trainees from college or from older, more experienced workers.

Like WorkPlus, this project includes multiple sites. Like WorkPlus, it envisions a performance/skill standards and certification system. Like WorkPlus, the certificates are built on the industry standards developed by CHRIE and SCANS. Like WorkPlus, this project seeks to help each enrollee reach a career ladder. Unlike WorkPlus, the impetus for this effort comes from the private sector and is directly connected to the firms' career ladders. This project is more serious about changing the schools. Finally, this project, although it will recruit from at-risk communities, is unafraid of "creaming" to obtain the best candidates.

Each site represents a partnership of schools, students, parents, and business, with clearly defined responsibilities. Schools agree to provide teachers and counselors and give them time to attend corporate training programs, incorporate business-defined competencies into school curricula, recruit and help the corporate partners select students, and, finally, give students the scheduling flexibility to go to the worksite training programs. Businesses agree to provide their apprentices a paid work experience and structured worksite learning, including internal training from entry through management levels, establish competencies and provide curricula to the schools, provide a site coordinator or counselor, and provide a set of standards and certificates.

Each site expects to recruit 600 students and orient them to the career possibilities in the consumer industry (*see* Fig. 6.4). Of these, 150 are expected to pass the initial assessment and seek to join the program. One hundred of the 150 will, however, probably need to enter a summer preemployment program in order to reach the standards set by McDonald's. The summer program will introduce the students to the industry. It will teach them how to gather and refine information to clarify and, ultimately, solve problems. All 150 will take a McDonald's-designed course, Business Management I, at their schools.

The 150 16-year-olds will then go through a series of McDonald's interviews for hiring and apprentice selection by restaurant managers. At that point, the 150 will be split into three groups of 50. One group will be selected for apprenticeship at McDonald's, one for student mentoring, and the third for other work-based learning. All three groups will go on to the sequence of Business Management (BM) courses at their schools.

The apprentices enter McDonald's Crew Training system in the second semester of their sophomore year while taking BM II. By the end of the semester their crew and workplace skills are assessed at the job and at school. That summer they receive credentials in both areas.

In their junior year, apprentices take two modules of BM III at school and three modules of McDonald's Management Development Program. The MDP basic course includes operations, management

FIG. 6.4. EXPECTED STUDENT PARTICIPATION IN EACH PROJECT SITE

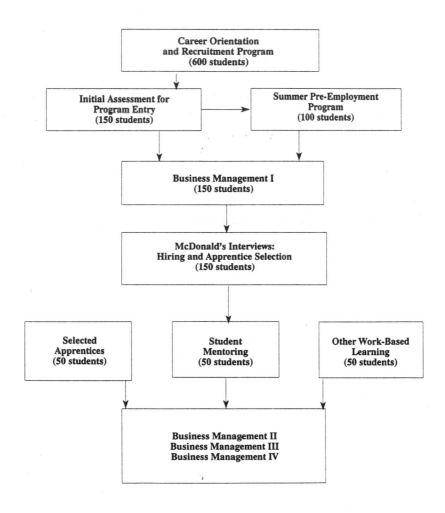

skills, leadership, managing special situations, time planning, and crew recognition. The intermediate course covers store leadership, recruiting and retaining crews, and decisionmaking. The equipment course focuses on equipment technology and planned maintenance.

Apprentices are certified as a Crew Leader in the first semester and Swing Manager in the second semester of their junior year. (That is, they can "open" and "close" a store.) In their senior high school year, and through 2 years of postsecondary education, they continue to take the Business Management courses at school and McDonald's Management Development program at work. They may take further McDonald's training at Regional Training Centers. Those who stay with the program through their first year of college should receive an interim certification as Assistant Manager. They would then be eligible to attend Hamburger University and take their 2-week Advanced Operations Course. That curriculum includes accounting, equipment service, and marketing. A major focus is interpersonal skills such as communications, personnel management, and human relations.

The full sequence takes a youngster through five levels — crew member, crew team leader, swing manager, assistant manager, and manager. The apprentices are certified in the relevant SCANS competencies at each level. By the time they finish the program, graduates should be assured of a career path that includes at least modest salaries and decent benefits. Assistant managers start at $19,500 annually and 1st assistant managers average about $27,000. Managers average about $35,000. By the year 2000, McDonald's expects to fill over 5,000 management jobs annually. Some apprentices will advance further in the McDonald's corporate structure or as entrepreneurs. About one-third of the current group of McDonald's Owner/Operators began as crew people.

CHALLENGES

Creating communitywide partnerships that will survive over a period of years is the foremost challenge. McDonald's will have to overcome the skeptics in the education community who see these as "hamburger flipping" jobs in the so-called secondary labor market. Parents and some students are also likely to share this bias. The program will also have to overcome the reluctance of other companies to sign on to a "McDonald's" program. This problem may be compounded by McDonald's reluctance to work with other fast food companies. McDonald's intends to include noncompeting corporate partners such as Walgreen's and Marriott.

If the program is too small, it may face resistance from the schools who will be reluctant to establish curricula for a small percentage of their students. Moreover, if too few employers are involved students may be reluctant to work for a Certificate that they perceive as valuable only within the McDonald's organization. Getting to scale presents a different challenge. The program expects 1,000 apprentices in 1995. Adding new sites will be difficult unless the genius of McDonald's franchising expertise can be brought to bear.

LESSONS LEARNED

The program began operations in the summer of 1995. Its launch alone proves that a university-corporation (Northern Illinois and McDonald's) partnership could spawn a meaningful program. The lesson that school-to-work is good business should be instructive for many other employers *if* the research demonstrates that such projects can be managed and that they pay off at the bottom line.

SERVICE-LEARNING

MARYLAND'S STATEWIDE SERVICE-LEARNING REQUIREMENT

BACKGROUND — A NEGLECTED OPPORTUNITY BECOMES A MANDATE

On July 29, 1992, the Maryland State Board of Education (MSBE) took a bold step — it became the first state board of education to require service-learning for high school graduation. The mandate took effect in the fall of 1993, affecting the graduating class of 1997.

This action came as the culmination of efforts began in 1983, when then State Superintendent of Education David Hornbeck responded to a report of the State of Maryland Values Education Committee by proposing that students engage in community service activities prior to high school graduation. Hornbeck believed that such service would build good citizenship. The program was to emphasize both service and learning; not teaching about service or only volunteering to serve.

In 1985, MSBE issued an "opportunity mandate," requiring that all school systems offer credit-bearing opportunities for community service — at the rate of 66 hours for a half-credit or 132 hours for a full credit. To support this, the Maryland Student Service Alliance (MSSA) was formed in 1988 as a public-private partnership between the Student Community Service Foundation, Inc. and the Maryland State Department of Education. MSSA's mission was to provide training and technical assistance to schools and school systems involved in service-learning projects. Few students took advantage of the opportunity, but after MSBE was confident that school systems had developed capacity under the opportunity programs, it made the service-learning a requirement in 1992.

GOALS — ACTIVE CITIZENS AND SUCCESSFUL STUDENTS

The goals of the service-learning requirement are simply stated in the Maryland Student Service Alliance's (MSSA) report to the State Board of Education: to create active, engaged citizens and successful students. In a public relations question-and-answer sheet, MSSA shows how children will benefit from the requirement:

> Service-learning will help awaken students to the great potential that they have to make a difference in their schools and community. It will help them develop the character and acquire the skills necessary to act as responsible, contributing citizens.
>
> Students involved in service-learning demonstrate social, personal, and intellectual growth and development. Students involved in service increase their teamwork and problem-solving skills, as well as leadership and initiative. Their self-respect increases as they see that they can tackle tough problems and succeed.

PROGRAM MODELS — 24 SCHOOL SYSTEMS PRODUCE 24 PROGRAMS

To meet the State Board of Education requirement, every high school student in Maryland must complete one of the following:

- ◆ Seventy-five hours of student service that includes preparation, action, and reflection components and that, at the discretion of the local school system, may begin during the middle grades; or

♦ A locally designed program in student service that has been approved by the State Superintendent of Schools.

All 24 school systems in Maryland decided to design their own programs, which resulted in 24 different program models. These programs fall into three categories:

♦ **Infusion**: 23 of the 24 school systems in Maryland infuse service-learning into existing courses as all or part of their plan. Teachers enhance their students' learning by adding experiential, community-based service activities to their existing curricula. In some cases, students complete all three components of service learning — preparation, action, and reflection — during the regular hours of the school day. In other cases, the preparation and reflection components are incorporated into the school day, while the students must perform the action after school or on weekends. Teachers track their students' hours of service and report them, or the students' failure to accomplish them, along with the students' marks for the course.

♦ **Independent Service-Learning Programs**: Students in 8 of Maryland's 24 school systems conduct independent service projects to fulfill all or part of the requirement. Teachers give their students guidelines identifying appropriate organizations and time requirements for service. School systems vary in the amount they help students to find service opportunities. Some have coordinators at each school who act as placement agents and record the number of hours served. School records generally include reports from a supervisor at the service site and students' essays about their experience.

♦ **Site-Based Management**: 3 of the 24 school systems provide guidelines to their schools, but allow the faculty of each school to tailor their approach to the local community and the resources and traditions of the school. System guidelines in all three cases include both infusion and independent program components. The school systems also provide technical assistance in the form of staff training and resource fairs. Finally, the school system monitors each school's plan and implementation.

The Maryland Student Service Alliance (MSSA) has expanded to provide teacher training, curriculum development and technical assistance throughout the state.

CHALLENGES

Implementing a service-learning requirement throughout a state is not easy. As with any state mandate, monitoring and coordinating the efforts of several independent school districts is an onerous task. It is not surprising that an administrator at MSSA identified one of the biggest challenges as "helping school districts develop their own guidelines to meet their own needs, without standardizing the twenty-four different programs."

Public relations present another demand. The popular rhetoric of "forced volunteerism" often conjures images of child exploitation or the justice system's community service programs. A MSSA administrator reports that, "Educating teachers, students, parents and the public about what service-learning is — how it's different from traditional community service and volunteerism, and why it's a valid educational method has been difficult." Related to this, she says, is the challenge of ". . . making explicit the links between service-learning and other education reform areas, such as school-to-work . . . and cooperative learning."

Finally, a challenge with the infusion model is integrating service-learning into the curriculum without diminishing the action component. Getting teachers to lead their students in service, not merely teach about service, remains a challenge.

LESSONS LEARNED

As with most initiatives, providing adequate training and support to the frontline staff is vital. MSSA's report to the State Board of Education states that ". . . districts that have requested and received training for all involved staff experience a smoother implementation of the program."

Given the diversity of programs both across and within districts, MSSA visits sites to observe implementation. This gives them a clear image of how a program runs, and helps them share information from one site to another and across districts.

The gradual implementation of the requirement was a wise choice. The opportunity mandate required that all school systems provide the opportunity for students to earn academic credits through service-learning. Under this mandate, school districts developed systems to plan, implement, and record service activity on a relatively small scale. The mandate also pushed the state to determine what it would need to coordinate the efforts of the school districts. This resulted in the creation and development of MSSA and the eventual universal graduation requirement.

MAGIC ME, INCORPORATED
UNITED STATES, ENGLAND, AND FRANCE

Imagine that you are one of 15 sixth-graders called to an isolated classroom for a mysterious meeting. After you are seated, a stranger enters the room and begins disfiguring you. She tapes your arms together, puts cotton in your ears, and places a pair of petroleum jelly-coated glasses over your eyes. She then invites you to accompany her to a nursing home. After an hour's discussion of real versus imaginary fears, the frustrations elderly people face when their bodies do not function properly, and how you can make a difference in the life of an elderly person, are you and your classmates ready to accept her invitation? You have just been introduced to MAGIC ME.[3]

BACKGROUND — 15 YEARS OF PROGRAM DEVELOPMENT

"MAGIC ME is an international non-profit organization dedicated to bringing to life the power of service-learning." Thus begins one of MAGIC ME's brochures. And MAGIC ME certainly has a history that bears this out. Founded in 1980, in Baltimore, Maryland, as a trial project with 20 participants, MAGIC ME has grown to include 27 sites across the United States and in France and England. During this 15-year period of development, MAGIC ME has been praised by former presidents Reagan and Bush, Britain's Prince Charles, and Maryland's Governor Schaefer, as well as the Governor's Drug and Alcohol Abuse Commission, the Juvenile Justice Advisory Council, and the Health Facilities Association of Maryland. More recently, MAGIC ME was one of 40 nonprofits selected by the Corporation

---

[3] This introduction was excerpted from Kirsten Strand, "Serving to Learn, Learning to Serve," *The Journal of the Michigan and Ohio Associations of Teacher Educators*, January, 1993:51–53.

for National Service as a multistate program, making MAGIC ME eligible for volunteer service from AmeriCorps members.

GOALS — MOTIVATION AND EDUCATION THROUGH COMMUNITY INVOLVEMENT

MAGIC ME's mission statement reads: "To motivate and educate adolescents by involving them in long-term service with elderly and challenged persons in their communities." They break this down into four primary goals:

◆ To enable youth to provide needed community service.

◆ To help youth realize their own power, abilities, and purpose.

◆ To create links between community service and academic learning.

◆ To provide companionship to isolated elderly and challenged individuals.

PROGRAM MODEL — PARTNERING YOUNGSTERS WITH THE ELDERLY AND DISABLED

MAGIC ME works at several levels to achieve its goals. At its most basic level, MAGIC ME is a service-learning program for middle school students. Cooperation between a middle school and a nursing home facilitates the pairing of sixth grade students with elderly and challenged "partners." When youths and elders come together, activities may include arts and crafts, games, oral history projects, or poetry writing. Some activities are designed to involve the entire group, while others aim to build the relationships between young and elderly partners. School-based preparation for and reflection on the students' experience with their partners enhances the learning. Students are asked to keep a journal, write occasional essays on their experience, and plan activities for themselves and their partners. Often, teachers use the school-based learning to meet curricular goals in language arts, art, history, or social studies. This partnership between a student and an elderly person, intended to last from sixth through eighth grades, is the heart of MAGIC ME.

At the college and graduate levels, MAGIC ME sponsors internships, practice, and field placements, in which students synthesize theory and practice by leading or supporting MAGIC ME groups, or working in program research, development, or administration.

While these college and graduate students gain many of the same benefits as do their middle-school counterparts, they also learn how to implement service-learning, how to conduct a program evaluation, and/or how to work with children. Thus, the involvement of college and graduate students benefits the program, by lightening the staff's workload or adding something to the program that would not otherwise be available, and by spreading the word of the benefits and methods of service-learning to up-and-coming human services professionals.

MAGIC ME is part of the AmeriCorps national and community service program. AmeriCorps members make a 1-year commitment in exchange for a living allowance and an educational award. At MAGIC ME, members increase the capacity of the organization by establishing new partnerships and recruiting and training teachers, agency staff, and college interns to conduct MAGIC ME.

MAGIC ME is also an affiliates program. MAGIC ME affiliates form a dynamic network, sharing opportunities for professional development and idea exchange. Affiliates operate much like franchises. Affiliation is a legal agreement between MAGIC ME and organizations interested in conducting the program. Affiliate membership is available at three levels:

- The Project Level is a partnership between a middle school and a care facility, where a teacher and a staff member run one or more MAGIC ME groups.
- At the Program Level, MAGIC ME is under the auspices of another nonprofit agency, and at least one full-time staff member conducts the MAGIC ME program in multiple sites.
- At the full Affiliate level, an independent MAGIC ME is formed, with a volunteer board and §501(c)(3) status.

Regardless of level, MAGIC ME works with affiliates to adapt the curriculum to meet participant and local needs. In exchange for an initial licensing and certification fee, and annual dues, MAGIC ME provides initial and ongoing training and technical assistance, and complete program materials.

Finally, MAGIC ME has a considerable research and development agenda. They are interested in developing and refining techniques for meeting their goals. MAGIC ME affiliates are encouraged to develop new approaches that meet the needs of their participants and communities. The national organization collects and disseminates best practices by incorporating them into training materials and publications such as a quarterly newsletter and the *MAGIC ME Program Manual*. Given the diversity of MAGIC ME affiliates, which include probation departments, community theaters, mental health agencies, private industry councils, as well as middle schools and nursing homes in a wide variety of communities, there is great room for innovation.

MAGIC ME and the University of Maryland are currently conducting a 6-year multistate research evaluation. The pre- and post-tests assess the impact of the program on the quality of life of service-site staff and clients, and the relationship between program participation and students' self-esteem, prosocial behavior, and attachment to school.

CHALLENGES

Implementing MAGIC ME is challenging. A school's norms and expectations sharply contrast with those of a nursing home. A great deal of time is devoted to preparing the youth, elders, teachers and staff prior to starting the group. The group leader must carefully plan activities that will link youth and elders, while holding the attention of both age groups.

There are challenges inherent in any endeavor that is based on partnerships. When two or more schools or organizations are involved, coordinating schedules is the first challenge. For example, schools often schedule core classes in the morning, which is also the best time of day to work with the elderly. Elders may be disappointed by breaks in service when schools are on vacation.

Transportation is often an issue, since many school districts have limited transportation budgets and strict regulations regarding transporting students in parents' or teachers' cars. This can be particularly important in rural areas, where there can be great distance between schools and service sites.

Staff turnover is another challenge. Once the group is underway, the loss of a key teacher or staff member can disrupt the program.

Changing teachers', staff's and participants' mindsets can be one of the greatest challenges. The magic happens when people, young or old, discover that they can accomplish something beyond their own expectations. For this magic to happen, teachers and staff must believe it possible. They must give youngsters and elders the opportunity to join MAGIC ME, then work with them to set aside their self-limitations. As many of the other case studies demonstrate, this premise of learning by doing is often in conflict with teacher-driven educational approaches.

LESSONS LEARNED

MAGIC ME capitalizes on its diversity of sites by encouraging affiliates to innovate and share their experiences with each other. MAGIC ME is a learning organization, and the lessons learned are incorporated into the program approach, training and publications. At the same time, core aspects of MAGIC ME, such as the creation of intergenerational partnerships and respect for participating youths and elders, are constant whether one is working in Nebraska or London. To maintain consistency, MAGIC ME leader certification must be earned through participation in training and technical assistance. This training and technical assistance also lays the groundwork for an ongoing relationship between the national and local organization.

MAGIC ME has also learned that it can make extensive use of emerging communication technology and infrastructure to improve communication among affiliates and the national staff. MAGIC ME is currently experimenting with videoconferencing and electronic discussion groups, and is looking into the possibility of putting some of their training and technical support materials on interactive CD-ROM.

By extending the MAGIC ME partnership web to include local service organizations or colleges, in-kind contributions of supplies, transportation, volunteer or intern hours can provide the elements needed for a successful program.

7

INTEGRATED PRACTICES

INTRODUCTION

School-to-work programs are about a work context for education, a learning environment for work, and connections between them. The practices described up until now focused on either learning-rich work or work-rich education, with varying degrees of connections. The seven practices described in this section have struggled with the difficulty of connecting work and learning practices, without compromising either. One point stands out: when properly integrated, the sum is greater than the parts!

Some have been initiated by schools with an eye toward where their students go, some by employers with a concern for where their employees come from, and others by communities concerned for the economic and social well-being of their individual residents and the community as a whole. Most importantly, they have realized that no one agency or institution can successfully facilitate their constituents' educational and employment development alone. The synergy among these diverse partners is encouraging to those who aim to break down the barriers between the realms of work and learning. It has created a diversity of promising approaches.

SIEMENS-LYMAN-SEMINOLE
SEMINOLE COUNTY, FLORIDA

BACKGROUND — THREE STRONG PARTNERS,
ALL COMMITTED TO EXCELLENCE

School-based learning, work-based learning, and connections — youngsters in Seminole County in central Florida get a chance to see all three. Seminole boasts the highest per capita income in the state. Part of the wealth arises because it is located about 30 miles from Orlando and Disneyland. But Mickey Mouse is not evident. Instead, one sees corporate facilities of high-tech firms, such as AT&T and Siemens Stromberg-Carlson, one of AT&T's important suppliers.

High School

The best place to start is Lyman High School in Longwood. The school is a nationally recognized School of Excellence.[1] Many of Lyman's graduates go on directly to work; others first attend community colleges such as Seminole Community College, while others go on to Central Florida University or other colleges.

It is hard to say which is more impressive, Lyman's "Blueprint for Career Preparation" or Carlton Henly, the crusty former principal who fought the defenders of the status quo to make a living structure from the blueprint. Henly, who was a school administrator for 30 years, dominated his high school's campus and everything that happened on it. He had the vision that shaped the school's philosophy. He pushed curriculum change and saw to staff development and technology acquisition. He obtained waivers from the state's Education Department and about $1 million in grants from the government to invest in change. He redesigned facilities and schedules and negotiated changes with the teacher union. He dealt with the school board and worked with the parents. Henly clearly ran Lyman high school until his recent retirement.

Community College

Seminole Community College (SCC) is one of the places where Lyman students go for further education. Located in Sanford, Florida, SCC is a well-equipped, handsome institution that offers a comprehensive set of programs for a variety of purposes and clients. Youngsters looking for the first 2 years of a 4-year college program and senior citizens looking to improve their leisure time activities attend SCC.

But SCC's forte is economic development. It gives short courses to architects wanting to keep up with the latest in computer-assisted drafting (CAD) or mechanics who want to learn and be certified

---

[1] "Blueprint for Action," Lyman High School, Longwood, FL.

in the newest Mercury Marine engine. SCC's Business and Industry Support Center appeals to firms looking for special short-term training programs to be conducted on site.

Work-Based Learning

Stromberg-Carlson is an electronics firms with a long history. Fifty years ago, many American living rooms sported large console-type radios, some of which are displayed in the Siemens reception room. Bought and sold a number of times in recent years, Stromberg Carlson is now owned by Siemens and is now known as Siemens Stromberg-Carlson.

The Siemens plant in central Florida is a state-of-the-art manufacturing facility for telephone switch gear. When Stromberg-Carlson built radios, telephone messages were "switched" at a local facility so that caller and the called party could be connected. Today the electrical-mechanical switching gear has been replaced by electronic equipment. The equipment is not supposed to fail and the computer-driven plant is designed to produce total quality components for AT&T. When equipment does fail, troubleshooting must be done quickly and efficiently. Thus, Siemens needs well-trained field service representatives, equipment servicing technicians, and instrumentation technicians.

Siemens is a German firm whose chairman champions the German Training System at home and abroad. John Tobin, a retired New York City high school principal (Brooklyn Technical High School), manages the national program in the U.S. A Master Instructor (or Meister) is among the contributions that Siemens makes to the program.

GOALS — PREPARATION FOR CAREERS AND CONTINUING EDUCATION

Principal Henly believed that Lyman's purpose was to prepare students for later life. "Students who graduate . . . will be prepared to begin a career and continue their education . . ., " reads Lyman's mission statement. The statement concludes with the following operational injunction: "Only those courses and programs that will contribute significantly to the mission statement will be continued or implemented."

SCC and Siemens support Lyman's mission. They both want entrants to their institutions to be well-prepared upon arrival. They strive to keep them prepared, as the students or employees work their way through the SCC curriculum toward graduation and employment or further education, or as they face rapidly changing technological and management systems once they are employed at Siemens.

PROGRAM MODEL — TECH PREP, INTERNSHIPS, AND A SCHOOLWIDE FOCUS ON APPLIED LEARNING

High School

Lyman's approach to school-to-work affects the entire school. This is not a "pull out" program for those not going to college or for students with special characteristics. Instead, the program applies to all the students and teachers in this comprehensive high school. The most far-reaching change is in the roles of students and teachers. Students are no longer spectators. Rather, they do the work. Teachers are no longer dispensers of information. Instead, they guide the students as the youngsters work at learning.

Midterm report cards have been replaced with a report on progress. "Incomplete" has replaced a failing grade — Lyman's students will meet the standards, if not sooner, then later. Evaluation is the school's rationale for testing policy. The Lyman Blueprint states: "Testing measures what a student has learned" and "indicates to a teacher what material needs to be reviewed or retaught."

Henly's goal was to realize Lyman's mission of preparing students for careers and further education. He had to apply it to teaching philosophy and strategy, to curriculum, and to the daily experience of students, teachers, and staff at Lyman — and to the students' parents. The school is not responsible for making the student learn or do his homework. The students and parents are.

The school's responsibility is to assure that graduates have the know-how needed in the new workplace. Henly, quoting the SCANS work frequently and favorably, has reorganized his school to meet this responsibility. "Traditions of the last 100 years" that do not meet the purpose are changed. For example, the 30-student, 50-minute, lecture class, meeting daily, was eliminated.

Lyman students, in groups of 250, attend six, 60-minute, presentations every Monday. These presentations are carefully and jointly prepared by a team of teachers. The presentations lay out the theory that will be applied in the problem-solving sessions during the week,

First, however, students, in groups of 80 this time, attend clarification lectures for three 2-hour periods on Tuesday (subjects 1, 3, and 5) and another three on Wednesday (subjects 2, 4, and 6). On Thursday and Friday, working in teams of six or seven, they apply the theory to solve problems.

In redesigning curriculum, Henly's goal was to eliminate the escape hatches, the routes by which students could avoid rigorous work. "Liberal Arts Math" and "General Math" were abandoned and "Applied Math I and II" were added. In Art, "Fabric and Fibers" was abandoned and "Basic Principles of Graphic Communication Technology" was added. "Principles of Technology" was added and "Physical Science" was abandoned.

Workplace know-how and career preparation are now emphasized. "Every student will go to work, only some will go to college first," is the philosophy. Every student receives two 30-minute career counseling sessions weekly, if not by a counselor then by a teacher. Each student maintains a "Career Planner" during his 4 years at Lyman. The inside front cover records the student's career interests and career plans, extracurricular and community activities, awards, and work experience. The inside back cover contains his academic record. Inside the folder are the results of his action plans:

◆ Vocational aptitude tests to be shared with parents;

◆ A 4-year plan related to his career choice and articulation requirements to access that career;

◆ The results of career investigation based on completing the "Holland Self-Directed Search" and a writing assignment that is also presented in a classroom setting;

◆ A completed "Micro Choice Module" booklet and a research paper on one possible career choice;

◆ Analyses of "help wanted" advertisements, including the requirements and salaries offered in the careers chosen;

◆ PSAT, SAT, ACT, and NASVB scores; and

◆ Copies of the forms required for college and to apply to work.

Lyman has designed school-based learning around the connections between school and work. The contents of the folder are only a small part of Lyman's 5-year (8th to 12th) career plan, a description of which goes on for 29 pages of action plans, which include such items as:

- Appointments with advisors and parents to discuss career choices and the steps required to realize the choice;
- Visits to a Career Center and presentations by Occupational Specialists in conjunction with science teachers;
- Closed circuit and other media presentations about careers;
- Speakers from the business community, including minorities and women who have been successful in business;
- Visits from colleges, Rotary, and the Armed Services; and
- Meetings with counselors and Teachers as Advisors.

Finally, staff development and teaching strategies are built on sound research: cooperative learning and learning in the context of workplace applications. Lyman has arranged schedules so that teachers have time for training, for planning, and to prepare lessons. They are given the opportunity to learn to become career Teachers as Advisors. Time is also made available so that teachers can learn how to use technology, which is there in profusion as a result of the school's successful pursuit of grants.

The result is the infusion of workplace know-how throughout the curriculum — all teachers and all courses are involved in insuring that all students are prepared for work *and* further education.

Community College

Seminole Community College is deeply committed to Tech Prep, a 2+2 cooperative program of study with six local high schools including, of course, Lyman. SCC offers Tech Prep in six career clusters: Electronics, Drafting, Business, Health Services, Automotive, and Child Care.

The Drafting program leads to careers as diverse as interior design or civil engineering technology. While the student begins with the traditional drafting board, she soon progresses to wonderfully sophisticated CAD equipment. State-of-the-art equipment is also available in the business cluster which leads to careers such as financial services, office management technology, and computer systems analysis.

Needing up-to-date equipment for school-based learning, SCC works hard to develop close connections with industry. The desire to provide their students with employer-based certificates is another reason why SCC seeks close connections with industry. The business cluster already teaches network engineering, the ability to connect computers on a local network of electronic wiring. SCC is negotiating with Novell, one of the largest firms in this business, to produce certified "Novell engineers." In many localities that certificate is as valuable as a 4-year degree in Electrical Engineering.

The Automotive Program clearly demonstrates the connection between SCC and employers. This program is designated by Ford as one of their Asset Programs, one of only 62 in the nation. Asset students at SCC learn their trade on a new line of cars that they receive every year from Ford. The Asset program has a placement rate exceeding 90% and most of the graduates go on to work for a Ford dealer.

In addition to the cars, Ford provides curriculum and books. Ford helps the teaching staff keep up with the state of the art by financing staff trips to Detroit. Ford also empowers SCC to certify students in 13 of the 19 competencies that define a full-fledged Ford mechanic. It usually takes a working mechanic a week to acquire one of these competencies. Hiring SCC- trained personnel, therefore, saves the employing dealer a substantial amount in wages and expenses (compared to sending one of their own staff to school).

Courses include such standbys as *AER 1123, Automotive Steering and Suspension* and *AER 1120, Automotive Brake Systems.* Students also, however, learn to apply more generic workplace know-how in a dealer repair and maintenance shop. In one exercise, students allocate space to design a repair facility. In the process, they come to understand the cost of acquiring tools and equipment, learn about the information systems needed to maintain inventory, and acquire the interpersonal skills that underlie customer service.

SCC's tech prep agreements with its participating high schools are directed to the six career clusters noted earlier. The technical electives in high school, for those in the automotive cluster, could include as many as three automotive courses. To provide the basis for their technical electives, students might study Applied Mathematics and Principles of Technology, as well as other science courses. These high school students will also take English and History so as not to foreclose their going on to a 4-year degree.

Telecommunications Engineering Technology is one of the most interesting SCC tech-prep programs, especially because of its relationship to the Siemens Electronic Technician Program. In the "Work and Wages" section of SCC's tech prep page, this degree is associated with a salary range of $18,000 to $28,000 annually. Possible positions include field service representatives, equipment servicing technicians, instrumentation technicians, and printed circuit layout designers.

High school students in the Electronics Tech prep program choose Principles of Technology I and II, Applied Mathematics I and II, and two courses in Basic Electronics as their electives. Their first-term college courses will include College Algebra, Digital Circuits, and Electronic Instrumentation. Naturally, Lyman High School offers this tech prep option along with a number of others. Lyman, too, is connected to the Siemens Electronic Technician Program.

Work-Based

The SCC Electronics Technician Program specializes in Equipment Engineering (Test Technician) and Telecommunications Technology (Installation Technician). The Apprenticeship program for college students lasts for 2½ years. Additionally, there is a 1-year Pre-Apprenticeship program for high school students. High school students spend 6 hours each week job-shadowing in the Siemens plant and 20 hours in high school taking their tech-prep courses. Siemens pays the minimum wage for the 6-work-based learning hours.

Subsequently, students move on to community college (SCC in this case). Students spend 20 hours weekly at the plant and another 12 hours weekly at SCC, doing the academic work referred to before. Siemens starts them at a stipend of $450 a month. The stipend increases to $800 month by the last term. Additionally, Siemens loans each student enough for all tuition, lab fees, and books. The loan is forgiven if the student graduates and spends 1-year working for Siemens.

Students must maintain a GPA of 2.5 (2.75 in Math) to get in and stay in the program, and must promise to work for Siemens for 1 year after graduation. The learning at the plant is both work- and classroom-based. In the factory, classroom students learn about electronic logic and build a logic tester. They learn circuit theory and then build a personal circuit tester that they will use on the factory floor. They learn metalworking and use these skills to build the casing for their circuit tester. Students spend time in the room where operators receive calls about system malfunctions and help engineers troubleshoot the problem over the phone. They troubleshoot malfunctioning equipment that has been returned to the factory (using the circuit tester that they had built earlier).

Students study the complex computer-driven factory operation and make suggestions for improving the process. One co-op student tested how much gold was needed to make a contact and found it was only a fraction of the amount that Siemens was using. The production process was changed, saving Siemens a considerable amount.

If all works as planned, the Lyman student who has gone on to Seminole Community College, while involved in the Siemens Apprenticeship program, has made the successful transition from school-to-work. She has a high school diploma, an Associate degree, certified work experience, and a job with Siemens Stromberg-Carlson. At the end of the first year of work, Siemens will forgive the loan they made to her for tuition. She has also earned a good sum while going to school. If she wants, she can continue on for a baccalaureate degree at Central Florida University.

Tech Prep and Apprenticeship

	9th	10th	11th	12th	13th	14th
School-Based	*Lyman*	*Lyman* Applied Math I	*Lyman* Principle of Tech I Applied Math II Basic Elect. I	*Lyman* Principle of Tech II Basic Electron. II	*SCC* College Algebra	*SCC* Digital Circuits Electron. Instruments
Work-Based				*Siemens* 6 hrs/week Job-Shadow	*Siemens* 20 hrs/week	*Siemens* 20 hrs/week

CHALLENGES

Challenges arise when these innovative programs begin. The change agent must overcome resistance at many levels. Carlton Henly had to convince his faculty and their union before he could institute the schedule changes for teacher training. He had to convince the state to provide the waivers to change class schedules and other traditional procedures. He had to wrangle grants from the federal government and foundations.

Once established, viability becomes the biggest challenge. Can they survive the changes in funding and policy emphasis that occur from time to time? More importantly, can they survive the loss of the original change agents, such as Carlton Henly or John Tobin? Only time will tell.

Making connections among various programs presents another test. Clearly, a great many connections have been made to put the student on a path from Lyman to SCC and Siemens. Counselors and teachers at Lyman have to know and communicate the opportunities in electronics apprenticeship. They also must let the student consider other possibilities in, for example, construction or fire sprinkler systems (two high-demand fields in central Florida). Helping students examine other careers is not easy. It requires convincing business people to come to Lyman to explain the opportunities in their fields.

LESSONS LEARNED

The Lyman-SCC-Seimans experience demonstrates that the start-up obstacles can be overcome if vigorous and determined change agents want it. The experience also demonstrates the synergy of complementary programs. This synergy is built on networks with nodes such as these three institutions but which include other high schools, other community colleges, and other employers. A single path would be less flexible and, paradoxically, harder to build than the network.

For example, Lyman and SCC "connected' to build the tech prep program that helps students obtain their associate degree a little sooner. But Lyman students need not go to SCC in order to benefit from the innovations. Those who go directly to work or on to Central Florida University also benefit. The same can be said of the connection between Lyman or SCC and Seimans. These schools make the Siemans school-to-work program, but they also work closely with other employers. SCC was one of the draws in the county's economic efforts that brought Siemens here. Siemens Master Instructors and other staff work with the instructors at SCC to integrate the school-based and work-based learning. The same statement, however, also describes SCC relationships with other firms such as Ford auto and Mercury boat engines. If the network is not "seamless," at least the seams are neatly finished. There were no gaping hole through which students could easily fall.

PARTNERSHIP FOR ACADEMIC AND CAREER EDUCATION
(PACE)
ANDERSON, PICKENS, AND OCONEE COUNTIES, SOUTH CAROLINA

BACKGROUND — BUILDING A CONSORTIUM AROUND AN IDEA

In 1985, just prior to the publication of Dale Parnell's book, *The Neglected Majority*,[2] Dr. Don Garrison, president of Tri-County Technical College (TCTC) convened a meeting with several of his staff and business and education leaders from Anderson, Pickens and Oconee Counties, the region served by TCTC. Because of a close, long-standing professional relationship with Dr. Parnell, Garrison knew what the upcoming book would say. He took the challenges to heart and wanted to work with his community to address them. Garrison focused on the tech-prep model to remedy the general failure of the community college to work effectively with secondary education.

Garrison knew that TCTC had a strong relationship with the region's industries. The college worked with them, tailoring curriculum to prepare students for local careers, as well as developing training programs for incumbent workers at specific factories. But what of the younger side of the equation? Garrison saw many high school students enrolled in traditional vocational/technical programs who were unclear about postsecondary education and career opportunities. Indeed, many of these students were preparing for careers about which they knew little or nothing. Dr. Garrison was concerned that they were receiving insufficient training for the high-performance, highly complex workplaces he saw coming to the region.

The Tri-County region has a 95% employment rate, thanks largely to its booming manufacturing industry. Manufacturers report that they are attracted to the area, in part, because of the training support offered by TCTC. But once there, they must compete with each other for skilled technicians. This reinforces their commitment to work with TCTC to develop a skilled workforce. The combination of strong leadership on the education side, a need for a skilled workforce on the employment side, and a spirit of cooperation between the two,

---

[2] Dale Parnell, *The Neglected Majority*, Washington, DC: Community College Press, 1985.

created and maintains an atmosphere of innovation in the region's education and training systems.

Thus, between 1985 and 1987, Garrison was able to get industry and education to begin developing "2+2/Tech-Prep/Associate Degree" programs, as proposed by Parnell. In May of 1987, the Partnership for Academic and Career Education (PACE) was established. The original partners included the five Anderson County school districts, the School District of Pickens County, the School District of Oconee County, the National Dropout Prevention Center at Clemson University, the ACCTion Consortium, Tri-County Technical College, and three industry partners representing major manufacturing companies in each county. TCTC provided startup money, office space, and operational support for the PACE administrative staff.

Since 1987, PACE has grown to include all 16 high schools in seven school districts, and more than 50 businesses. Although focusing on tech-prep in the Tri-County region, their efforts have supported other applied academic programs and apprenticeships, including developing and disseminating materials nationally. To date, nearly $2 million in funding for PACE and/or consortium-wide activities have come from a variety of sources, including grants from the Departments of Education, the South Carolina Employment Security Commission, the South Carolina Commission on Higher Education, the Appalachian Regional Commission, the American Association of Community Colleges, and the Sears, Roebuck Foundation. Additionally, all seven school districts and TCTC have received state and/or corporate grants to support programs on their respective campuses.

GOALS — GETTING AND KEEPING REWARDING EMPLOYMENT

PACE strives to provide students with the education and training, both at school and at work, that they will need to get and keep rewarding employment. They provide meaningful academic and career education with the promise of accessible employment and continuing education. Through applied academics, they motivate more students to complete high school and continue with postsecondary education. Their mission statement, revised in 1992, reaffirms their commitment to tech-prep, including:

♦ A viable and challenging blend of academic and occupational coursework;

♦ An integrated curriculum that is articulated at both entry points (middle school) and exit points (postsecondary); and

♦ a comprehensive guidance program for grades 6–12 that emphasizes understanding and preparation for midlevel technologies, as well as alternative routes to baccalaureate study.

Their mission includes expanding the tech-prep model to develop apprenticeship and other work-based learning programs and to better articulation between the technical college and senior colleges.

PROGRAM MODELS — EXPANDING AND CUSTOMIZING THE TECH-PREP MODEL

PACE is a consortium of independent institutions and no one program model applies to all partner institutions. Rather, the PACE office at TCTC provides training and technical assistance and coordinates the efforts of participating schools, school systems, and business partners to develop tech-prep, apprenticeship, and related programs.

School-Based Learning: The Tech-Prep Model

The PACE model for tech-prep (*see* Fig. 7.1) spans the years from middle school through postsecondary education and into the workforce. At the middle school level, students are exposed to midlevel technology careers through visits to local employers, guest speakers in the schools, and, in some cases, applied academic courses.

In ninth grade, tech-prep students take an "Introduction to Technologies" course. A combination of counseling and academics, this course lays the foundation for tech-prep participation. It systematically builds awareness of careers in technologies, highlighting the interplay between academic and technical education in preparing for these careers.

After ninth grade, students build their academic and technological bases through a combination of applied academic and college preparatory courses, and applications. These applications may include visiting lecturers from PACE's business partners, job-shadowing, apprenticeships, or courses at the vocational education centers. Many schools in the consortium have adapted their daily schedule to facilitate off-

FIG. 7.1. TECH-PREP CURRICULUM PATHWAY OPTIONS

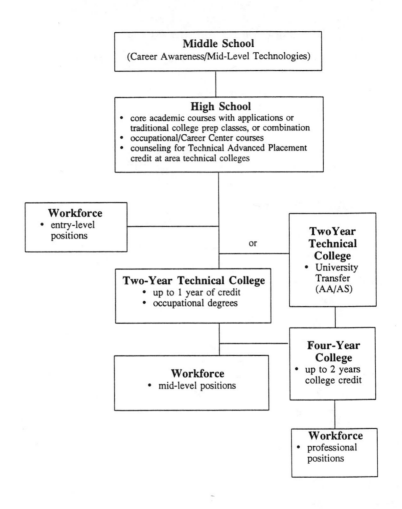

campus trips or because apprenticeships may overlap with school hours, or because students may split their time between the comprehensive high school and the vocational training center. For example, Wren High School in Piedmont, SC, developed a four-period, A/B schedule. Most classes meet every other day for 90 minutes, rather than every day for 45 minutes. Students take all of their college prep and applied academic courses on 1 day, or 1 full day and the morning of the next. They go to the vocational education center, or to their apprenticeship venue, for the afternoon of the second day. Ninety-minute classes also allow more flexible college prep and applied academic courses. Students have time to complete projects or laboratory assignments in 1 period. Teachers can go into greater depth in the traditional lecture/discussion format.

The PACE model integrates applied and academic training. PACE has worked with partner schools to develop applied academic courses which begin with application. Students then see how the applications demonstrate a more universal theory. Students see theory in action and understand the value of what they are learning. As one student said, "These classes are more fun. I think they teach just as much (theory), but I am more interested." One high school teacher who teaches both applied and traditional science courses observed that her students learn more in the applied course because they become more involved.

By coordinating technical training with the community college and establishing articulation agreements, PACE and its secondary education partners have created the opportunity for many students to enroll at TCTC with credit toward their associates degree. Like traditional advanced placement courses, students can earn credits toward their postsecondary degree by taking advanced courses at the vocational education centers. This "technical advanced placement" allows students to finish their associates degree in less than 2 years, or to earn both the associates degree and an advanced certificate during 2 years.

Work-Based Learning: Apprenticeships

From the start, PACE has counted industry among its partners. The scarcity of skilled manufacturing technicians convinced several employers to sponsor internships. As with their school partners, PACE's business partners represent several autonomous entities. PACE provides training and technical assistance to employers who choose to sponsor apprenticeships, job shadows, summer internships for teachers, or visits to schools, and helps them coordinate their efforts with the academic partners. Although more business partners contribute in other ways, apprenticeship is a key component of the PACE model.

PACE sees apprenticeship as a logical outgrowth of the tech-prep curriculum. Figure 7.2 illustrates one sequence that is used to integrate apprenticeships with academics in Machine Tool Technology. Aside from the limitations that child labor laws place on youth apprentices under the age of 18, no distinction is made at the workplace between youth apprentices and adult apprentices. Successful apprentices leave the program with a high school diploma and vocational certificate, an associate degree, and Department of Labor or local apprenticeship credentials, often including a journeyman's certificate.

The Pickens County Youth Apprenticeship Initiative (PCYAI), with support from the PACE office and Jobs for the Future, developed an apprenticeship program that starts at the beginning of the twelfth grade, after a student has gone on several job shadows and completed most of the high school tech-prep curriculum. The responsibilities of the employer, educational partners (secondary and postsecondary), parents and youth apprentice are outlined in the Training Agreement (Fig. 7.3).

PCYAI places students in a variety of workplaces, ranging from school district offices, where apprentices maintain and program the computers for the district office and the school system, to Ryobi Motor Products, where apprentices participate in machine tooling. The varying needs of the apprentices and workplaces requires flexible education partners. Initially, apprentices planned to spend their mornings with teachers at the B.J. Skelton Career Center, and their afternoons at the worksite during their senior year of high school. However, some of the employers preferred to have the apprentices at the worksite for full day shifts, so some apprentices alternate days between the Career Center and the worksite.

The Bosch Corporation has an existing adult apprentice program extracted from the company's German roots. Their desire to model the youth apprentice program after the adult program led them to scale back the duration of the apprenticeship from 3 years to 2 years, starting after high school graduation. In the same spirit, they chose to place apprentices on their payroll for a full 40-hour week, to be split between the workplace (20 hours) and attendance at Tri-County Technical College. With their full-time employee status, apprentices get the insurance and other benefits offered to all full-time employees.

(Text continues on page 198.)

FIG. 7.2. MACHINE TOOL TECHNOLOGY (MTT) APPRENTICESHIP OPTIONS

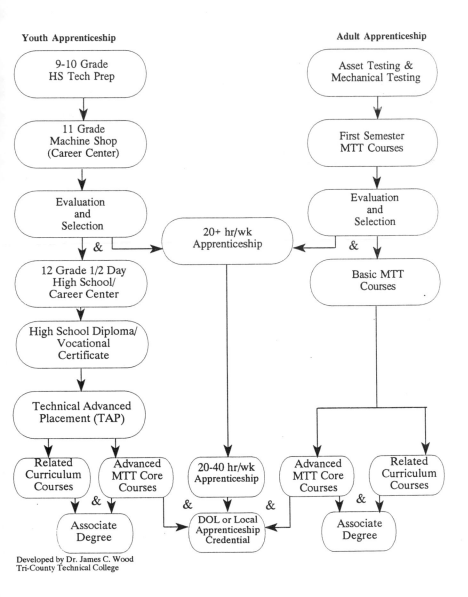

Developed by Dr. James C. Wood
Tri-County Technical College

FIG. 7.3. PCYAI TRAINING AGREEMENT

Training Agreement

The Pickens County
Youth Apprenticeship Initiative

_____
Student (Youth Apprentice) Name

_____
School Year

As a part of a comprehensive Tech-Prep program developed to improve school-to-work transitions, the _Pickens County Youth Apprenticeship Initiative_ is designed to benefit the students, employers, schools, and colleges. In a collaborative effort to achieve a successful educational program all parties jointly agree to:

Business/Industry Site

1. Provide apprenticeship opportunities for the above-named student enrolled in the _____ program during the senior year of high school and during the postsecondary segment.

2. Assist educational agencies (secondary and postsecondary) in designing the curriculum for the _____ program.

3. Provide the youth apprentice paid work experience and guided learning opportunities of the total manufacturing enterprise.

4. Provide the apprentice with a mentor and participate in appropriate training for workplace mentor/supervisor(s).

5. Monitor progress of the apprentice and work with all partners in evaluating effectiveness of the initiative.

Instructor/Coordinator - Career Center

1. Provide student with technical instruction related to apprenticeship and work with postsecondary institution to obtain maximum articulation of course work.

2. Coordinate adequate staff development for all parties.

3. Provide adequate counseling and advice to apprentice and to all participants including parents.

4. Monitor progress of apprentice and assist mentor as requested.

5. Act as contact/liaison for all parties named in this agreement.

Postsecondary (Technical College)

1. Participate in the design and/or refinement of the Pickens County Youth Apprenticeship Initiative.

2. Expand opportunities and ensure smooth transition into postsecondary curriculum.

3. Provide flexible scheduling as appropriate to support apprenticeship activities.

4. Participate in joint staff development programs and assist in the development of activities to support the initiative.

5. Assist partners in development of secondary workplace curriculum and assessment documents.

Training Agreement *(Page Two)*

Parent(s) /Guardian

1. Grant permission and give support for the apprenticeship participation.

2. Inform instructor/coordinator of facts vital to the performance and success of the youth apprentice.

3. Provide transportation for the youth apprentice.

4. Attend any meetings or activities designed to promote or assist the Youth Apprenticeship Initiative

---

Student (Youth Apprentice)

1. Be regular and prompt in attendance at school and at the workplace.

2. Obey all rules and regulations at school and at the workplace.

3. Maintain scholastic averages acceptable to school and the workplace.

4. Communicate **honestly** with workplace mentor regarding job performance.

5. Communicate to Apprenticeship Coordinator or Instructor any concerns or conditions that are interfering with your progress at school or at the workplace.

NAME OF BUSINESS/INDUSTRY   Business/Industry Representative

Career Center Instructor   Youth Apprenticeship Coordinator

Career Center Director   Postsecondary Representative

Parent(s) / Guardian   Student (Youth Apprentice)

Date

The School District of Pickens County does not discriminate in regard to
race, color, national origin, or handicapping condition.

Connecting Activities

Connecting all the partners involved in a comprehensive school-to-work transition program can be an onerous task. Fortunately for the partners, the PACE administrative offices have been very helpful in coordinating their activities. The connections between the secondary education partners and TCTC are well-articulated. With all partners participating in the development of the tech-prep model, and the articulation agreements that it includes, students have an almost seamless transition from secondary to postsecondary education. Many of them achieve advanced standing upon entry to TCTC because they have taken "Technical Advanced Placement (TAP)" courses that TCTC has agreed to recognize. Regardless of TAP status, students know that they will be well-prepared for TCTC because the high school and community college tech-prep curriculum was designed as one continuous curriculum.

Connections between the schools and employers of apprentices, however, can be a bit more cumbersome. The schools need to accommodate the scheduling requirements of the worksites. For their part, the worksites agree to assign a mentor to each apprentice who will be responsible for their end of the communication. To support this communication, PACE and PCYAI developed reporting forms so that worksite mentors can report what the apprentice is learning and the level of competency achieved to the school faculty.

Accomplishments

PACE has become a national model for tech-prep, as well as school-to-work systemic reform. As evidence of their accomplishments, TCTC's Annual Report documents that, during the 1993–94 school year:

♦ 5,766 students were enrolled in applied academics courses across the consortium.

♦ 17 companies sponsored youth apprenticeships, some of them committing to a 3-year period of employment during which time apprentices are paid as full-time employees with full benefits, while they work half-time and attend TCTC.

♦ PACE conducted 22 staff development programs, in which approximately 300 teachers, counselors, and school administrators upgraded their own skills. Many of these were developed and run jointly by college and high school faculty.

♦ Nearly a dozen new materials were developed, including workshop materials and a parents' brochure on tech-prep and midlevel manufacturing careers, a workbook on designing Youth Apprenticeship, operational handbooks, and a guide to area business speakers.

♦ Materials, over 7,000 items in total, were distributed to 345 educators from 33 states, Washington, DC, and abroad.

♦ PACE held a national conference for more than 300 registrants from 22 states. The 27 sessions were all conducted by PACE participants, teachers, business partners, and administrators.

CHALLENGES

School reform is difficult and the PACE experience is no exception. Administrators, echoed by teachers and students involved with tech-prep, report that PACE is identified with traditional vo-tech. As a result, the program must fight the bias that many hold against vo-tech education: that it recruits and trains a strata of students who would not be able to succeed in college. PACE has worked hard to develop materials explaining to students, parents, and even teachers, that tech-prep and college prep are not mutually exclusive, that tech-prep is both academically and technically rigorous, and that students from tech-prep programs can and often do go on to 4-year colleges.

Another challenge arose when Wren and other high schools changed from 45-minute to 90-minute periods. One rather candid student at Wren reported that, at first, the change did not seem to be working. Teachers did not know how to use the time well, and students got restless. By the second year, however, he reports that all parties had learned to make good use of the time. Now, a lab project can be completed in 1 period, and another period can include lecture, application, and discussion — a combination that is well-suited to applied academics that would not be feasible in a 45-minute period.

Another difficulty is keeping abreast of the activities of all the partners in PACE. Their regular meetings and newsletters do not provide information on a timely enough basis. For example, several businesses complained that they would negotiate their participation with a coordinator from one school, only to have another school's representative knocking on their door the following day. In response,

Diana Walters, PACE's Executive Director, hopes to set up an electronic bulletin board to facilitate communication among the guidance counselors and tech-prep coordinators at all the high schools.

The reporting and dissemination requirements of their various grants slow the development of materials and other supports for the consortium. Walters says that she is often behind schedule on curriculum development or other projects because she spends too much time reporting what the consortium has done. She has learned to carefully review these requirements when applying for funding.

On a similar note, she has had to deal with the effects of PACE's growing reputation. Because PACE has developed a strong following both within South Carolina and across the country, she is often asked to donate her time or contract with other agencies attempting to create similar partnerships. "We have to keep in mind that our mission is to serve the Tri-County area. We could easily become a state technical assistance agency, and fail to sufficiently serve our local constituency. If we let this happen, it would be to the detriment of our consortium, and our local success would not continue."

LESSONS LEARNED

PACE succeeded because partners from all sectors (community college, high schools, vocational centers, and employers) were involved at the start. They all had input into developing the mission statement, goals, and methods of meeting those goals. All partners feel ownership and, therefore, are committed to making it work. Furthermore, because PACE is not the property of any one entity, its chances for longevity are good regardless of the future involvement of any one partner.

PACE demonstrates that systemic change requires continual communication. As noted earlier, communication among the partners is one of the major challenges of PACE. But without it, much of the partners' efforts would be redundant or counterproductive.

The Apprenticeship Director at Ryobi Corporation, who hosts several of the apprentices and provides in-service training for teachers and school staff, feels that the consortium does not include enough of the area employers. He justifies Ryobi's involvement in the consortium as reducing later training costs. If, however, only a couple of the region's employers make this investment, then they could easily lose the benefits to nonparticipating companies. Ryobi could invest a great deal of training in youngsters who could then go to other employers. Only if Ryobi were able to hire employees who have done their PACE apprenticeship at other businesses, could he justify a large-scale investment in PACE.

Finally, PACE is a consortium, not a regulatory agency. PACE administrators must get the school districts, technical college, and businesses within the consortium to share their vision. They cannot force any one model on any of the partners. To do so would risk alienating the partners, and it would leave little room for creative implementation that best suits the partners' needs. Rather, PACE shares their vision, provides technical assistance, mostly in the form of curriculum materials and training, and coordinates the efforts of the independent partners within the consortium. At times, they also use the successes of one school or district to cajole another into trying what was once thought impractical.

PROTECH HEALTH CARE
BOSTON, MASSACHUSETTS

BACKGROUND — CIVIC-BUSINESS OUTREACH
TARGETED TO CITY SCHOOLS

ProTech traces its beginning to the Boston Compact, a business/ school consortium organized in 1982. Member companies agreed to give the city's public high school graduates hiring preference, in return for progress by the public school system in curtailing dropouts and achieving improved measures of academic performance. In 1989, the Compact's commitment to the schools deepened. Businesses pledged to stress high-skilled jobs, and to help city educators develop programs which would equip Boston's young people to qualify for them.

ProTech originated in 1991, when a United States Department of Labor grant helped create a school-to-work pilot project. Affiliated with selected urban-core high schools and coordinated by the Boston Private Industry Council, the project combines paid youth apprenticeships, and structured worksite exposure rotations related to the school curriculum, with clustered applied-academic courses. A health occupations focus was launched in Fall 1991; a financial services sequence was added 2 years later; and a utilities and communications cluster is now in the startup stage. Currently, ProTech Health Care has about

180 participating students, admitting 35–40 eleventh-grade students each year.

ProTech is one of the nation's largest active school-to-work programs, bolstered by substantial government and nonprofit support. Career focus options offered through the program have become more widely available and diversified in recent years. Program administrators are committed to sustaining this expansion. The health occupations sequence is the largest and longest-running.

ProTech runs health programs in three large city schools — Boston, English, and Brighton High Schools. These schools enroll about 1,000 students each, but the ProTech cohorts are clustered in small groups of 25–30 students who take most of their classes together. Program participants reflect their schools' high minority composition. Nearly half the healthcare youth apprentices are African-American and about 30% are Hispanic. Seventy percent of the enrollees are female.

GOALS — INCREASED POSTSECONDARY ENROLLMENTS AND IMPROVED JOB READINESS

ProTech targets high school students "who are unlikely to enter and/or complete postsecondary education without the structure of a youth apprenticeship program." Participating students range from high achievers to some at serious educational risk, including a few who had already dropped out of school but reenrolled to join the program.

High school students enter ProTech at the beginning of their junior year. They receive an intensive job readiness upgrade along with increasingly focused career preparation during eleventh and twelfth grade. Two years at a community college generally follow. Most students will finish with an associate's degree, but there is a baccalaureate option.

ProTech Health Care students are assured part-time and summer jobs at participating hospitals through the entire 4-year duration if they remain in good standing. The program's work-based component is integral to its mission on several counts. Students are drilled — pushed hard if need be — to master the conceptual, communication, and self-presentation skills that define a desirable employee. Applying these skills in an authentic work setting motivates the students and enhances their self-esteem, especially on payday. Students who show they can handle responsibility, and are fortunate enough to connect into the right situation, may actually make their part-time jobs the first rung on a career ladder. A number of the program's early graduates have moved into full-time employment with their original employers.

PROGRAM MODEL — HEALTHCARE APPRENTICESHIPS SUPPLEMENT A 2+2 PROGRAM

ProTech utilizes the 2 + 2 design: an academic and career preparation foundation in the final 2 years of high school, leading to associate degree study at a community college. Students can expect to complete the program as certified health technicians or medical assistants. Some choose to pursue more advanced objectives, such as nursing.

ProTech is administered by an independent agency set up by the Private Industry Council. The agency hires program coordinators, based in participating schools, who provide liaison among students, school staff, and employers. A designated intermediary handles routine matters and addresses difficulties as they arise, reassuring educators and employers who can see the benefits of a program like ProTech in theory, but do not want to add to their workload or complicate their customary duties.

Starting in the eleventh grade, ProTech upgrades students' academic skills to establish basic work readiness. Classes in English, math, and science have no explicit vocational or technical component, but teachers are encouraged to tailor their presentations to be occupationally relevant. Teachers have the opportunity to visit workplaces and meet with employers. *The Private Industry Council employs consultants who brief teachers on making the education-employment link.* This feature is very unusual for any school-to-work program.

Students who encounter difficulty mastering the core academics have access to tutoring services. Each eleventh-grade ProTech entrant is paired with a twelfth grader in the program to provide peer perspective and guidance. Personalized remediation, coaching, and support is no mere addon, but an essential design feature. The program's expectations are challenging, but students receive plenty of encouragement and assistance. This intensive reinforcement can be crucially important to at-risk students.

Students who meet grade and attendance requirements begin working at a paid part-time job in the second semester of their junior year. Typically, students will work for a couple of hours each weekday afternoon. If scheduling permits, the job may be for 1 full day per week. Additionally, apprentices in good standing work full-time for 8 weeks each summer while they are in the program. Wages run approximately $5.50–$6.00 per hour in the high school years, rising to about $7.00 per hour during postsecondary years.

At work, each student has a designated personal mentor, an adult employee. The mentor's function is to sharpen the apprentices' awareness of appropriate, responsible workplace demeanor, rather than to provide specific skills instruction. The mentoring illustrates how ProTech is designed to give students as much individual support and guidance as possible.

In the twelfth grade, ProTech students delve more deeply into career development and college preparation. If possible, they take one course each semester at a community college. While continuing in their part-time paid jobs, they also expand their workplace exposure through clinical rotation sequences. These observation sessions at participating hospitals give students the chance to see a range of procedures which take place in different parts of a hospital. Program designers originally hoped to integrate the rotations into the school curriculum in a comprehensive fashion, and actually contracted with educational consultants to develop a structured clinical rotation-class instruction format. However, according to an evaluation done for the U.S. Department of Labor,

> These ambitious plans were scaled back . . . to more ad hoc exposure to activities in particular hospital departments, arranged for an individual or small groups of students by a department supervisor. Planners made this change after hospitals reported that the structured training plan required more staff time, energy, space, and equipment than hospitals could commit.[3]

ProTech divided the work experience component into two distinct segments — paid part-time jobs and unpaid clinical rotations. Most part-time jobs did not provide adequately focused or thorough learning. Also, when the program started, there were insufficient paid

---

[3] Walter Corson and Marsha Silverberg, *School-to-Work/Youth Apprenticeship Demonstration Preliminary Findings*, Mathematical Policy Research, Inc., June 1994:82–83.

slots available for all eligible students, and some had to wait up to a year to be placed in a part-time job. According to ProTech administrators, that has been ironed out, and students now obtain jobs promptly.

Although fully integrating the school curriculum with clinical rotation sequences proved infeasible, ProTech leaders remain devoted to making classroom work relevant to employment. Within an applied academic course framework, teachers are urged to relate class material to the specific job contexts students encounter in their part-time jobs and clinical rotations.

CHALLENGES

As noted, ProTech readjusted its work-based component from the initial plans. The students' paid jobs are still a vehicle for instilling employability skills and responsibility. The chance to earn money remains a major attraction of the program. But to fulfill the goal of substantive career preparation, a sequence of unpaid clinical rotations had to be added. That design also had to be modified. Program planners first conceived the rotations as a logical progression fully integrated with classroom material. However, implementing such a comprehensive format was too complicated. ProTech's operation represents a noticeable scaling back of expectations.

The students' paid jobs vary widely in quality and pedagogical potential. In the best cases, students who master basic skills encounter receptive situations which generate valuable, increasingly responsible workplace experience. For example, a high school senior placed at Boston's Deaconess Hospital sorted blood samples and verified lab test orders for the hematology unit.[4] Conversely, a few students complained to a U.S. Department of Labor evaluation team that they only received low-level tasks like photocopying or cleanup.[5]

Some minor problems appear to stem from misunderstanding or faulty communication. The program coordinator at one school criticized details of students' dress and mannerisms in a way some found demeaning and meddlesome. There is a nuanced distinction between helpful instruction about appropriate, mature workplace

---

[4] Erin Martin, "Making the Grade," *Deaconess Magazine*, Spring 1993.

[5] Corson and Silverberg, *op. cit.*, p.37.

demeanor and nitpicking micromanagement. In this instance, the students felt they were needlessly treated like young children. Another communication misfire occurred when some of the first cohort of apprentices were preparing to enter community college. Some students found the program's tuition reimbursement provisions less comprehensive than they had expected. Employers pay tuition for specific career-related courses, but not for a student's entire post-secondary education. Students then had to explore the ordinary range of financial aid options available from channels outside the ProTech program.

The screening process for new entrants to the program may need refinement. Preliminary admission standards are far from rigorous. A ProTech staff person characterized the recruitment process at one high school as taking "practically anyone who raised their hand."[6] But once they are in the program, students are required to maintain a C+ average and 85% attendance. As a result, there has been up to 30% attrition from initial ProTech sign-ups in some schools. This compares with 10–20% at most other programs studied, although almost all programs are new and data is scarce. Instituting very strict admissions standards would, however, undercut ProTech's mission to serve as a last-chance resource for reclaiming the potential of disadvantaged or marginal students.

ProTech students are clustered in core academic and career-prep classes, spending substantial stretches of each school day together as a group. In each high school, about 25 or 30 ProTech students take most of their eleventh and twelfth grade classes together. Clustering lets teachers maintain a contextual focus. Most of them agreed that the clustering enhanced students' mastery of the material taught. On the downside, they felt that so much time almost exclusively in the company of their own small group limited their social life, and made it hard for them to participate in schoolwide extracurricular activities.

LESSONS LEARNED

ProTech is still in the early stage of implementation. The 1991 cohort of high school juniors who were its first apprentice class should receive associate degrees by summer 1995. The program continues

---

[6] *Ibid.*, p. 29.

evolving, as planners and directors seek to identify the most effective elements and approaches. Anecdotal examples strongly suggest that some marginal or at-risk students have been able to positively reorient their lives by participating. But rigorous assessment of Pro-Tech's impact must await further time and research.

The program receives strong community support and multiple sources of grant funding. When Massachusetts was awarded federal implementation money under the 1994 School-to-Work Opportunities Act, ProTech (all program sequences, not just healthcare) garnered $1.22 million. This money assures the program's viability and enables employers to receive a $1,000 subsidy for each hired student. These factors underlie ProTech's ability to expand. The number of students participating in the healthcare youth apprenticeship has grown impressively: 108 in 1992, 160 in 1993, 184 in 1994. The number of Boston hospitals taking on student workers increased from seven in 1993 to 10 in 1994. Such figures substantiate predictions that hands-on transition programs can be steadily scaled up. As Neil Sullivan, executive director of the Boston Private Industry Council, remarked on the occasion of ProTech's latest grant award,

> It's not just about pilot programs anymore. What we're talking about is taking the entire district system and working with area employers to create education and job experiences for thousands of young people. We've got dozens of good pilot programs, but we've never been able to take excellence to scale for all students.[7]

Impressive as ProTech's growth has been, the fact remains that it serves but a small fraction of the thousands of Boston high schoolers who could plausibly benefit from such a program. Even its present level of operation is dependent on government and foundation funding, which could be precarious.

ProTech offers a credible demonstration that the combination of applied academics related to a job context, along with generous amounts of individual attention and support, elicits improved student achievement. Young people ostensibly not earmarked for success

---

[7] *Boston Globe*, August 12, 1994. The new infusion of federal school-to-work money will enable the various ProTech programs to offer an aggregate 400 youth apprenticeship slots in 1994–95, up from 220 the previous year.

are capable of succeeding. But a program which draws out their full potential is not easy or cheap; it takes assiduous and sustained effort with no shortcuts.

BOEING
WASHINGTON STATE

BACKGROUND — A GIANT CORPORATION'S GROWING INVOLVEMENT WITH WORKFORCE TRAINING

The Boeing Company, based in Seattle, is the number one aircraft manufacturer worldwide and a leading player in related high-tech aerospace developments. Its main concern is not solvency, but rather maintaining its competitive edge.

What motivates a multibillion-dollar concern like Boeing to get involved in work readiness and school-to-work transition programs? Probably, a combination of long-term preventive maintenance (taking steps to assure and improve the quality of the incoming workforce), good community relations, and a chance to have broad influence on the structure of education.

It doesn't hurt that Boeing is the largest employer in the State of Washington. People around Seattle take great pride in Boeing's presence; they identify with its achievements and are rocked when it faces adversity. Sporadically adverse economic conditions and the inevitably cyclical needs for aircraft replacement have spurred massive layoffs at the giant firm several times since the early 1970s. Downturns have serious repercussions throughout the region. A dominant employer is a welcome bulwark for the local economy, but dependence on its prosperity creates vulnerability. Boeing's interests strongly color the greater Seattle region's civic culture and much of its politics.

Like many large corporations, Boeing traditionally devoted the bulk of its educational outreach and support to 4-year college programs. This orientation began to shift in the late 1980s. The reason is twofold and familiar: recognition that a majority of young people will not receive 4-year degrees, and too many new workforce entrants lack the increasingly complex skills needed to succeed.

As Boeing Vice President and General Manager Bill Selby characterized the company's entrance into high school and community college work preparedness programs, "Pay now or pay later." If the company is able to organize and shape the education of its future entry level workers, it can expect measurable savings in on-the-job training and attrition costs. Moreover, Boeing's move into this sphere gives the company leverage to influence the development of education standards for the manufacturing workforce on a more general scale.

GOALS — COMPANY-SPONSORED TRAINING PROGRAMS LEADING THE WAY TO A RECOGNIZED SYSTEM OF MANUFACTURING SKILLS AND STANDARDS

Boeing's corporate clout empowers it to shape school-to-work transition well beyond the pilot project level. The manufacturer has consciously parlayed its school-to-work programs into a major role in guiding legislation and education policy for the manufacturing industry. Boeing's involvement has been seminal in the drive to establish a set of skills standards for entry-level employment. Developing these standards continues as a manufacturing-industry collaboration with modest government support.

The story begins in late 1992 with the formation of an ad hoc group of members of state and regional business and education associations, along with major area industries. Original members included Boeing, Hewlett Packard, Simpson Timber Company, the Eldec Corporation, and others. Several more companies, notably Kaiser Aluminum, joined later. The participants soon formalized their association as the Manufacturing Technology Advisory Group (MTAG). The initial meeting began a joint industry-education effort to "develop a common core of competencies and standards for preparing a high performance workforce in manufacturing technology." This continues to be the consortium's prime focus.

The term "competencies" should ring a bell, and, indeed, the adopted standards format uses the SCANS concepts. Assembling and implementing a set of manufacturing-employee standards is a long, painstaking process. A $500,000 federal grant to MTAG moved it forward in 1994. (*See* Chapter 5, "Community Colleges," for a discussion of a national program in which Boeing and South Seattle Community College play a part.)

PROGRAM MODEL — AN EXPANDED AND FLEXIBLE TECH-PREP
BASED ON MANUFACTURING STANDARDS

While the standards project is an ongoing long-term effort, Boeing already has a hand in setting up model school-to-work training programs. An early watershed came in 1991, when the Washington State Legislature approved the Community and Technical College Act. This statute regularized the requirements for a 2-year postsecondary "technical degree," and effectively merged the state's existing technical institute and community college systems. It also guaranteed efficient, nonredundant articulation among various programs of instruction.

Boeing provided seed grants to 59 Washington high schools to develop technical curricula. It set up a small student summer internship program, sponsored teacher education, and contributed financial support to participating community colleges. The fruit of these efforts was a new 2-year college degree in Manufacturing Technology.

The program adheres to the traditional tech-prep concept. Sufficiently advanced junior and senior year courses (11th and 12th grade) at an approved technical high school are certified for community college credit. Most students seek an associate degree following 2 years of postsecondary instruction. But this actually represents 4 years of substantive technical training, beginning in the eleventh grade. The program also includes an option for transfer to a 4-year institution (initially Western Washington University) to complete a baccalaureate degree.

Training is described as "rigorous;" however, the program's statement of purpose notes that the 2-year postsecondary timeframe should not foreclose the possibility of success for students unable to complete the requirements in that duration: "Students [should be allowed] to progress at their own pace, leave and reenter at various points in their progress, and continue until the industry-defined competencies are mastered."

The manufacturing technology curriculum is based on the premise that future employees should achieve the SCANS foundation skills (basic academic grounding, thinking, and personal skills) as a condition of high school graduation. During high school and community college, specific manufacturing applications — such as measurement, layout, product, and process control — are introduced, eventually forming a "technical core" of manufacturing knowledge. More specialized applications, like computer programming, electronics, or machining, come in the final community college courses, or in a bachelor's degree program.

The pilot curriculum is tied to the standards development process. Manufacturers in the standards-setting consortium rated the relative importance of several dozen manufacturing-relevant skills, and reported at what point (e.g., in high school, in community college, or on the job) they believe a worker should master each capability. Skills covered ranged from understanding how to work in a self-directed, cooperative team to knowing the metric system to being able to understand and comply with EPA and OSHA regulations. Based on these ratings, MTAG continues to compile and refine its competency standards. In turn, the evolving standards feeds back into the Manufacturing Degree curriculum.

CHALLENGES

Boeing expects its several-million dollar backing of Washington's tech-prep program to show a positive cost-benefit return within a few years. This projection calculates expected tangible benefits, such as reduced training costs and greater employee retention and productivity. Other, less quantifiable benefits, like influencing education legislation and curriculum development, or simply higher company morale and good public relations, are noted but not counted in a return on investment calculation.

Nevertheless, the main argument in favor of revitalized technical education should probably not rest on grounds of short-term cost effectiveness. Efforts by Boeing and other manufacturers to promote improved school-to-work transition programs evince both self-interest and civic-mindedness, which does not necessarily strike an easy balance. Sustaining the effort requires an inherent commitment to educational involvement and improvement. But no automatic formula ensures that a specific investment in upgraded technical training will produce a predictable return. Projects like this tend to acquire their own momentum, and the community good-will they generate makes furthering them a priority.

Boeing and the other MTAG companies recognize that competitive job readiness concerns and overall quality of life issues are interconnected, although their relationship is not expressible in an algorithm.

As MTAG's inaugural statement of purpose pronounces, there is a need

> . . . to develop and maintain a highly skilled and flexible manufacturing work force. This need is driven not only by industry, but also by the recognition that high skill, high wage jobs are the backbone of a healthy economy in our State. It is imperative that we develop more effective educational programs that provide advanced technical skill training for our youth and existing workforce if we expect industry to locate and remain in our State. It is also critical to the health and welfare or our State that we assure our work force the opportunity for high skill, high wage jobs.

Moving from rhetorical goals to a functioning system that achieves them is a long process. Boeing's vision of more effective school-to-work transition hinges on the formation of industry-approved technical education standards. Concomitantly, success hinges on how clear, rigorous, and usable the standards turn out to be.

LESSONS LEARNED

Program sponsorship by giant companies like Boeing bespeaks a serious business commitment to collaborate with schools in upgrading the preparedness of the future workforce. Bringing about better articulated technical education which utilizes manufacturer-developed standards is an ambitious task by any reckoning, but the task has considerable corporate muscle behind it. At present, manufacturing technology associates are just starting to come out of the community colleges and industry standards are still in the formative stage. A reasonably definitive evaluation of the project's success is probably several years away.

However, to conclude on a sobering note, even an enormous firm like Boeing will have only modest direct impact on student placements. Boeing's summer internship program (paid work-based learning for tech-prep enrollees) began in 1993 with only 25 students. It is projected to reach maximum scale in 1997 with only 300 interns at four locations in the greater Seattle area. Presumably, the manufacturing technology degree will be a valued credential in the eyes of other employers, so it is hard to gauge the tech-prep initiative's overall employment effect. The most germane inference may be that the largest employers are capable exemplars and an important resource for program innovations — but industry giants alone cannot cause systemic educational reform or the entire community's transformation to high performance workplaces.

CRAFTSMANSHIP 2000
TULSA, OKLAHOMA

BACKGROUND — STATE AND INDUSTRY PROMOTION OF REVITALIZED TECHNICAL EDUCATION

Craftsmanship 2000 centers around a youth apprenticeship in metalworking. It originated in a fortunate confluence of circumstances — employers willing to make long-term commitments to a promising innovation, matched with state educators determined to sharpen the occupational focus in the schools and expand the reach of relevant vocational programs. On the employer side, Tulsa-area metalworking firms launched the apprenticeship in response to prompting from executives at the local division of Hilti, Inc., a multinational construction-fastener manufacturer based in Liechtenstein. On the school side, Oklahoma's Department of Vocational and Technical Education was already pursuing systemwide curricular reforms. A modern technical campus, offering both adult and youth education, was available.

A 1993 status report on implementing youth apprenticeships in Oklahoma[8] describes the need for a system of postsecondary education and training for the majority of students who will not obtain a 4-year college degree. It emphasized that there are more college graduates than jobs which require a baccalaureate credential;[9] but almost all worthwhile jobs now demand some formal education or training beyond high school. Improved vo-tech, community college, and youth apprenticeship programs lead to career development for every student. Beyond reducing the incidence of high school drop-

---

[8] Roy Peters, Jr., *Building a Youth Apprenticeship System: The Oklahoma Edition*, Oklahoma Department of Vocational and Technical Education, August 1993.

[9] *Oklahoma Counselor's Guide to Tech Prep* (1994) cites U.S. Department of Labor statistics that 25% of those with bachelor's degrees are not in jobs which require 4 years of college, with that proportion projected to increase to 30% by the turn of the century.

outs and undereducated high school graduates, the report recommended that the entire educational system be restructured to provide options better tailored to realistic employment opportunities. The Tulsa metalworking apprenticeship effort provides one such option.

Craftsmanship 2000's germination dates to around 1990. Andre Siegenthaler had recently been transferred from Switzerland to become human resources vice president for Hilti's Tulsa branch. Mr. Siegenthaler realized that entrants to the local manufacturing workforce were less well-equipped than their European counterparts with the conceptual and technical skills that would effectively complement their evident eagerness to work. In Switzerland and Liechtenstein, line-workers readily troubleshoot minor production problems on their own. Similar glitches in Tulsa would necessitate calling an engineer. Mr. Siegenthaler promoted the idea of industry-sponsored youth apprenticeships developed cooperatively with the educational system. Through such a project, companies could both upgrade young workers' preparedness and bolster community relations. Industry would also get the chance to team with educators in formulating more work-relevant instructional programs — admittedly an investment of time, effort, and resources which U.S. companies are not accustomed to making. But as a long-term dividend, employees who need less on-the-job training to do high-quality work without close supervision significantly boost productivity.

GOALS — TECHNICAL TRAINING COMBINED WITH SOUND ACADEMICS

As a motto on state vo-tech department notepads declares, the objective is "making the pieces fit" to achieve "schools that work." Oklahoma has become an educational leader in offering applied academic courses. The state school system has taken substantial strides in breaking down the barriers and status distinctions between academic and vocational programs. An increasing portion of the Oklahoma high school curriculum consists of applied courses which fully meet baccalaureate entrance requirements, but equally well serve the many students who will pursue an associate degree or technical certificate. An ongoing curricular review process strives to eliminate gaps or redundancies and to improve articulation between secondary and postsecondary programs.

Oklahoma's vo-tech division has also expanded its reach into middle schools, presenting an innovative Technology Education package to sixth through tenth graders. This course introduces students to four technology systems — communications, construction, manufacturing, transportation — in a manner designed to complement the regular curriculum and to assist students in their early exploration of career opportunities and career preferences.

In Spring 1990, at Mr. Siegenthaler's invitation, the mayor of Tulsa and a group of upper-echelon Chamber of Commerce officials got a personal introduction to the European apprenticeship system by touring Hilti's Liechtenstein facilities. Hilti organized similar visits for state vocational education administrators and staff. A bandwagon effect ensued as Hilti continued to spearhead the effort. The upshot was a group of Tulsa-area firms agreeing to sponsor a metalworking youth apprenticeship program. By 1993, seven local employers — a range of manufacturers along with American Airlines — were participating. Hilti originally conceived the project as a youth apprenticeship in machining, but the venture was reformulated under a broader metalworking theme following input from the other employers, who are not primarily engaged in the machine-tools industry.

The program aims to produce technical trainees with a very sound academic foundation. Its 4-year format is evenly split into secondary and postsecondary components. Instruction combines a broad-based classroom curriculum with progressively more advanced workplace experience. Students receive an employer-paid stipend.

PROGRAM MODEL — A EUROPEAN-STYLE METALWORKING APPRENTICESHIP

Given the novelty of cohesive school-to-work youth training in this country, it is not coincidental that a European-based company led the way in instituting Craftsmanship 2000. Manpower Demonstration Research Corporation, in a January 1994 study of school-to-work transition programs, noted that for the Tulsa project, as well as other new youth apprenticeship programs, "A European connection makes it easier to recruit and motivate employers."[10] A receptive education system is the other element in the equation, and circumstances were

---

[10] Susan Goldberger, Richard Kazis, and Mary Kathleen O'Glanagan, *Learning Through Work: Designing and Implementing Quality Worksite Learning for High School Students*, Manpower Demonstration Research Corporation, January 1994:24.

equally auspicious in this regard.

Craftsmanship 2000 is administered by a nonprofit agency expressly organized for this purpose under Chamber of Commerce aegis. In addition to the corporate sponsors, Tulsa public schools, Tulsa Area Vo-Tech, Tulsa Junior College, and the local Chamber of Commerce have a voice in the program's structure and content.

The Craftsmanship 2000 model uses a flexible array of articulation options built around an intensive applied academic core. Its 2 + 2 design provides for industry-specific metalworking training to commence in the junior year of high school. A community college associate degree is the typical concluding credential. However, the program accommodates options for lesser or greater levels of postsecondary study.

Continuous feedback between employers and teaching staff emphasize making classroom material as workplace-relevant as possible. Applied math, communication, and science classes meet the requirements for admission to 4-year colleges, but are presented with a practical workplace orientation. The apprentices' class schedule differs radically from traditional high school curricula. Instruction takes place at the area vo-tech campus, a site for adult, as well as secondary, level technical education. Classes last longer than the standard daily high school fare of 50-minute periods — perhaps 2 hours, even 4 hours for a lab session. Classes generally meet only two or three times weekly for each subject.

Craftsmanship 2000 demands considerably more time than either ordinary high school or most work-preparation programs. Students take part in either classes or worksite training for 8 hours per day, 220 days of the year. Time-on-task is thus 60% longer than a conventional school schedule based on 180 6-hour days. Apprentices who make this commitment and fulfill program requirements receive stipends, paid in progressively larger increments, totalling approximately $30,000 per student over the 4-year program term. The stipends are not tied to hours spent at work. At some companies taking part in the program, unions would not agree to young trainees being paid hourly wages. Craftsmanship 2000 youth apprentices have an additional incentive to excel in the classroom, the possibility of a several-hundred-dollar bonus awarded for achieving outstanding grades.

When the apprentice-students are not in class, they are at the worksite. Initially, the students rotate through brief workday sequences at a variety of companies. After gaining exposure to multiple enterprises and receiving progressively more detailed introduction to particular crafts, they gradually focus on training for specific skilled jobs.

Apprentice recruitment occurs by soliciting applications from interested students in area high schools. A panel of business represent- atives and educators, weighted toward employers, screens the appli- cants and admits about 20 students per year to the program. Accepted trainees transfer to the area vo-tech campus. The 20 eleventh-grade youth apprentices chosen for the 1994–95 school year came from approximately 55 applicants, so there is competition for program admission. Nevertheless, there is no overwhelming crush of applicants for this modest-sized program. The recruitment and selection process seems to be functioning effectively. Attrition runs about 10%, reason- ably low for a school-to-work regimen both highly innovative and quite demanding.

Although official state vo-tech education policy encourages fe- males to consider nontraditional careers, Craftsmanship 2000 does not appear to explicitly seek out female applicants. The selection process is nominally gender-neutral, but so far the apprentices have been overwhelmingly male.

CHALLENGES

Craftsmanship 2000, the state's first youth apprenticeship, is a small, but important, element in Oklahoma's larger workforce development strategy. The state seeks broad-based preparedness for high-skill, high-wage jobs that will propel the state economy. In fiscal 1993, Oklahoma vocational-technical enrollments totaled some 293,000 — 102,000 secondary school students and 191,000 in adult education. Fields of study include business, marketing, health occupations, home economics and consumer education, agriculture, trade and industry, and technology. Tech-prep programs — defined by state educators as similar to youth apprenticeship in general orientation, but without an explicit work experience component — are ongoing in 10 pilot projects, involving 60 school districts, 10 vo-tech schools, 10 community colleges, and 3 state universities.

Craftsmanship 2000 is heralded as a demonstration of extensively remodeled vocational education. Its linchpin is inducing employers to make a formal commitment to years-long apprenticeships, a fairly alien concept in the U.S. If the youth apprentice program model catches hold in America, the impact would resonate significantly. But these are very ambitious goals for a project whose scale is limited to about 20 entrants annually.

Launching a youth apprentice program requires a sizable investment. The 2-year planning process for Craftsmanship 2000 cost $75,000–$100,000. Training mentors cost another $20,000. Industry representatives spent about 2,000 aggregate hours on curriculum development.[11] Although the Craftsmanship 2000 concept is now being loosely replicated in other sections of the state, education officials acknowledge that the spinoff programs are considerably less well funded. In fact, the Tulsa endeavor, despite its prestigious status as a flagship youth apprenticeship model, had to scale back the stipends pledged to students considerably — from $50,000 to $30,000 over the 4 years of training — to persuade enough employers to participate.

The program's intense schedule and commitment to a specific craft demand a level of maturity that may be extraordinary for high school students. In a study commissioned by the U.S. Department of Labor,[12] some Craftsmanship 2000 apprentices — along with trainees in other "cluster" programs — expressed regret at being largely separated from the bulk of their peers attending "regular" school. Yet, there was widespread agreement among students in all such programs that the design does foster effective learning. Certainly some teens seize the opportunity to be treated more like adults. As one Tulsa student put it, "The program makes you more mature because you have to do everything yourself."[13]

Since Craftsmanship 2000 is an employer-initiated program, the administrators anticipating upcoming workforce needs are actually those closest to the hiring process. Uncertainty about whether training has real job relevance is greatly reduced. Conversely, preparation for a narrowly defined position means that the trainee must

---

[11] Walter Corson and Marsha Silverberg, *School-to-Work/Youth Apprenticeship Demonstration Preliminary Findings,* Mathematical Policy Research, Inc., June 1994:110.

[12] Corson and Silverberg, *op. cit.,* p. 38.

[13] *Ibid.,* p. 36.

depend on that job remaining in demand. Those who acquire expertise in tubing manufacture may not be able to transfer their expertise automatically to another field. How education reacts to changing labor markets poses a tangled question for overall school-to-work transition development. The Craftsmanship 2000 cohorts' future careers will help determine how good a fit can emerge between a detailed job-preparation focus and long-term, remunerative job security. On the positive side, the Tulsa program emphasizes the state vo-tech department's commitment to sound academic and conceptual grounding for all secondary-level students. That is a vital asset for any worker's career adaptability and prospects for advancement.

LESSONS LEARNED

The positive response to Craftsmanship 2000 has encouraged startup of other youth apprenticeship programs in different parts of Oklahoma. Four of these were operating by 1994, with others in the planning stage. However, attracting sponsoring employers and coordinating the school-work interface to meet both business preferences and educational requirements can be difficult.

In the long run, the value of school-to-work transition efforts will be adequately established only when completion of a program confers a generally recognized "portable" credential that certifies a young worker has skills for which employers will pay good money. At present, Oklahoma's youth apprenticeships and other technical preparatory programs represent a collection of individual agreements between local school districts and participating businesses. Articulation agreements — for instance, the decision to grant community college credit for advanced high school technical classes — are also decided on a district-by-district basis. But a mechanism for coordinating the certification of technical programs on a statewide level is in the offing. The Business Association of Standards and Excellence (BASE) is an industry-education consortium organized by the state vo-tech department to promote uniform standards and business-approved in-school training materials.

Recognizing successful employment as the surest indicator of effective education, the state welcomes employer involvement in designing high school and community college courses. Ivan Armstrong, Oklahoma's Supervisor for Trade and Industrial Education, sees the current challenge as a search for balance. Implementing curricular innovations and hands-on training programs calls for considerable local flexibility and autonomy in both schools and among the employers who agree to sponsor work-readiness initiatives. At the same time, state administrators are responsible for maintaining credible uniformity of content and exercising central oversight.

Craftsmanship 2000 occupies a rather specialized niche. It constitutes a major departure from customary school scheduling, with craft-specific training, rigorous classroom work, and a heavy time commitment. It does not promise to serve all students, but to serve a limited group of students exceptionally well.

BROOME COUNTY YOUTH APPRENTICESHIP PROGRAM
BROOME COUNTY, NY

BACKGROUND — EMPLOYERS COOPERATE WITH
SCHOOLS IN A MODEL YOUTH WORK PROGRAM

Cornell University's Department of Human Development and Family Studies organized this youth apprenticeship pilot in the Binghamton area of New York State in the Fall of 1991. Ten local employers agreed to hire and train young workers, whose paid work experience combines with concurrent high school and community college studies to form an integrated career preparation learning program. Apprenticeships are sponsored in three broad occupational areas: manufacturing and engineering technology; administration and office technology; and healthcare. These fields were chosen for their importance in the regional and national economy.

The program is modest in scale, admitting about 20 high school juniors each year. The apprentices reflect the ethnic and educational background of the general community, which is 95% white. Most of the apprentices' parents are high school graduates who did not attend college. Employers who sponsor apprenticeships generally see their participation as an exercise in civic responsibility and good community relations, although they hope to acquire reliable long-term employees through the process. The project draws a considerable portion of its support from foundation grants.

GOALS — IMPROVED COHESION BETWEEN SCHOOL AND WORK FOR MIDDLE-ACHIEVING STUDENTS

Designers of the Broome County program consciously borrowed guiding principles from the German apprenticeship model. They seek more cohesion between schoolroom learning and workplace training than traditional American vocational education. The career goals these apprenticeships serve are described as best suited for someone with postsecondary education short of a 4-year baccalaureate degree.

The program targets "middle students, young people who probably would not enroll in college without an extra boost but who do not have severe academic or behavioral problems." A few of the apprentices are honor students, but more typically they have grades at about the B-minus level. The program directors would like to recruit a more at-risk student population. However, they intend to spend a few more years systematizing and streamlining the project before taking this step.

PROGRAM MODEL — STRUCTURED LEARNING THROUGH PAID WORK EXPERIENCE

The Broome County youth apprenticeships follow the usual 2 + 2 tech-prep paradigm: paid work experience integrated with classroom learning over the last 2 years of high school and 2 years of community college. Participants who complete the 4-year program will earn a high school diploma and an associate degree, along with "expert job skills derived from extensive work experience." The program's directors are attached to Cornell University, about 50 miles away, but work out of a local Binghamton office.

Employers involved in the Broome County program range considerably in size. Ten employers participate, including IBM, the Anitec Division of International Paper Corporation, the Security Mutual Life Insurance Company, Blue Cross, and a local hospital and nursing home. Notwithstanding the diverse sizes of sponsoring employers, the apprentice experiences themselves all provide one-on-one mentoring. This personal workplace "coaching" — in real, not make-work, situations — is repeatedly cited by the young participants as the most valuable and empowering part of their training.

After an initial 3-month probationary period, the apprentice rotates through various departments. Managers generally assign the mentors, also known as coaches, to a student when she comes into the department for her rotation. A student may have more than one coach, depending on the setting and the workplace tasks involved. School credit for their work is based on supervisor evaluations.

The coaches are usually quite informal. They instruct the apprentices in particular on-the-job procedures, but also provide them with a good background understanding of the workplace's overall function. The mentors have some administrative duties, such as completing evaluation forms, which can be bothersome. Yet, almost all of them enjoy personal contact with the students and consider the overall experience enriching. On the few occasions when friction arises between mentors and apprentices, or apprentices act inappropriately, school officials, supervisors, and perhaps parents discuss the situation at specially scheduled meetings.

While legislative mandates in some states, notably Wisconsin and Oregon, fostered the creation of more or less uniform, preapproved school-to-work transition programs, Broome County takes a "bottoms-up" rather than "top-down" approach. The Binghamton endeavor has no formal recognition from the New York State Department of Labor, although a state youth apprenticeship accreditation mechanism exists. Program sponsors and developers are sanguine about the lack of formalized status; they prefer to forgo certification procedures until they compile a longer record of proven success in the field. Ultimately, directors intend to register the program with the Federal Committee on Apprenticeship, an advisory body to the U.S. Department of Labor.

CHALLENGES

Program staff maintain that "securing employers' participation is the most challenging aspect of our project and of youth apprenticeship generally." This difficulty stems from the absence of a tradition to lifetime employment tenure in the U.S., as mentioned in the discussion on apprenticeships in Chapter 6. Why should companies invest in training and nurturing workers when the likelihood that those workers will remain with that employer over an entire career seems remote? Economic arguments for investing in a better trained workforce sound reasonable if one takes the longer view, but are less compelling than the next quarter's bottom line. Civic responsibility and good community relations probably provide more effective immediate motivation for employer participation.

Apprenticeship U.S.-style, to be realistic, may always be a relatively small-scale endeavor. But coordinators of the Broome County project express guarded hope that the scale can be increased slightly from present proportions, which they admit are minuscule. The key to such an increase is employers *collectively* deciding to set aside a few training slots apiece. Apprenticeships today are sponsored on a very scattershot, individual basis. An avowed policy commitment by many employers to provide apprentice positions, even on a small scale, would help maintain a presence and sense of continuity in the community.

The Broome County apprentice program is a pilot project whose wider implementation depends on employers taking proactive interest in youth training, and on significant institutional and philosophical modifications in American education. These are not small changes, and even the most optimistic advocates have a slim basis for predicting their imminent fruition.

Meanwhile, the logistics of combining a "normal" school schedule with work are quite cumbersome. The Broome County apprenticeship coordinators give very high marks to local school officials for being understanding and going the extra mile to accommodate apprentices. Nevertheless, sometimes unresolvable conflicts arise. Certain courses are required for high school graduation. Some small rural schools in the program offer few if any multiple classes in these mandatory subjects, and work schedules may be given short shrift in view of this constraint. Students, teachers, and employers have also mentioned that the quality and availability of certain advanced science courses could be upgraded.

Regulated workplaces impose other limitations. For example, a healthcare apprentice became accustomed to "doing almost everything" that the professional technicians did in the phlebotomy lab. But when she was transferred to the physical therapy unit, her status was restricted virtually to that of an observer.

In general, school-work coordination efforts encounter difficulty in making academics and work as mutually relevant as possible. Many programs which combine school-based and work-based components boast of how these elements are integrated. But the validity of the claim tends to hinge on how loose a definition of program integration one is willing to accept. Tight linkages seem more feasible in theory than practice is usually able to bear out. It is a trial and error process, with some progress being made.

LESSONS LEARNED

Broome County's program is explicitly designed to assure that apprentices and potential apprentices get the best possible overview of "career pathways" in their chosen field. The counseling component seems particularly strong. Young people entering or considering the program are well-informed about what opportunities they can compete for with a high school diploma, or an associate or bachelor's degree. The small, personal scale of the program helps ensure that participants don't get locked into something they don't understand, or feel lukewarm about. In one case, coordinators helped arrange a transfer from manufacturing to the office-administrative sector for a dissatisfied apprentice.

The Broome County program displays a number of encouraging possibilities for an improved school-to-work transition system. Students who might have been regarded as average at best, have shown the desire and capability to excel. Although the scale is small, employers have been successfully recruited in an intensive — but not overly expensive — effort by the apprenticeship coordinators. The mentoring experience is most heartening of all, in terms of making workplaces meaningfully "learning-rich." Almost randomly chosen mentors enthusiastically and competently rose to the occasion when presented with the chance to take part in a serious educational endeavor.

SEATTLE/KING COUNTY YOUTH FAIR CHANCE INITIATIVE
SEATTLE, WASHINGTON

Young people here have dreams like everyone else. They want to go to college, get a good job, have a nice family. . . . What they need is for someone to expose them to all the opportunities and guide them on an individual basis.

— *Southwest Seattle resident and parent*

BACKGROUND — AN UNDERSERVED, HIGH-RISK URBAN AREA

Southwest Seattle and the adjacent neighborhoods across the city line form a high-crime, high-poverty area. The neighborhoods are isolated from each other and from the rest of the region by jurisdictional, geographic, transportation, and other barriers. Their dropout, unemployment, crime, and teen pregnancy rates are higher than the rest of the region. Many of their residents are from a wide variety of minority ethnic and racial populations — and many are immigrants who speak little or no English. The area does not foster high aspirations in its youths. Rather, when asked about their goals, many youths in the area respond, "To not get killed."

Over the years, several community groups have conducted needs assessments in an attempt to leverage local, state, or federal programs to address these problems. Despite their best efforts, the area remains underserved by education, training, and social service programs. Poor public transportation, that isolates the neighborhoods from services offered elsewhere in the region, compounds the problem.

In early 1994, the Seattle/King County Private Industry Council saw an opportunity in the United States Department of Labor's (U.S. DOL) Youth Fair Chance Initiative. The U.S. DOL was seeking proposals for programs that would build on and integrate education, training, and supportive services for previously unserved or underserved youths and young adults (under 30 years of age) in impoverished communities.

As the local administrative entity for federal Job Training Partnership Act programs, the Private Industry Council (PIC) has an established working relationship with many of the region's education, training, and social service agencies, the business community, and local government. Therefore, the PIC was well-placed to coordinate efforts of these agencies and bring a comprehensive program, like Youth Fair Chance (YFC), to Southwest Seattle.

On March 18, 1994, after a frenzied schedule of focus groups and meetings with representatives from the community, its schools, local government officials, and the region's business and social service leaders, the Private Industry Council submitted its proposal to give Southwest Seattle's youths a "fair chance." The proposal outlined an array of services for in- and out-of-school youths and young adults. It included a comprehensive school-to-work transition program for the area's two high schools and a "one stop" career center for out-of-school youths. The U.S. DOL-funded Seattle's proposal, and implementation began in the Fall of 1994. At this writing, the House Appropriations Committee of Congress has recommended eliminating funding for the Youth Fair Chance Initiative effective July 1996. This narrative documents the initial planning and startup of a very promising approach to education and training in impoverished areas. If YFC survives this fiscal crisis, we should learn a great deal about the impact of a neighborhood-based saturation approach to school-to-work transitions and youth employment and training.

GOALS — COMMUNITY DEVELOPMENT FOR YOUTHS

It is instructive to look at both the national YFC goals and Seattle's local goals. The Academy for Educational Development (a technical assistance provider for YFC) identifies six national objectives of YFC:

+ To saturate impoverished communities with an integrated array of services which will allow young people to find jobs and develop careers;

+ To guarantee access to appropriate education, training, and supportive services to all youth residing in the target community;

+ To increase participation of previously unserved or underserved youth residing in the target community;

+ To integrate service delivery in the target community, including systems of common intake, assessment, and case management;

+ To increase the rates of high school completion and enrollment in advanced education or training and employment; and

+ To determine the feasibility of offering these services nationwide.

The first and second of these goals set YFC apart from most previous approaches. By saturating impoverished neighborhoods with job opportunities, the U.S. DOL hopes to improve the economic prospects of the whole target area, not only a few youths within it. Thus, the youths will not face increased employment opportunities in isolation, but hopefully they will garnish moral support from their friends and neighbors whose opportunities are also increased.

Second, the integration of services (goal #4) should provide for a more coordinated approach. With proper coordination, agencies will be neither redundant nor hit-or-miss in meeting their clients' needs.

Implicit throughout Seattle's goals, objectives and strategies are the six goals of the national YFC initiative. However, Seattle defines separate goals and objectives for their in-school and out-of-school programs. For in-school youth, the desired outcomes include broad, schoolwide effects, such as:

♦ Increased graduation rates and decreased dropout rates at the two targeted schools;

♦ Improved attendance for all ethnic groups;

♦ Fewer disciplinary actions;

♦ Improved standardized test scores;

♦ Improved transition to postsecondary training and apprenticeships; and

♦ Improved transitions to the labor market in jobs with career potential.

For out-of-school youths and young adults, the desired outcomes include:

♦ Skill attainment: increases in the SCANS foundation skills and competencies;

♦ Educational credentials: GED, high school diploma, or high school credits to reenter secondary education institutions; and

♦ Transitions to employment: finding and keeping employment.

PROGRAM MODELS — A TWO-PRONGED APPROACH

There are two principal components to Seattle's YFC program: a school-to-work transition program for youths enrolled at Evergreen (Highline School District) and Chief Sealth (Seattle) High Schools, and a one-stop career center for youths and young adults who are not in school. The in-school component looks like a fairly typical comprehensive approach to school-to-work transitions, including school-based learning, work-based learning, and connections. However, when you add the out-of-school component, it would better be called a school *and* work transitions program. The overall program focuses on keeping youths in school or employment if they are there, and getting them there if they are not.

YFC integrates and supplements services that already exist. It is not out to create a new program or set of programs, but to strengthen the way that existing programs operate, and to fill in the gaps in services where they exist. This should result in a stronger, more cooperative approach to providing services that outlives the YFC initiative.

In-School Youths

The program for in-school youths at both high schools includes school-based learning, work-based learning, and connecting activities. However, implementation strategies reflect the different services, staff, organizational and community characteristics of two schools in separate school districts.

The model (*see* Figs. 7.4 and 7.5) begins at the transition from middle to high schools. The schools have adopted an academy format wherein students are grouped in teams and instructed by teams of teachers. This integrates course material and permits a more adaptable schedule for special projects or field trips. The more intimate atmosphere means students get to know their classmates and teachers better and should develop stronger attachments to school. Ninth graders at Evergreen high school are also required to take a career awareness class, which integrates career assessment and counseling with exposure to a variety of career possibilities. Teachers are trained as mentors, and community mentors are brought in to provide additional support for personal and career development. In ninth grade, students begin to develop career portfolios, documenting their interests, aptitudes, and, in subsequent years, work experiences.

As students progress through high school, they are provided a variety of services. Career Information Centers at each school build on existing counseling services. An integrated core curriculum encourages learning the SCANS skills and competencies, while continuing the benefits of the ninth-grade academy format. Guest speakers representing a variety of professions give seminars to both teachers and students to develop career awareness and to assist teachers in developing real-life applications for their classroom exercises. Academic and vocational courses are integrated to break down the distinctions between academic and applied learning — and between college prep and career prep curricula. This includes an expansion of the existing Tech-Prep programs at each school.

This school-based learning is supplemented with work-based learning in a variety of forms. Business partners, coordinated by the PIC, the King County Labor Council, and the International Association of Machinists and Aerospace Workers, provide opportunities

FIG. 7.4. YFC IN-SCHOOL PROGRAM FLOW

Program Entry/Middle School Transition

- Career awareness, interest and aptitude assessments
- Placement in teams of students and teachers
- Connections with other support
  - Cities In Schools mentors
  - Home liaison
  - Team leader/mentor

Menu of Services

- Career Information Center
  - Interest/aptitude testing
  - Information/resource library
  - Computer assisted career planning
  - Career portfolio development

- Integrated Core Curriculum

- Portfolio/SCANS foundation
  skills and competencies

- Seminars/training from workers
  in many field

- Career Exploration/Work Site
  Learning Off Campus
  - Job shadowing
  - Internships
  - Work experiences
  - Vocational exploration
  - Field trips

- Integrated academic/vocational
  training courses

- TECH PREP

Career Development Outcomes

- Career plan and portfolio
- Mastery of SCANS competencies and
  foundations skills at a work ready level
- Graduation
- Post secondary education
- Apprenticeship
- Employment

FIG. 7.5. YFC IN-SCHOOL PROGRAM DEVELOPMENT TIMELINE

Year	School/Program	# Served	% of Total	Program Activities/Changes
94/95	Chief Sealth (total)	600	67%	• 9th & 10th grade teacher training on integrated instructn • Implement career portfolio
	• Career Center	600		• Begin work site development
	• Mentoring	500		• 9th & 10th grade team teaching • Begin integration of core courses with career developmnt • Expand tech prep
95/96	Chief Sealth (total)	750	83%	• Teacher release time for work site visits • Employer/parent/school curriculum review board
	• Career Center	750		• Course changes to integrate with career development
	• Mentoring	700		• Begin workplace learning • Most 9th & 10th grade have a work experience • More students access tech prep
96/97	Chief Sealth (total)	900	100%	• Work-based learning for subject-specific credit • Well developed business partners
	• Career Center	900		• Students career portfolio fully developed
	• Mentoring	900		• Complete integration of core courses w/career develpmnt
94/95	Evergreen (total)	450	50%	• Twenty-one 9th grade teachers train as mentors • Change "resource period" to career develpmnt team class
	• Career Center	450		• Plan outreach for work sites & for mentors
	• Mentoring	300		• Implement student career portfolio • Integrate Washington History with career development
95/96	Evergreen (total)	700	64%	• Train community mentors for 10th grade students • Large increase in work sites for students
	• Career Center	700		• Develop system for accrediting work-based learning
	• Mentoring	600		• More core courses integrated • Community members teach seminars, mentor, etc. • Implement customer satisfaction survey
96/97	Evergreen (total)	900	82%	• Continuous mentor training • Develop articulation of tech prep program
	• Career Center	900		• Supplement work-based learning for core courses
	• Mentoring	850		
97/98	Evergreen (total)	1,100	100%	• Implement and expand tech prep models • Complete integration of core courses w/career devlpmnt
	• Career Center	1,100		• All students have some type of work experience
	• Mentoring	1,100		

for job-shadowing, field trips, and internships. Other work experiences are provided through the PIC's Job Training Partnership Act (JTPA) programs (primarily the Summer Youth Employment Program, also slated for disappearance in July 1996).

By the end of high school, students should have a strong academic and applied education, clear career goals, and a plan to achieve them. They will have benefited from systematic career aptitude and interest testing and counseling, applied and academic coursework, and a variety of worksite and on-the-job experiences. Their development will have been supported by caring, competent mentors, and documented in career portfolios.

Out-Of-School Youths and Young Adults

YFC's primary mode of service to out-of-school youths and young adults is through a Community Career Center (CCC). It should be noted, however, that because many nominally "in-school" youths spend more days out of school than in, the CCC's services are available to all youths, regardless of their official school enrollment status. The CCC is designed on a holistic model. In addition to job training and placement, services include counseling, recreation, child care, and other services aimed at reducing barriers to returning to school or other training programs, or gaining and keeping employment.

The CCC draws heavily on the PIC's experience in running career training centers. While its operation is contracted to a community-based organization (Southwest Youth and Family Services), the PIC provides technical assistance, staff training, and development. The center, funded with both Youth Fair Chance and JTPA funds, is part of the PIC's larger youth and adult training system. The CCC is staffed by 22 full- and part-time employees, including seven AmeriCorp members, three teachers, three case managers, two employment specialists, intake, outreach, and career development specialists, a Center Director, administrative assistant, and receptionist.

The CCC's clients range from 14-year-old high school dropouts who have little or no exposure to work, to 30-year-olds with a wide variety of employment experiences and needs, including high school graduates and dropouts, and unemployed and underemployed persons. This variety of clients will have a variety of needs. The CCC provides a large menu of services, including intake assessment and case management to help their clients make best use of the services. Figure 7.6 lists offered services. Basic services will be available to

FIG. 7.6. YFC COMMUNITY CENTER PROGRAM FLOW

```
                    ┌─────────────────────────────┐
                    │    Program Entry/Intake/     │
                    │       Pre-assessment         │
                    └─────────────────────────────┘
                                  │
┌───────────────────────────────────────────────────────────────┐
│                      Menu of Services                           │
├───────────────────────────────────────────────────────────────┤
│  BASIC SERVICES                  CUSTOMIZED SERVICES            │
│                                                                 │
│  •Employment Counseling          •Case Management               │
│  •Vocational Assessment          •Intensive Assessment          │
│  •Community Resource Referral    •Support Services              │
│  •Career Resource Seminars       •Drug & Alcogol Counseling     │
│  •Educational Options Exploration                               │
│                                                                 │
│  •Job Search Skills Training     •Basic Skills Training         │
│  •Job Finding Resources          •GED                           │
│  •Job Placement                  •Credit Retrieval/Re-Entry     │
│                                                                 │
│  •Short Skills Courses           •Longer Pre-Voc Skills Training│
│  •Parenting Classes              •Work-Site Training            │
│  •Other Life Skills Classes      •Occupational Skills Training  │
│  •Support Groups                                                │
│                                                                 │
│  •Recreational Activities                                       │
│  •On-Site Child Care                                            │
└───────────────────────────────────────────────────────────────┘
                                  │
                    ┌─────────────────────────────┐
                    │  Career Development Outcomes │
                    ├─────────────────────────────┤
                    │   •Skills Attainment         │
                    │   •Career Decision Making    │
                    │   •Continuing Education      │
                    │   •Quality Employment        │
                    └─────────────────────────────┘
```

everyone, but the more advanced "customized" services are available only to those interested and assessed as needing them. Staff are trained to continually assess whether clients could benefit from other services offered at the CCC. For example, a person may drop into the center to inquire about a GED course. Discussion with staff may reveal that he or she lacks clear career objectives, and would benefit from a more intensive assessment, after which other customized services may be offered in addition to the GED class. During its first quarter in operation, the CCC served 247 clients.

CHALLENGES

A community saturation program that integrates and supplements existing services is not easy to get off the ground. Challenges abound, among them:

- **Forming partnerships** among agencies that have historically competed for funds, clients, and even staff.

- **Developing assessments** and methods of documentation that will be recognized by diverse stakeholders, including two school systems, a Community Career Center, employers, youths, young adults, and parents.

- **Staffing** a program (or system of programs) while developing them. For example, much of the CCC staff were hired before the building and its office space were available.

- **Managing a variety of unstable funding sources**, including YFC and "matching" contributions from the school systems, community organizations, unions, JTPA funds, and others. Each of these sources has its own funding cycle and duration of commitment. The difficulties in coordinating these resources is further complicated by the drastic reduction in YFC and JTPA funds.

- **Getting participation during the day of caring, competent adults**. Common sense dictates that the best people to help others get jobs are already successful at getting jobs themselves. To YFC, this means that the best mentors, class speakers, or other volunteers for YFC programs are already busy. Their schedules may be flexible or not. They may already be overextended with work, family, and other obligations. Whatever the case, YFC has had difficulty finding competent, caring adults to support their programs.

LESSONS LEARNED

Although YFC is still new, its planning and initial implementation offer hope that a diverse coalition of agencies can cooperate successfully if they focus on their common goals and complementary strengths. Planning YFC in a way that achieved this was not easy. A PIC planner reported,

> You cannot sit in the office and develop a plan that will work. You have to first listen to your prospective clients and all the partners and potential partners in the program. And some of them won't have a voice to tell you what they need, so before you can even listen to them, you have to help them develop a voice.

On a more specific note, he warned, " . . . and don't hire your staff until you have a place to put them."

When designing a set of programs to be implemented in more than one setting, flexibility is paramount. The same set of goals and objectives require very different management and staffing patterns at the two different schools. Similarly, the diversity of clients, especially at the CCC, requires great skill and flexibility in customizing services.

PART III:
SYSTEM BUILDING

8

"LEADING EDGE" STATE SYSTEMS

INTRODUCTION

Local programs operate within state systems which can either support or thwart local efforts. All the stakeholders have an interest in seeing that state systems are built to foster school-to-work. Yet, system building is hard work. And the educational enterprise has been bombarded with demands for systems reform for the past two decades. How to teach Johnny to read; how to keep him from dropping out of school; how to make sure he'll become a healthy, productive and contributing member of our society; how to govern schools and change the decision making process to better reflect the needs of the students. More and more of society's demands and needs have focused on the schools as family and community support systems have slowly eroded.

The most recent pressures come from the growing recognition that our students must compete with students from around the globe for good jobs in this global economy. Hence the demands for skill standards, academic competencies and a working partnership with employers and employees at the workplace. Building these new relationships and standards takes trust, time, patience, and leadership.

Promising practices, however promising, do not constitute systemic reform. There are reasonable differences among both policymakers and practitioners as to where to begin in building a successful and interactive career connections system. Is it better to seed the district with a dozen pilots, monitor, evaluate, and then gradually merge them into what passes for a systemic approach to new forms of learning? Or does it make more sense to start with the big picture, invest in "visioning," curriculum redesign, and staff development and then implement pilot projects? States are taking both approaches, sometimes in combination, as will be seen in the following section. Those at the local district level as well as at individual schools will readily see why decisions made in their state capitals are important to their own efforts.

The attention of every state in the nation has been directed to the workforce development strategy known as School-to-Work. Much of the impetus has emanated from the bully pulpit of the White House, reinforced by small planning grants (approximately $300,000) distributed by the Departments of Labor and Education to every Governor beginning in late 1993. The heat turned up when, shortly thereafter, the two departments announced a competitive implementation grant process offering the challenge and incentive of 5-year multimillion dollar venture capital grants. The commitment of the country to this reform effort was extended by the passage and funding of the School-to-Work Opportunities Act in late Spring 1994.

But what is school-to-work? Is it "fixing up" the vocational education system? Is it youth apprenticeship? Is it more tech-prep? What should a career opportunity system look like? What is the role of employers? How do we move to scale and reach all kids? Federal support, state responses, and local divisions will answer these questions.

The state implementation grant proposals demonstrate that much work lies ahead in order to realize the potential of this new initiative. The first task is to improve the understanding and breadth of the vision. Simply stated, the vision of school-to-work is a *redefinition of learning*. A broad collaborative effort is needed among major stakeholders to change the system and redefine learning. The change requires answering questions like learning for whom — all students? Voc-ed students? Learning in what environments — the academic classroom? The vo-tech center? The workplace? Who decides what to teach? The academic curriculum committee? The employer community? Do skills competencies guide curriculum development? What skills competencies? How will they be measured? How will the requisite collaborations and communications be brokered, facilitated and nurtured?

Eight states were selected for implementation grants out of the 22 state proposals submitted in the 1994 first round. Another 39 states applied for second round funding in Summer 1995 of which 21 were successful grantees. Their success could be attributed to the way in which some of the questions listed above were addressed. We will examine a representative sample of the winners to try to tease out useful approaches and perspectives.

OREGON

Oregon's vision of a statewide School-to-Work Opportunities System has been evolving over the past 3 years, stimulated largely by the 1990 publication of *America's Choice: High Skills or Low Wages*. Several significant legislative initiatives soon followed, creating an infrastructure for a comprehensive human resource investment system. These laws were:

♦ Oregon Educational Act for 21st Century — outlines a comprehensive systemwide reformation of Oregon's educational system.

♦ Workforce Quality Act — creates the Workforce Quality Council, the state's human resource investment council, and 15 local counterparts.

♦ Workforce 2000 Act — requires agencies to administer workforce education and training as a coordinated strategy.

♦ Youth Apprenticeship Act — creates pilot apprenticeships for 100 students.

♦ Oregon Benchmarks — provides quantifiable goals to measure progress toward its vision for integrating economic development with workforce and educational reform.

During the 1993 legislative session, all these initiatives became a system under Senate Bill 81 (*see* Fig. 8.1).

Undergirding this school-to-work system is an education reform strategy of high-quality statewide standards and assessment instruments leading to a Certificate of Initial Mastery (CIM) and Certificate of Advanced Mastery (CAM) — both designed for all students as they make a transition from school to productive lives of work and further learning.

The CIM recognizes the achievement of six foundation skills very similar to the SCANS skills, and five core applications for living

FIG. 8.1. OREGON'S SCHOOL-TO-WORK OPPORTUNITIES SYSTEM UNDER SENATE BILL 81

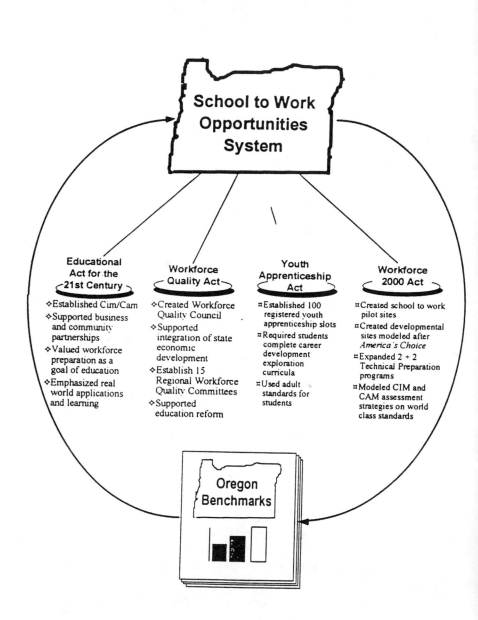

which include understanding diversity, interpreting human experience, positive health habits, applied science and math, and deliberations on public issues. Uniform statewide assessment criteria and performance standards are in the development stage for the CIM, utilizing a variety of formats (tests, portfolios, work samples, etc.).

The CAM must provide students with *contextual* learning opportunities in one or more career major cluster areas, and focuses on advanced applications such as Create and Use Knowledge, Improve Processes, and Enhance Performance of a System.

The contextual learning opportunities described are closely linked to the economic development environment of Oregon. Oregon's six "endorsement areas" or "career majors" are Arts and Communications, Business and Management, Health Services, Human Resources, Industrial and Engineering Systems, and Natural Resource Systems. These "endorsement areas" reflect the key, internationally competitive, industries which offer the high paying jobs that are vital to Oregon's economic viability.

Oregon recognized that successful school-to-work transition for all kids depended on the state's ongoing education reform effort. In Oregon, school-to-work will not be an "add-on" series of program models, but an integral part of its comprehensive, legislatively mandated strategy for educating and training its youth to world class standards.

There are eight essential elements that provide a framework around which all Oregon schools can design and implement activities. Local flexibility and creativity are encouraged. The framework tells local systems *what* they must do, but does not dictate *how* they should do it. They must:

- Provide career awareness at the elementary and middle levels that introduces students to the world of work;

- Provide career exploration and counseling for students pursuing the CIM (culminating around grade 10) that exposes them to a variety of career options through worksite experiences;

- Provide structured work-based learning opportunities for students pursuing the CAM, utilizing individual learning plans that guide and assess students' experience at the workplace. When possible and appropriate, these work-based learning experiences will be paid;

- Integrate and coordinate academic and occupational instruction as well as school-and work-based learning;
- Recognize diverse needs of students and provide multiple learning strategies;
- Award credentials for both academic and occupational skill mastery that are recognized by postsecondary institutions and employers;
- Employ a governance infrastructure that represents a broad coalition of employers, teachers, students, parents, local policy leaders, and labor; and
- Conduct continuous evaluation to measure program effectiveness as a basis for modification and continuous program quality improvement.

There are many exemplary school-to-work *programs* around the country, some of which were highlighted in previous parts of this book. Going to scale is the challenge that faces every state. Oregon proposes a regional "rollout strategy" to stage implementation and assist localities in their implementation. Before local implementation can be funded and implemented, localities must comply with a set of "readiness criteria" including evidence of:

- A working partnership of key players from the public and private sectors, including employers, government, community-based organizations, secondary schools, Education Service Districts, parents, community colleges, and other postsecondary institutions;
- Administrative structures capable of carrying out planning, fiscal, and evaluation activities;
- Inclusion of all schools in the region as part of a rollout over the grant period;
- Assurance that all local programs meet all standards outlined by the state, including a strategy to ensure inclusion of all students;
- Evaluation and continuous improvement process; and
- Registration of grant funds as venture capital accompanied by a description of the local plan to institutionalize the School-to-Work Opportunities System by the end of the grant period.

Once readings criteria are met, the state plans the following roll-out:

♦   Year 1: Five regions will implement; five will receive planning grants.

♦   Year 2: Five additional regions will implement; five remaining regions will receive planning grants.

♦   Year 3: Five remaining regions will implement.

♦   Year 4: Initial five regions are reduced to 50% funding, moving toward self-sustainment; 10 regions receiving full allocation of implementation funding.

♦   Year 5: Initial five regions fully self-sustained; second set of five regions are reduced to 50% funding; final five receive last full allocation of implementation funds.

Governance, management, and the role of the private sector are key challenges that all states face. Oregon has decided on a "joint venture" approach between the state's legislatively created Human Resource Investment Council (called the Workforce Quality Council) and the State Board of Education. Together they will appoint an advisory steering committee made up of key stakeholders and agencies, and an operational interagency management team.

Oregon recognizes and commits resources for the critical role of teacher, administrator, and employer training in systemic reform. Opportunities will be provided for teachers to experience the workplace outside of school, and teacher training institutes will be encouraged to examine and revise classroom climate to reflect the new thinking and new direction. Oregon's plan provides for training worksite staff — mentors, trainers, and supervisors — for their new coaching roles with adolescents in the workplace.

Every state who receives a 5-year venture capital grant must prepare for the "sixth year." Oregon's rollout plan is one attempt to ease out from federal support. Others are devices to increase employer involvement upfront and hopefully gain financial support in the out years. For example, state lottery dollars are proposed as an incentive to involve employers in the evaluation of student skills, development of credentials, and curriculum framework. Those employers who get fully involved and provide paid structured work experiences will be eligible for support in training their *existing* workforce, a real win-win innovative strategy.

The state, for its part, plans to use federal Perkins funds to build a stronger infrastructure for the school-to-work system. This will include the kind of staff development and technical assistance needed throughout the educational enterprise to refocus the mission and develop appropriate technical tools for implementation. Although Oregon required $9 million for its ambitious agenda, it was awarded only $3 million for Year I of its 5-year grant. Its sequenced plan for statewide rollout has proven to be a valuable management tool.

NEW JERSEY

New Jersey's vision for its future is a world-class workforce ready and able to compete in the global economy. Well before the passage of the School-to-Work Opportunities Act in Spring 1994, New Jersey, like Oregon, had established both legislative and administrative groundwork. In 1990, the Governor and the Legislature created the State Employment and Training Commission (SETC) to provide coordinated policy guidance on how New Jersey educates and trains its workforce. In 1992, this bipartisan public/private partnership created the Unified State Plan for the New Jersey Workforce Readiness System with the cooperation of all key state agencies, business, and labor. This plan provides the blueprint for the full development of a school-to-work system. Before the new federal funding became available, the New Jersey legislature had earmarked $2 million of state funds for 10 school-to-work pilots. Additionally, New Jersey's unique Youth Transition to Work Partnership Act redirects $4 million from JTPA, Perkins, and special state resources for local youth apprenticeship programs.

New Jersey is building strongly on these pilots, funding 90 more school-to-work partnerships throughout the state with the new federal funds. This strategy will pilot test diverse approaches and activities and serve as a catalyst for change in the existing educational system. In the new state school superintendent's view, school-to-work is "an integral part of a broad effort to improve the school system, not just a part of vocational educational improvement. There should be no distinction between college-bound and work-bound — *all are work-bound students!*" Therefore, New Jersey will require all training and education funds provided or supported by government assistance to include a strong school-to-work component. As in Oregon, the local pilots will be organized by local labor market-based partnerships, modeled on the State Employment and Training Commission. Two of these Workforce Investment Boards (WIBs) are already funded and in place with the intent to go statewide through the grant implementation period. Until then, existing Private Industry Councils (PICs) will provide the local coordinating role, ensuring that school-to-work decisions are based on the demands of the labor market:

♦ Using the best available market information to construct a strategic plan.

♦ Assisting local employment, training and educational programs and institutions to become more capable of responding to both short- and long-term labor market needs;

♦ Serving as a mandated part of the approval process of the local plans for specific funding streams such as the Perkins Act, JTPA, Wagner Peyser, and Adult Literacy; making specific recommendations on how these resources are used;

♦ Bridging local workforce readiness activities with direct state services provided within the WIB's (PIC's) jurisdiction;

♦ Fully involving the business community in the workforce readiness system; and

♦ Developing a strategy to meet the needs of significant segments of the population including dislocated workers, new entrants to the labor force, the economically disadvantaged, minorities, women, welfare recipients, persons with disabilities and at-risk youth.

Governance is clearly articulated and directly involves the Governor's office. A state level Executive Branch Work Group has the responsibility to ensure that implementation activities are on target. The needed implementation activities spell out action steps over a 5-year workplan, with assignments designated to lead agencies although interagency activities are required across the board. A few examples give the flavor of the New Jersey approach (Fig. 8.2).

New Jersey's stated intent is to ensure that all students attain the SCANS skills, combined with comprehensive career education, applied learning, and worksite opportunities in order to allow them to understand the value and relevance of their educational experience.

The SETC will study high performance workplaces, identifying the broad occupational clusters and the competencies required for success. Skills certificates will document competencies learned. Merrill

FIG. 8.2. EXAMPLES OF THE NEW JERSEY APPROACH

Example of Action Steps for Program Year 1994–95	*Convening Agency*
◆ Develop opportunities for sharing human resources, equipment, and written material between school, college, business and industry, and community.	Commerce
◆ Identify high demand occupations through a collaborative team from relevant state agencies.	Labor
◆ Review and revise high school graduation requirements as necessary to assure inclusion of the competencies and foundation skills.	Education
◆ Develop a system to provide all students with documentation of skills and competencies achieved in school. The attainment of these skills will be reflected in high school graduation credentials and portfolios and made available to prospective employers at the student's request.	Education
◆ Develop teacher and counselor in-service training to provide the knowledge and skills needed to conduct a comprehensive career development program.	Education

Examples of Action Steps for Program Year 1995–96	*Convening Agency*
◆ Provide support services for all students attending public schools and their families. Expand educational support services to single parents.	Human Services
◆ Assure high school dropouts, up to age 22, access to alternative programs, such as the New Jersey Youth Corps.	Education
◆ Coordinate services and programs such as JTPA, the National Community Service and Trust Act, the Education Opportunities Program, and the Tuition Assistance Program, with existing as well as new school-to-work initiatives.	Education

Lynch, New Jersey Bell, Merck, Johnson and Johnson, and DuPont are some of the businesses involved in this activity and other New Jersey school-to-work activities, including an extensive system of personnel exchanges. Along with the identification of standards and competencies, New Jersey's proposal recognizes the need for new assessment tools to measure the requisite SCANS skills: critical thinking, use and allocation of resources, interpersonal skills, use of information and technology.

New Jersey recognizes the need to have school-to-work permeate the educational experience of all children, and not be just an add-on high school activity for a few. Therefore, New Jersey has career education activities under development that are suitable for every age/grade level:

+ Beginning in **kindergarten through fifth grade**, students will develop an awareness of self and the value of work and be exposed to careers and technology.

+ **By grade six**, students — with the help of the teachers and parents — will assess personal aptitudes, abilities, and interests and relate them to careers. They will also learn the role of technology in the world of work and be offered the opportunity to participate in a community service activity.

+ Students in **grades seven and eight**, with parental involvement, will set career-oriented goals and develop 4-year career plans for grades nine through twelve. These plans may change as they are reviewed annually, but it sets students on a course and provides a basis for curriculum selection.

+ During **high school** a new "applied curriculum" will make academic concepts relevant to the workplace, especially in communications, math, and science. Vocational courses are coordinated with academic instruction. WORKLINK, a computerized interactive program, will be introduced as a tool to gain access to the workplace.

+ **At the end of tenth grade**, students will have reached a level of competency that will allow them to choose a Career Major with broad exposure to a cluster of related occupations.

+ **During the eleventh year**, students will have greater career exposure through job-shadowing, internships, community service, or employment. Summer employment will become an integral part of the student's education. By the end of twelfth grade, all students will have had a direct learning experience in the workplace.

♦ Students will have the opportunity to choose **postsecondary** education programs to advance within their fields or change career direction. These opportunities include vocational technical centers, community colleges, and universities.

♦ **Community service** will be incorporated into the work requirement for youth who are not involved in paid employment opportunities. These community service projects will emphasize work skills and rules, and, when possible, provide stipends.

♦ Educators will intensify efforts to share information and to involve parents throughout the educational process. Business, organized labor, and community-based organizations are crucial in the partnerships that must be constructed.

Several supportive networks are either in place or planned. The existing School-Based Youth Centers will become counseling and activity centers for all youth and their families, as well as reconnectors for dropouts to the New Jersey Youth Corps and Service Corps. A network of one-stop career centers is being implemented to:

♦ Disseminate information and promote the school-to-work opportunities system to the employer community and identify work-based learning sites that are available to students;

♦ Provide technical assistance and/or direct services to school counselors and youth in the areas of assessment, employment counseling, career development, labor market information, and job training opportunities;

♦ Provide job analysis and recommendations for curriculum modification to schools, which will assist in integrating academic, occupational, and work-based learning; and

♦ Assist youth with job placement.

The Educational Testing Service will use its technology expertise to expand communication networks linking schools and enabling learners to work collaboratively with students in other schools and communities on research and school projects; gather information about careers, their own preparedness, and educational opportunities;

and obtain on-line help with homework.

Both teacher and counselor preservice and in-service training programs will be redesigned. Consideration is being given to ending the permanent lifetime certification for education staff. Reflecting its philosophy of incorporating school-to-work into lifelong learning, New Jersey will expand options for learners to continue to acquire skills while employed. Arrangements are being made with Thomas Edison State College to credential student knowledge gained in the workplace so that experience-based knowledge can be transferred into college credits.

After federal support ends, New Jersey plans to totally redirect all appropriate federal and state educational funding for school-to-work, including Adult Education, Perkins, and JTPA.

New Jersey received $6 million for Year 1 of its 5-year implementation grant.

NEW YORK

New York recognizes the enormous challenge of the School-to-Work Opportunities Act. The task is integrating existing programs, resources, networks, and coalitions to create a comprehensive system, not adding a new program. Furthermore, New York knows that building such a system is beyond the ability of any one agency. Therefore, high on New York's strategy for implementation is putting a considerable effort and resources into a massive outreach to parents, students, employers, and employees to increase understanding of systems-building and gaining broad support for the effort.

New York has important "pieces" of the system in place: the state's K–12 education system, the area Vo-Tech Centers, the higher education system, including the vast network of community colleges and the broad existing infrastructure for continuing education, job training, and economic development. The entities who operate and govern these systems need to buy into the overarching goal. A chart illustrating many of the activities essential to a school-to-work system and how they are arrayed across a student's life from kindergarten to adulthood, both in school and at work is found in Figure 8.3.

As in Oregon, New York's political leaders and chief policymakers were heavily influenced by *America's Choice: High Skills or Low Wages.* "A New Compact for Learning," New York's blueprint for educational reform, contains a well-stated and unusually insightful analysis of

FIG. 8.3. SCHOOL-TO-WORK OPPORTUNITIES ACTIVITIES

School-to-Work Opportunities Activities

- Field Trips/Worksite Tours for Career Awareness
- Community Service
- Career Exploration
- Job Shadowing
- General Work Experiences
- Internships/Clinical Experiences
- Cooperative Occupational Education
- Apprenticeships
- Mentoring/Advising from Adults in Workplace and School
- Career Majors
- Tech-Prep Education
- Career Academies
- Vocational/Technical Courses
- Essential Workplace Skills
- Career Development
- Academic Courses

Education Levels: K 1 2 3 4 5 6 7 8 9 10 11 12 13 14+

Elementary   Middle   Secondary   Postsecondary   Adult

the current system and the challenges ahead.

> The problem is not that the legions of dedicated people who work in our schools are limited or uncaring, nor that they are unwilling to exert themselves to serve our children. On the contrary: the schools are filled with intelligent, conscientious, even idealistic people eager to be effective. The problem is that the system they are caught in — schools as we still organize and run them, prevailing notions of curriculum and instructional methods, the existing allocations of responsibility and authority — has become obsolete. Either we will make now the fundamental changes needed in the ways we raise and educate our children, or we can begin the slide into a darker and less prosperous time. Tinkering with the status quo is not enough. We must change the system so that we may achieve the results we need. And we are running out of time: either we will make the changes that a new century and a new era require, or we will sink into mediocrity.

After absorbing the story of *America's Choice*, the former Governor assigned the Lieutenant Governor, who also served as vice-chair for the Job Training Partnership Council, to head up a taskforce to develop implementation strategies for New York State. Another important document emanated from that effort — "Education That Works: Creating Career Pathways for New York State Youth."

By the time of grant award, a political and policy commitment was made to fold school-to-work into systemic educational reform. Four broad strategies undergird New York's plan:

♦ *Integrating workplace knowledge and skills into the curriculum for all students.* High content and performance standards, and a set of career majors will be the basis for the curriculum framework. Woven into all of this will be the essential SCANS skills and competencies. If students change career majors, their SCANS skills will easily transfer to a new "language context," *e.g.*, from a health context to a business context.

♦ *Integrating skills standards, skills assessment and skills certificates into the state's new Performance-Based Assessment System.* A system of both state program assessment and local student assessment is planned. New York considered and rejected the CIM and CAM approach suggested in America's Choice in favor of an Assessment of Initial Mastery (AIM). The AIM measures of academic and workforce skills will be required for graduation from high school for all students. Business and labor organized into Career Major Panels, working in conjunction with the National Skill Standards Board, will develop skills standards.

♦ *Preparing teachers, counselors, and administrators to implement new curriculum, instruction, and assessment strategies.* New York's current professional development activities have been too scattered and brief to bring about real change. New York's approach to this problem is unique among the grant proposals submitted. Almost a million dollars is reserved to establish a state research, development, and dissemination center. The center will collect information about successful models from around the state and country, develop training materials, develop certification criteria, develop manuals of work-based learning strategies, etc. — all organized around career development, workplace skills, and work-based learning. An established statewide network of Teacher Centers, organized by the Teachers' Union, will disseminate the information. The Teacher Centers will also receive funding to assist in research and development.

♦ *Involving parents and employers and other community members in shared decisionmaking.* Local partnerships will establish and maintain communication among all the local stakeholders. To receive subgrants, each partnership will be expected to communicate the new vision, the scope of changes that will be enacted, and develop a process for shared decision-making.

New York plans to secure employer commitments in a two-step fashion. After the Career Major Panels identify occupational clusters, specialties and competencies, partnerships with major business associations will be pursued. Their mission will be to develop large numbers of work-based learning opportunities for students. Two hundred thousand dollars of the funding will be dedicated to statewide technical assistance in support of this effort.

New York has developed a set of five principles regarding work-based learning:

♦ Existing work-based learning opportunities must be incorporated into a coherent system.

♦ Mentoring and coaching must be built in and fostered. Many adults are natural coaches and mentors. They can be enlisted as trainers and supporters of other adults.

♦ Work-based learning must be carefully planned and monitored to assure that it builds young people's competence and reinforces their school-based learning.

♦ Work-based curriculum must be organized around occupational areas and specialties within those areas. Technical, personal, and social competencies must be specified for each occupational area, providing both the learning objective and standards for certification.

♦ Implementation must proceed simultaneously from the top down (*e.g.*, state and national skill standard setting) and from the bottom up (e.g., agreements between school and local employers).

New York intends to build a system of local partnerships that is flexible enough to allow different players to assume leadership roles in different parts of the state, while at the same time maintaining quality and consistency. The State School-to-Work Advisory Committee will establish guidelines for membership and delineate responsibilities of the local partnership. The Private Industry Councils (PICs) will be asked to take a lead role in helping the State convene the appropriate partnership in their geographic area.

The State will put the full force of its state aid to schools ($8 million each year) to support a system that comprehensively prepares all students — both in and out of school — with quality school-to-work opportunities. Additionally, the resources of the Perkins Act, JTPA, a State Health Personnel Grant ($5.7 million), and Governor's School and Business Alliance ($1.7 million) will be dedicated to developing career majors and structured work experience for students.

New York is planning to start local implementation with a variety of targeted pilots — including:

♦   Incentive grants to 10 local partnerships to place elementary
    school counselors on a shared service basis,

♦   Enabling 100 middle schools to benefit from the on-site tech-
    nology developed by the Department of Labor's work station
    project; and

♦   Incentive grants to local partnerships that commit to fully
    integrating all out-of-school youth and adult programs
    operating in their area into their overall school-to-work
    opportunities strategy.

New York anticipates that this comprehensive top-down and
bottom-up quality school-to-work opportunities system will take
10 years to put in place. For this effort, the State received $10 million
for Year 1 of its 5-year implementation grant.

WISCONSIN

By virtue of winning three prior federal demonstration grants,
Wisconsin had a substantial lead in developing a school-to-work
system. National attention had focused on their Youth Apprenticeship
model and a statewide systemic institutionalization of tech-prep.
The Wisconsin vision is undergirded by state legislation supporting
Youth Apprenticeship, tech-prep, Education for Employment Standards, employer training grants for youth apprenticeship, career counseling and postsecondary enrollment options, all of which mesh together into a structured school-to-work system.

In 1992, Wisconsin approved skill standards for youth apprenticeships in printing. The next year financial services was added. These
are being implemented in 10 high schools across the State. Standards
are being developed in seven other clusters that will enroll approximately 400 youth apprentices. Wisconsin's goal is to organize 30
industries with skill standards and new statewide curricula, enrolling
at least 10% of its annual youth cohort by the end of the 5-year implementation grant.

Wisconsin's approach seems closer to the classic structured European model than most other states. The hallmark of Youth Apprenticeship is the combination of classroom work with structured work-
based learning provided through workplace mentors. The integration
of academics with work-based learning leads to both a high school
diploma and a certificate of proficiency in a specific industry. State-

wide industry associations working with the support of organized labor have been directly involved in defining the skills that entry level workers need to know and do across broad occupations in the industry.

The industry sectors to be included:

♦ Must have strategic value to substate regional economies.

♦ Offer strong potential for entry level employment leading to careers.

♦ Call for higher skills that require preparation and development.

♦ Offer wages that reflect skill content and high performance employment.

A similar process has been underway to institutionalize tech-prep as a foundation for higher academic and technical skills. Rather than existing as a series of pilot programs, as in many states, the Wisconsin legislature directed that tech-prep was to be a statewide effort, existing in all 427 school districts. Wisconsin's definition of tech-prep is also distinctive. It is not a system of study for a definable group of students. Wisconsin's initiative has developed "Quality Components" for continual improvement of integrated school-based programs for *all* Wisconsin high school youth that incorporate: higher standards and higher levels of achievement; integrated curricula; hands on learning; enhanced career guidance; career mapping — written plans for career goals and strategies to achieve them; exposure to technical subject matter; and postsecondary articulation possibilities.

The Wisconsin school-to-work system includes a network of community based counseling centers, modeled on the German system, "The Bundesanstalt fur Arbeit." These centers organize access to labor market information, opportunities for job-shadowing, career exploration, and access to the private sector for all students. The State funded three communities to operate these centers in the Fall of 1994. This will grow to 10 regional centers within 3 years and will complement the existing network of 22 one-stop job centers that currently exist. It is one of the important connecting links between school and work and school and the community.

Starting in 1985, the Education for Employment standard required all K–12 students to have access to Education for Employment programs that included applied instruction, work experience, career exploration, etc. A curriculum guide for middle schools includes "Exploring Life's Work" modules. Wisconsin requires every school participating in a local partnership to design and implement a plan, *complete with staff development*, that infuses the Education for Employment curricula and Exploring Life's Work concepts into the classroom.

A strong developmental guidance model reinforces this curricular approach. School-based personnel, parents, and business and industry representatives provide guidance services. Community members meet students in a structured K–12 guidance and counseling program that is managed as an integral part of the learning process.

Like many leading edge states, Wisconsin recognizes the value of other existing education, employment, and training programs in the development of a comprehensive school-to-work system. The State is supporting a "conversion strategy" for upgrading existing cooperative education, summer youth, and JTPA-funded efforts to incorporate all the major elements outlined in the School-to-Work Opportunities Act.

Wisconsin also recognizes that to expedite these changes, teachers need an enormous amount of retraining and ongoing staff development. They have developed a unique train-the-trainer approach. The State Tech-Prep Management Team started with a cadre of teachers who were trained in applied/integrative curriculum. After a period of practice, they are given the opportunity to share their new learning with their colleagues and enhance their own skills. The train-the-trainer model will:

♦ Help educators develop a deeper appreciation of the value of the applied/integrative curriculum;

♦ Implement a statewide process for training teachers to identify, write, and implement applied/integrative instructional tasks;

♦ Prepare teachers to help their colleagues identify, write, and implement applied/integrative instructional tasks so that these strategies become an integral part of the system employed by their schools; and

♦ Create an environment where students learn to transfer knowledge from one application and knowledge base to another.

In February of 1994, 500 educators were trained to write authentic integrated tasks that can be used by individual classroom teachers to help students make connections between subject areas and recognize and appreciate the relevance in learning activities. A plan for mentor training to be provided through the technical college system is also underway. One of those colleges has developed a comprehensive mentor training curriculum which is being shared by the system and widely used by employers.

The linchpin in Wisconsin's design is a competency-based admission criteria for the state university system. Currently, the University of Wisconsin is developing such criteria to supplement its traditional freshman admission policy. Within a few years, admission to the university system statewide will be based on competency attainment. Work-based learning will be valued as much as the current seat-based Carnegie Units.

The Governor is creating a School-to-Work Commission, representing all the major stakeholders, public and private, to integrate all the elements and entities in the State that currently make independent policy decisions in this arena. A school-to-work cabinet will mobilize the public side of the team, giving "operational roles" to each agency. (*See* Fig. 8.4.)

Local partnerships will be organized using the geographic maps defined by the technical college districts and will receive grant funds to carry out duties and responsibilities comparable to the state. Particular attention is given to Milwaukee, where the majority of the state's disadvantaged students live. The Milwaukee public schools superintendent, working with a diverse group of stakeholders, envisions a major school reform effort that includes the Milwaukee public schools, universities, technical colleges, labor, employers, parents, and community. Milwaukee will provide every student with a combination of school-based and work-based learning, new integrated curricula with real-world applications, career counseling, and work experience. Milwaukee and the State are working together on implementation and funding coordination.

Wisconsin expects that by the year 2000:

♦ One out of five high school seniors will have earned or will be in the process of earning a state skill certificate in an industry area and such skill certificates will be available in 30 industries;

FIG. 8.4. GOVERNOR'S COMMISSION FOR SCHOOL-TO-WORK TRANSITION

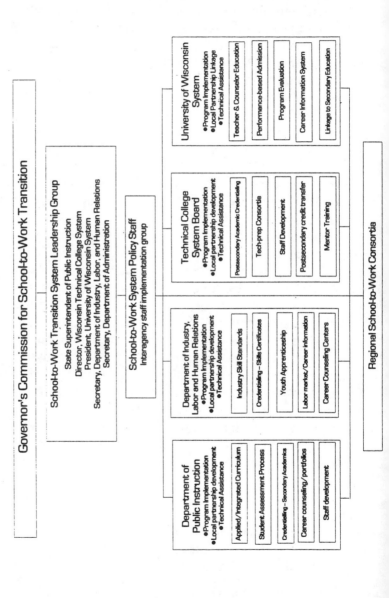

♦ One of three graduating seniors will have a career major linked to an associate degree with plans to go on to a technical college, and 90% will have achieved basic skills mastery against challenging national academic standards at the high school level;

♦ All students will have at least some exposure to the workplace and all students will have a career plan.

Wisconsin received $4.5 million for its first year of funding under the 5- year grant.

9

CONCLUSION: WHAT DO WE KNOW?

Although the School to Work Opportunities Act was not signed into law until May, 1994, many innovative initiatives linking classroom students to the workplace had already been underway across the country. The challenge is moving from the innovative initiative to systemic change. The new legislation officially recognized that preparing all students for productive roles in society, including the ability to earn a living, is a legitimate and necessary mission for American educational institutions. To some academicians, that may seem like heresy. "Learn for the sake of learning," and, "knowledge is its own reward," have been their credos. Implicit in this philosophy is the belief that learning is almost exclusively a school-based enterprise.

But the ground is shifting. Labor market demands are shaped by competition from a global marketplace. Family and community support structures have changed, and in many cases eroded. Financial support for schools is uneven and often inequitable. Too many kids are still dropping out of our schools, prepared for nothing constructive, but filled with unrealistic expectations about "getting a job." And employers are complaining about the inadequacies of the students who do graduate. The stage is set for a comprehensive and comprehendible *system* connecting school and careers for all students, including the college bound.

As such systems are being built around the country, it may be useful to review what we have learned from the pioneering pilots described in this book and what we know about school and work. The prospect of having a successful career is a profound motivator for young people to work harder, achieve more, and modify their behavior to accommodate workplace expectations. We have learned that linking school-based and work-based learning initiatives can provide those incentives. Those student-workers are learning the "why" of schooling, the connection between school and work, and, therefore, the relevance of school work. Most importantly, as a result, they are learning to value school more. We have learned that the labor market is confusing even for mature and experienced job seekers. Young people, starting on career paths, need advice and guidance. They must have up-to-date information in order to make informed choices. All students deserve career and labor market information comparable to the information about college entrance requirements now available at most school guidance offices

Employers must see the connection between school performance and achievements at the job. A recent census bureau survey of 3,000 employers ranked academic performance, teacher recommendations, and school reputation at the bottom of a list of qualities that count with employers. This must change to convince students that school is the pathway to careers, and end the purposeless drift through high school that characterize too many student experiences.

Employers must also be helped to recognize the key role they, their employees, and their workplaces play in developing this new learning enterprise. Across the country, we have seen a few private sector grants take the leadership. But to be successful and go to scale, the midsized and smaller companies need to be fully engaged in the effort. States with implementation grants will be well-advised to allocate resources for technical assistance to business associations to help local employers understand not only the "why," but also the "how," to play a meaningful role in the school-to-work system.

Work-based learning is emerging as a major new tenet in student education. Beyond the value implicit for students in the experience itself — reality-based, learning-lab, hands-on, behavioral adjustments, etc. — it involves employers in the learning enterprise. That involvement has the greatest potential for changing attitudes, curriculum, and educational outcomes. Work-based experiences clearly tied to classroom learning, form career connections in tangible ways for students, teachers, and employers.

We have learned that it is constructive to structure students' programs in a focused, integrated way, hence the call for "career majors." Career major clusters must be compatible with economic development activities and regional job opportunities. Career majors should convey the interrelatedness of groups of jobs or occupations so that students are equipped for a rapidly changing workplace. Preparation for specific occupations that may soon become obsolete no longer fills the bill.

To be credible, this new system must deserve and gain credibility. It must have standards of competencies for both the academic and work-based learning components. Employers must participate in developing the standards and measurements.

We have learned that career education may continue throughout a lifetime. Articulation agreements with institutions of higher education is critical to continuing the lifelong learning process. These articulation agreements should recognize applied academics and work-based learning competencies as part of admissions criteria.

We have learned that even though the need for change may be obvious, the ability to change institutional practice is slow and painful. Many partners need to come together, on a continuous basis, in a new collaboration if the learning experience is to be truly reinvented for all students. New interagency, public-private partnerships are emerging. They are planning and developing new educational systems that prepare students for high-skill, high-wage careers. Such sponsoring collaboratives, having the confidence of all the partners, can then assume joint ownership and joint custody of the new enterprise.

In summary, we have learned that the core elements of a school to work opportunities system must strive to *create a new pedagogy in a high performance learning environment by developing:*

♦ Rigorous skill standards;

♦ Valid assessment and measurement systems;

♦ Portable credentials;

♦ Work-based learning opportunities;

♦ Integrated academic and vocational curriculum in new career frameworks;

♦ Massive and sustained staff development strategies;

♦ New career guidance and counseling systems;

♦ Articulation with state and regional economic development activities;

♦ Articulation with higher education;

and must be coordinated by a network of interagency, intergovernmental, public-private policy and management entities.

Such a system has important implications for the key players:

For Governors: A state that will have a healthy economy into the next century must redefine what kind of learning takes place in its public schools. We know what needs to be done. Each state may well define its own way of getting the job done. As we have seen, leading edge states and localities have developed strategies — strategies that differ to some extent, but all include the core elements listed above. Governors must recognize the challenge, provide the leadership, support legislative underpinnings, demand interdepartmental collaboration, and enlist the private sectors as full partners.

For Business and Labor: Only quality products and services will remain competitive in the global marketplace. Business and labor must bring this idea to the worker-production process taking place in our schools. At the same time, they need to enlist the workplaces under their control in that worker-production process. Collaboration between workplaces and schools must take place on an unprecedented scale. The "Promising Practices" show how to make it happen and how to sustain the collaboration.

For State and Local School Districts: This is either the scariest of times or the most exciting. The possibility of engaging students in a new kind of learning process — one in which real world settings form the context for classroom experiences should be immensely rewarding. This means school personnel stepping beyond the school room door, recognizing the value of learning environments other than the classroom, and developing a common language for communicating with new workplace partners. Wisely, many states allow maximum creativity and flexibility at the local level as long as the core elements of a system are seamlessly woven together and measurable outcomes are achieved. The outcomes may vary from the traditional high school diploma to include portable skill certificates, portfolios, and work samples, all designed to propel youth smoothly along a career path. The state has a responsibility to engage all the stakeholders in a "rollout" strategy to go from pilot stage to scale and remain viable when the federal venture capital ends.

For Parents: A school-to-work opportunities system is not a traditional voc-ed program for noncollege bound students, but a true developmental activity starting in kindergarten. Eventually, every successful person goes to work. The traditional focus of education in this country has paid little heed to that fact except for limited programs for a handful of students. Parents must be included in outreach programs to make sure they understand and welcome this new kind of learning for *all* students.

For Students: Schools cannot succeed unless students appreciate the purpose of learning. This appreciation depends on employers becoming more interested in how students perform in school and giving students opportunities to develop and demonstrate skills at work. More will be expected of students in time, effort, and skills development. In turn, students can expect a more rewarding future.

PART IV:
SCHOOL-TO-WORK
PRACTITIONER'S
DIRECTORY

SCHOOL-TO-WORK
PRACTITIONER'S
DIRECTORY

(Entries are listed in the order they appear in the text.)

Elementary and Middle School Microsocieties
Mohave Middle School
5520 North 86th Street
Scottsdale, AZ 85250
>*Contact Person:*
>Peggy Eischen or Shari Just
>Phone: (602) 423–3700

Desert Sky Middle School
5130 W. Grovers Avenue
Glendale, AZ 85308–1300
>*Contact Person:*
>Patti Grossman (formerly at Desert Sky M.S.)
>Desert Mountain School
>35959 North Seventh Avenue
>Phoenix, AZ 85027
>Phone: (602) 581–7100

Washington Elementary School
300 East Myrtle
Independence, KA 67301
>*Contact Person:*
>Debra Toomey
>Phone: (316) 332–1875

Elementary and Middle School Entrepreneurial Projects
Smitha Middle School
2025 Powder Springs Road
Marietta, GA 30064
> *Contact Person:*
> Glenda Wills (Formerly at Smitha M.S.)
> Hayes Elementary School
> 1501 Kenesaw
> Kenesaw, GA
> Phone: (404) 424–9275

Jerome Lippman Jewish Community Day School
705 White Pond Drive
Akron, OH 44320
> *Contact Person:*
> Mike Currey or Rebecca Tolson
> Phone: (216) 836–0419
> Fax: (216) 867–8498

Lilburn Elementary School
531 McDaniel Street
Lilburn, GA 30247
> *Contact Person:*
> Laurie Harling or Rhea Oberholzer
> Phone: (770) 921–7707
> Fax: (770) 564–3962

Elementary and Middle School Media Publications
Bulkeley Middle School
Rhinebeck, NY 12572
> *Contact person:*
> Patrick Kern
> Phone: (914) 871–5550

Pacific Island School
PO Box 5047
Avalon, CA 90704
Contact Person:
S.E.A. Peterson
Isthmus Bee, The News
PO Box 5085
Two Harbors, CA 90704
Phone: (310) 510–1807

Knowlton Elementary School
801 West Shepard Lane
Farmington, UT 84025
Contact Person:
James Harris
Phone: (801) 451–1045
Fax: (801) 451–1048

Elementary and Middle School Construction and Manufacturing Enterprises
Shaker Junior High School
Latham, NY
Contact Person:
Rodney Wheeler or Craig Uline
Phone: (518) 785–1341

Fogelsville Elementary School
312 South Route 100
Allentown, PA 18106
Contact Person:
Winnifred Bolinsky
Phone: (610) 398–0331

Elementary and Middle School Workplace-Based Activities
Gleason Lake Elementary School
310 County Road 101
Plymouth, MN 55447
Contact Person:
Bonnie Hatton
Phone: (612) 476–3170

Mandalay Middle School
9651 N. Pierce
Westminster, CO 80021
Contact Person:
Maria Rask
Phone: (303) 430–1021
Fax: (303) 429–3395

Philadelphia High School Academies, Inc.
230 South Broad Street, 18th Floor
Philadelphia, PA 19102
Contact Person:
Natalie S. Allen, President
Phone: (215) 546–6300
Fax: (215) 546–9174

Roosevelt Renaissance 2000
Roosevelt High School
6941 North Central
Portland, OR 97201
Contact Person:
Rene Leger, Coordinator
Phone: (503) 280–5260

Smokey House Project
Box 292
Hilliard Rd.
Danby, VT 05739
Contact Person:
Lynn Bondurant, Executive Director
Phone: (802) 293–5121
Fax: (802) 293–5650

An Associate Degree in High-Performance Manufacturing
Institute for Policy Studies
Wyman Park Building, 5th Floor
The Johns Hopkins University
3400 N. Charles Street
Baltimore, MD 21218

Contact Person:
Arnold Packer or Elizabeth Mathias
Phone: (410) 516–4556
Fax: (410) 516–4775
E-mail: packer@jhunix.hcf.jhu.edu
Homepage: http://www.jhu.edu/~ips/scans

Montgomery College Tech-Prep
Montgomery College
51 Manakee Street
Rockville, MD 20850
Contact Person:
Joan Lautman, Tech Prep Coordinator
Phone: (310) 279–5026
Fax: (310) 251–7969
E-mail: jlautman@hamlet5.umd.edu

Summer Beginnings National Demonstration Project
Brandeis University
Center for Human Resources
60 Turner Street
Waltham, MA 02154
Contact Person:
Barbara McKay
Phone: (617) 736–3770
Fax: (617) 736–3773
E-mail: hn3676@handsnet.org

Maryland's Summer Youth Employment and Training Program
Maryland Governor's Workforce Investment Board
Summer Youth Employment Program
1414 Key Highway, 2nd Flr.
Baltimore, MD 21230
Contact Persons:
James E. Callahan, Executive Director
Mary L. Vrany, Policy Administrator
Phone: (410) 333–4454
Fax: (410) 333–4467
E-mail: aaua89a@prodigy.com

WORKPLUS
Public/Private Ventures
One Commerce Square
2005 Market Street
Philadelphia, PA 19103
  Contact Person:
  Carol Clymer, Senior Program Officer
  Phone: (215) 557–4495
  Fax: (215) 557–4469
  E-mail: ppvg@dolphin.upenn.edu

McDonald's Youth Demonstration Project
North Illinois University
Business and Industry Services
1520 Kensington Road
Oak Brook, IL 60521–2141
  Contact Person:
  Robert Sheets, Director
  Research and Development
  Phone: (708) 573–5070 ext. 229
  Fax: (708) 573–5075

Maryland Statewide Service–Learning Requirement
Maryland Student Service Alliance
Maryland State Dept. of Education
200 W. Baltimore Street
Baltimore, MD 21201
  Contact Person:
  Margaret O'Neill, Executive Director
  Phone: (410) 767–0358
  Fax: (410) 333–2379
  TDD: (410) 333–6442

Magic Me
2521 N. Charles Street
Baltimore, MD 21218
  Contact Person:
  Janet Salmons, Executive Director
  Phone: (410) 243–9066
  Fax: (410) 243–9076
  E-mail: jesmagicme@aol.com

Siemens–Lyman–Seminole
Lyman High School
865 South County Road 427
Longwood, FL 32750
Phone: (407) 942–6360

Partnerships for Academic and Career Excellence (PACE)
PO Box 587, Highway 76
Pendleton, SC 29670
Contact Person:
Johnny Wallace, Executive Director
Phone: (803) 646–8361
Fax: (803) 646–8256
E-mail: j.wallace@tricty.tricounty.tec.sc.us

ProTech Health Care
Boston Private Industry Council
2 Oliver Street, 7th Floor
Boston, MA 02109
Contact Person:
Lois Ann Porter, Project Director
Phone: (617) 423–3755
Fax: (617) 423–1041

Boeing Corporation
Department of College and University Relations
Boeing Corporation
PO Box 3707, MS 1F-05
Seattle, WA 98124–2207
Contact Person:
Dr. Carver Gayton, Corporate Director
Phone: (206) 655–1035
Fax: (206) 544–0111

Craftsmanship 2000
Oklahoma Department of Vocational–Technical Education
6601 Broadway Extension
Oklahoma City, OK 73116
Contact Person:
Ann Benson
Phone: (405) 743–5436
Fax: (405) 743–5541

Broome County Youth Apprenticeship
Cornell Youth and Work Program
Department of Human Development and Family Studies
College of Human Ecology
Cornell University
Ithaca, NY 14853
Contact Persons:
Steven Hamilton, Professor
Mary Agnes Hamilton
G62C Martha van Renselker Hall
Ithaca, NY 14853–4701
Phone: (607) 255–2535
Fax: (607) 255–3769

Seattle–King County Youth Fair Chance
Seattle–King County Private Industry Council
Market Place One, Suite 250
2003 Western Avenue
Seattle, WA 98121
Contact Person:
Renee Fellinger, Program Coordinator
Phone: (206) 448–0474
Fax: (206) 448–0484

Oregon State School-to-Work System
Oregon Department of Education
Office of Professional Technical Education
255 Capitol Street, NE
Salem, OR 97310
Contact Person:
Bill Braly
Phone: (503) 378–3584
Fax: (503) 378–5156

New Jersey School-to-Work System
New Jersey Department of Education
Office of School-To-Work Initiatives
CN 500
Trenton, NJ 08625

Contact Person:
Thomas A. Henry, Director
Phone: (609) 633–0665
Fax: (609) 633–0658

New York School-to-Work System
New York State Education Dept.
Office of Workforce Preparation and Continuing Education
Room 315 Ed.
Albany, NY 12234
Contact Person:
Cindy Lakes, Coordinator
Phone: (518) 474–4809
Fax: (518) 474–0319

Wisconsin School-to-Work System
Wisconsin Department of Industry, Labor &
Human Relations Office for Workforce Excellence
201 East Washington Avenue
Room 231X
Madison, WI 53702
Contact Person:
Orlando Canto
Phone: (608) 266–1103
Fax: (608) 266–7645

INDEX